Second Edition

DISCOVERING LINGUISTICS

AN INTRODUCTION TO LINGUISTIC ANALYSIS

Teresa Griffith
University of California, Irvine

Kendall Hunt
publishing company

Kendall Hunt
publishing company

www.kendallhunt.com
Send all inquiries to:
4050 Westmark Drive
Dubuque, IA 52004-1840

Copyright © 2009, 2011 by Teresa Griffith

ISBN 978-0-7575-8979-9

Contents

Detailed Contents

Preface

To engage in linguistic analysis is to engage in the scientific study of human language. This text undertakes precisely this type of study, using the English language as the primary but not exclusive exemplar of all human languages.

If English is your native language (or a language you speak well), embarking on the scientific study of English may strike you as an unusual (if not a trivial) pursuit. You may even say to yourself, "Well, linguistics may be of interest to grammarians, but it's of little concern to me. I already know all I need to know about English. I'm taking this course only to satisfy a General Education Requirement."

Such a pessimistic view arises in large part because our native language makes up so much of who we are and how we view ourselves that we tend to take it for granted. As a result, we effectively ignore just how remarkable a system human language is.

Linguists (along with many other scientists) consider language to be the most complex product of the human brain. That is, a language is not something that can be stuffed between the covers of a book entitled *Modern Spoken Cambodian* or *Intermediate College Latin* or *Russian for Everybody* (three books I happen to own). Instead, as we discover in this text, a language comprises a finite system of elements and rules which together enable the speakers of that language to construct a non-finite number of phrases and sentences. As a (mental) system, language forms an eminently appropriate subject for scientific study. The primary goal of this text is to provide some basic tools of linguistic analysis as a means of imbuing readers with both appreciation for and comprehension of this amazing mental system that we call "human language."

Mastering the tools of linguistic analysis requires practice. Each chapter beyond the first closes with a series of Practice Problems, designed to help you grasp the phenomena covered in that chapter. Answer Keys are provided at the end of the text, but I encourage you to work diligently through each problem before leaping to its solution. This last caveat is based on a simple fact: Seeing the solution before working through a problem never facilitates understanding. Additionally, linguistics brings with it a fairly large, technical vocabulary. Each chapter contains a list of the Key Terms and Concepts introduced there, and all of these are listed in the Index.

With these remarks in mind, let's begin to discover linguistics!

Acknowledgments

For their in-depth reading of various stages of this text, for their always pertinent and extraordinarily helpful comments, and (especially) for their overall clarity of mind, I thank Bernard Tranel and Francesca Del Gobbo. For their patience in explaining typos and unclear passages in the first edition to almost one thousand undergraduates over the last two years, I thank Jennifer Lindsay, Ben Mis, and Ray Mendoza. The two editions of this text would be considerably less readable without their input.

I extend special kudos to Linda Chapman and Jason McFaul of Kendall Hunt for their continuous support throughout the publication process.

Remaining errors are my responsibility. Readers can earn extra stars for their crowns in heaven by (politely) pointing out those problem areas which no doubt remain.

CHAPTER 1

ON LANGUAGE, SCIENCE, AND LINGUISTICS

Most readers likely come to this text with little knowledge of what linguistics is all about and what it is that linguists do. One way to fill in the blanks is to begin by dispelling two false impressions that some readers might have. First, a linguist is not (necessarily) one who speaks a host of languages, and studying linguistics does not automatically allow you to gain proficiency in many languages. While it may be true that a given linguist is a polyglot, there is nothing about the study of linguistics which requires this ability. Second, a linguist is not one who mandates "rules of correct usage" for a given language, and studying linguistics will not, in and of itself, help you write a better term paper.

Simply put, linguistics is the scientific study of Language—where the term Language (with an upper case "L") refers to a uniquely-human mode of communication. Linguistics is an intellectual endeavor, most often conceived of as one of the cognitive sciences, whose primary purpose is to understand the nature of Language in order to understand something about the nature of the human brain.

Linguists are scientists whose area of specialization is Language. One way to gain an understanding of Language is to delve into one or more of the approximately six thousand nine hundred languages (with a lower case "l") currently spoken on the planet: Arabic, Basque, Dyirbal, English, Guajarati, Navajo, Swahili, Zulu, and so forth. (The number of languages cited here comes from data compiled in SIL's *Ethnologue;* you can view the online version at http://www.ethnologue.com/web.asp.)

As scientists, linguists describe what they glean from native speakers in order to develop a theory of the language(s) under study. That is, linguists are descriptivists who adhere to the scientific method and view their functions as (a) describing a range of data from one or more languages; (b) making generalizations over those data; (c) posing, testing, and revising hypotheses to account for those generalizations; and (d) formulating theories to tie various hypotheses into a coherent structure. The resulting coherent structure is called the grammar of a language.

In contrast to the descriptive, scientific approach to language, those who are prescriptivists delight in mandating the "rules of correct usage." Prescriptivists are only too pleased to tell us various rules of English, such as: Don't end a sentence with a preposition! On this view, a preposition is simply not one of the words a sentence can end with. Prescriptivists deem

1

sentences such as *Who did you vote for?* to be "bad English" (or worse). But of course this sentence is perfectly natural and grammatical in English. Its non-prepositional-ending counterpart, *For whom did you vote?*, is grammatical, but it may sound "affected" or "snotty" to most speakers of the language.

Linguists' interest in Language stems in part from the ubiquity (i.e., pervasiveness) of languages: No 'language-less' human community has ever been discovered. Instead, except in extraordinary circumstances, every human being develops full command of a language, whether that language is spoken like English or gestured like American Sign Language.

Moreover, all humans acquire their native language effortlessly and without explicit instruction. Thus, even though newborns cannot effectively communicate with the adults around them, by the time children enter school, they have extensive vocabularies and have developed sufficient meta-linguistic awareness to make rhymes and tell language-based jokes.

Those of you who have studied a foreign language in high school or college realize that learning a language as a teen or adult is a difficult process. While you may become proficient in reading this other language, and may be able to write reasonably well in it, you will likely never become an accomplished poet in this language; and you will likely always speak this language with what native speakers would judge to be a "foreign accent." Yet you achieved fluency in your native language easily and perfectly. As the Italian physician and educator Maria Montessori once remarked, "The only language men ever speak perfectly is the one they learn in babyhood, when no one can teach them anything!"

We are able to acquire our native language so easily and readily because human beings are effectively 'hard-wired' for Language. That is, as part of our biological endowment, our brains come equipped with the chemicals, electricity, axons, dendrites, connections, and so forth that are necessary for producing and understanding Language. As linguists (and others) recognize, Language is arguably the most complex product of the human brain and is part of our nature as human beings.

Which language serves as our native tongue depends on our nurture, that is, on the language(s) spoken by those who surround us as we grow up. Those who are very fortunate are raised in environments in which more than a single language is spoken. These people generally achieve fluency in each of their nurturing languages and do so as effortlessly as those of us who are raised in mono-lingual environments achieve fluency in a single language.

Since Language is part of our biological endowment, all languages must be equal, in some sense, as all are the products of the human brain and all human brains are essentially alike. Now it is true that not all languages have the same social status; but it is simply not the case that those who live in "primitive societies" speak a "primitive language." Although it may be possible to define a "primitive society" based on some type of anthropological, sociological, and/or economic criteria, the term "primitive language" is meaningless. What is true is that any thought that any human being can entertain can be expressed in any one of the approximately six thousand languages spoken today on Planet Earth.

Moreover, it must be the case that, at some (perhaps abstract) level, all languages are essentially <u>alike</u>, as all are products of the human brain. Although it is certainly true that languages may differ from each other in certain respects, what is much more interesting is the fact that all languages share what some linguists call <u>fundamental design features</u>, as sounds, words, phrases and sentences, and meaning comprise the four key ingredients—i.e., design features—of all languages (excluding signed languages, where gestures replace sounds).

Here are two inter-related facts which are of great interest to linguists:

- We display a knowledge of our native language that is much richer than what we can glean from the conversation of those around us and from what we've been very carefully taught in school.
- We know all kinds of things about our native language that we have no conscious awareness of. This means that much of our knowledge of language is <u>tacit</u> or sub-conscious, rather than conscious, knowledge.

Four sets of examples are introduced below to demonstrate the tacit knowledge we have of English. The first set of examples relates to the sound system of English, the second set to the way words are formed in the language, the third to the order in which those words must occur, and the fourth to the interpretation of those words. These four sets of examples involve the phonological, morphological, syntactic, and semantic components of the grammar, the four components (or modules) which form the basis of the grammars of English and of every human language. Because every human language is composed of these four modules, they comprise part of the fundamental design features of Language.

As we consider the various examples, we see that these components sometimes interact in interesting ways with each other, although each component may at other times operate independently. More significantly, we see that each component is <u>rule-governed</u>; that is, each component has its own sets of rules and native speakers intuitively know of the existence of these rules and also how to apply them.

The label linguists employ when discussing the knowledge we have of our native language (or of any language which we speak well) is <u>linguistic competence</u>. Linguistic competence comprises both (a) our <u>creativity</u>, that is, our abilities to produce and to understand words, phrases, and sentences we have never before encountered; and (b) our <u>intuitions</u>, that is, our ability to make grammaticality judgments about those words, phrases, and sentences.

The Rules of the Sound System of English Exemplified

Consider the nonce (i.e., made-up) words in (1) below, none of which exists in English. While you likely sense that the words in (1a) might be perfectly possible words of the language, you likely also sense that those in (1b) are completely impossible if they are pronounced as they are spelled. The symbol " * " marks these strings as ungrammatical in English, where ungrammatical means "violates a rule of the grammar." (Ungrammatical strings are marked with asterisks throughout this text.)

1.

a	klume	plive	shroke	trute
b	*knong	*psaa	*sroke	*tboung

While we cannot ascertain the meanings of the words in (1a), we find them easy to pronounce. You might sense that you could invent a new product or develop a new process and then coin one of the words in (1a) to label that product or process. But you also sense that you would not be allowed to coin any of the words in (1b), as there is something decidedly amiss about the sequence of sounds each of these words begins with: The word-initial sequences <kn>, <ps>, <sr>, and <tb> are impossible. That is, as a native speaker of English, you have internalized something about the rules of the language which govern the sequences of consonants which can occur at the beginnings of words—though you have never been explicitly taught this.

The sound system of another language does not necessarily adopt precisely the same rules as does English. In fact, the words in (1b) are the Cambodian words for 'inside', 'market', 'country', and 'south', respectively.

These examples demonstrate that part of the knowledge of the grammar of English that native speakers possess includes knowledge of what strings of consonants are licit in word-initial position. Such knowledge is not explicitly taught—and cannot be taught about words you've never before encountered. Yet we have no difficulty in categorizing some words as possible words of English and others as impossible. This state of affairs follows on the approach to language taken here: Our abilities result from rules of the sound system of English; these rules are generated in our minds and represent part of our tacit knowledge of the language.

Chapter 2 explores the sounds of English, a component of the grammar called <u>phonetics</u>. Chapter 3 considers how sounds pattern together, in English and in a range of other languages; this component of the grammar is called <u>phonology</u>.

The Rules of Word Formation in English Exemplified

To form the plural of an English word such as *pot,* we add the plural marker (*-s,* for regular plurals) at the end of the word: *pot + s = pots.* That is, while the singular form *pot* consists of one piece of meaning, the plural form *pots* consists of two pieces of meaning.

Observe that there are actually four ways to string these two pieces of meaning together: We could add the plural marker at the beginning of the singular form; in this case, the result would be *spot*—a perfectly good word of English, but not the plural of *pot.* We could add the plural marker inside the singular form, before the final consonant; in this case, the result would be *post*—another word of English, but again not the plural of *pot.* Finally, we could add the plural marker inside the singular form, just after the first consonant; now the result would be **psot.* But as discussed above, the sequence <ps> is impossible in word-initial position in English, as it violates a rule of the sound system of the language. This is an example of interaction between the sound module and the word-formation module: To make a plural noun, we need to add -*s*, but we cannot add this -*s* just anywhere.

With more complex words, the number of possibilities for attaching various pieces of meaning multiplies. For example, the word *reactive* contains three pieces of meaning: *re, act,* and *ive*. Now note that *re* must come first and *ive* must come last in the word. If we switch the order of these pieces of meaning, the result is complete nonsense: **iveactre*. In fact, there are six ways these three pieces of meaning could be put together—but only one of these ways produces an actual word of English:

2.   reactive   *reiveact   *iveactre   *ivereact   *activere   *actreive

Certainly, we are not taught in school that **reiveact* or **iveactre* are impossible words of English. Nor have we ever encountered such words as we listen to the conversation of those around us. Yet we somehow sense intuitively that such words are simply not words of the language. What this finding means to a linguist is that the word formation component has rules for stringing pieces of meaning together to make words, and native speakers have tacit knowledge of these rules.

Linguists refer to the word formation component as the <u>morphological</u> component. The morphological component is detailed in Chapter 4.

The Rules of Word Order in English Exemplified

The basic sentential word order of English is Subject-Verb-Object (SVO). We interpret the noun which precedes the verb as the subject of the sentence (i.e., the 'doer') and the noun which follows the verb as the direct object (i.e., the 'done to'). If we switch the order around, as in (3a-b), we find sentences with different meanings.

3.   a.   The man killed the king.
     b.   The king killed the man.

Interestingly, while Modern English is an SVO language, this rigid word order did not always obtain. In Old English (the form of the language spoken until the end of the eleventh century) the three main elements of a sentence (S, V, and O) could occur in any of six possible orders. All of the following were perfectly acceptable sentences, and all meant precisely the same thing, as in each the man is interpreted as the killer and the king as the one who is killed:

4.   a.   [SVO]   Se   man sloh þone   kyning.
                  the   man slew the   king
                  'The man slew (i.e., killed) the king.'

b. [SOV]   Se man þone kyning sloh.
c. [OVS]   þone kyning sloh se man.
d. [OSV]   þone kyning se man sloh.
e. [VSO]   Sloh se man þone kyning.
f. [VOS]   Sloh þone kyning se man.

In (4a), the first line contains the actual words of Old English, the second line is the gloss or definition of each word, and the third line is a translation into Modern English. (This three-line format is used throughout this text.)

One thing you might notice about these examples is that there are two different words which are both glossed as the definite article 'the'. *Se* was the form which occurred with the noun that was the subject of the sentence (here, the killer); *þone* occurred with the noun that was the object (here, the one killed). The difference between *se* and *þone* reflects a difference in what linguists call morphological "case." The freedom in word order that was allowed in Old English resulted at least partially from these differences in morphological case, as speakers could identify killer and killed regardless of order of the words.

These differences between Modern English and Old English demonstrate that it's not only the words of a given language that can change over time (e.g., *se* and *þone* have disappeared from the Modern language, and both have been replaced by *the*). In fact, the rules of a given language can change over time (e.g., from "free word order" to rigid SVO). The changeability of rules over time illustrated here holds true of all living languages, though of course which rules change may be particular to a given language.

One rule that hasn't changed over time in English is the order of article and noun, as the former always precedes the latter: *the man* is fine, as was *se man;* *man the* is ungrammatical, as was *man se.*

It's also the case that we can understand sentences we've never heard before, such as the following:

5. a. Giant possums in pink velvet slippers sang in the sunshine.
    b. Colorless green ideas sleep furiously (Chomsky, 1957, 15).

Those of you who know something about possums know that some of them are big enough to qualify as "giant." But you also know that possums do not normally wear slippers (whether those slippers are made of pink velvet or not), that possums may snarl or grunt but don't sing, and that possums are nocturnal animals. Hence, slippered possums are most unlikely to sing in the sunshine. Thus, (5a) is not a sentence which would describe an event in the real world. However, it is fairly easy to imagine a scene in a fairy tale of some sort which the sentence in (5a) might accurately describe. If you can imagine such a scene, then you clearly understood (5a)—even though I'm relatively certain you have never encountered this particular string of words before.

Now think about the sentence in (5b). It shouldn't take you long to realize that (a) this sentence makes no sense at all, in the real world (or in any other world); but (b) it is still a "grammatical" sentence of English, as it follows the normal word order of the language. You can easily make up more sentences with the same word order that do make sense; cf. *Motherless black cats meow noisily; Muffler-less red cars pollute endlessly;* and so forth. Moreover, you can straightforwardly judge the following string as completely ungrammatical in English:

6.   *Green sleep furiously ideas colorless.

These last examples quite clearly demonstrate our linguistic competence in English by exemplifying both our creativity and our ability to make grammaticality judgments. What we, as speakers of English, have internalized is in large part the rules for combining words in English.

The component responsible for combining words into phrases and sentences is the syntactic component. Chapter 5 outlines a theory which accounts for a portion of the syntax of English.

The Rules of Interpretation of Phrases and Sentences in English Exemplified

Two phrases or two sentences which share the same meaning stand in what is called the paraphrase relation to each other; some examples follow:

7.   phrasal paraphrases
   a.   a bearded physics professor
   b.   a professor of physics with a beard

8.   sentential paraphrases
   a.   Homer borrowed some tools from Ned.
   b.   Ned loaned some tools to Homer.

The paraphrases in (7a-b) contain only some of the same words, as the second contains more words than the first. Note that the words which are shared by both occur in different orders; for example, *professor* occurs as the last word in (7a) but as the second word in (7b). The examples in (8a-b) have different verbs (*borrow* vs. *loan*), different prepositions (*from* vs. *to*), and different word orders (*Homer* precedes *Ned* in the first but follows *Ned* in the second). Yet, in each instance, we interpret both strings with precisely the same meaning, that is, with what philosophers of language refer to as the same "truth value."

Presumably, you had no difficulty at all in ascertaining that the phrases in (7a-b) and the sentences in (8a-b) share meaning. Now observe that this finding entails that we have tacit knowledge of not only the meaning of a given string of words, but also that we have the ability to compare different strings of words to ascertain if they have the same meaning (or different meanings)—and this is a remarkable ability indeed.

In Chapter 6, we explore the world of <u>semantics</u>, that component of the grammar devoted to the meaning of words, phrases, and sentences and to rules of interpretation.

So far, no mention has been made of what is perhaps the most salient function of our language and that is the host of communicative functions it serves. We use our language to transfer complex information; to solve complicated problems of all sorts; to cajole or persuade or order others; to ponder and discuss the meaning of events and consider their possible outcomes; to record and interpret (and perhaps re-interpret) history; to share our feelings and desires; to present a certain version of ourselves to others; and even to talk about languages and Language.

Some of these communicative functions are harnessed in this text, whose purposes include transferring complex information, solving complicated problems, and talking about languages and Language. Other linguistics courses delve into some of the other communicative functions outlined above. For instance, among other topics, socio-linguistics studies how we use our language to present a certain version of ourselves to others. Here's one simple socio-linguistic example: You decide to offer help to a stranded motorist, and you do so by saying, "Whacha need, bro?"—though you could alternatively have said "May I be of some assistance, sir?" Your choice of words in this situation is a direct reflection of the "version" of yourself you have selected to present to another individual.

The previous discussion has noted in various places that, as children, we acquire our native language effortlessly and without explicit instruction, though learning a second language as an adult can be a difficult process. This text remains silent on current theories and methodologies related to second language acquisition, leaving that for other coursework. However, because of the significance of first language acquisition to the theory of grammar we develop here, each of the following chapters concludes with a section entitled "A Note on Language Acquisition." These sections are short, in general highlighting only a few points relevant to the discussion of a given chapter, and are intended solely to whet your interest for future study.

In Chapters 2 through 6, our general task is to develop a set of analytic devices that allow us to understand part of the nature of English (but keep in mind that we use the English language as exemplar of human Language). The analytic devices, when put into a coherent whole, form (part of) a theory of Language, that is, a mental system of elements and rules needed to form and interpret linguistic expressions (words, phrases, and sentences), both familiar and novel. As noted previously, this theory of the mental system responsible for Language is what is called a grammar.

Why Study Linguistics?

The foremost reason for studying linguistics is this: It's fun! You can uncover many things you never knew that you knew about your native language, and you can discover many things about other languages that you previously knew very little about.

Linguistics makes a very useful minor, as it interacts with a host of disciplines, including but not limited to the following alphabetic list: anthropology, biology, cognitive sciences, communication sciences, computer science, drama, education, foreign language studies, history, logic, philosophy, pre-law courses, and sociology.

Linguistics helps prepare you for a range of graduate-level coursework, including not only all of the disciplines noted in the previous paragraph but also for professional programs such as library science.

Studying linguistics may open up job opportunities in the computer industry (in fields such as speech recognition, data mining, and artificial intelligence) or in education (classroom teaching of ESL or a foreign language and/or designing curricula and assessment tools). A background in Linguistics might help you find work as a translator or interpreter with the federal government or a private agency, as a technical writer or journalist in the publishing field, or as a lexicographer (one who works on developing a dictionary).

As an interesting aside, J. R. R. Tolkien was a linguist and for many years held the title *Rawlinson and Bosworth Professor of Anglo-Saxon* at Pembroke College, Oxford, though one of his first jobs was as a lexicographer for the *Oxford English Dictionary*. Tolkien went on to become the creator of Bilbo, Samwise, and Gollum—and of a host of languages, including two languages of the Elvish family, Quenya and Sindarin.

Many linguists find work in Hollywood, where studios often hire linguists to train actors, to help develop scripts, or to create whole languages. Marc Okrand, a linguist trained at the University of California, Santa Cruz, and the University of California, Berkeley, was working on the first close-captioning system for hearing impaired television viewers when he met the producer of Star Trek II. Before long, he had developed the Klingon language, complete with a dictionary, a grammar book, and an audio-tape of "conversational Klingon" recorded by Michael Dorn, the actor who played the Klingon character named Worf in the Star Trek series. Now that's fun!

KEY TERMS AND CONCEPTS

Language vs. language	descriptivist	a grammar
prescriptivist	nature	nurture
tacit knowledge	rule-governed	linguistic competence
(un-)grammatical	phonetics	phonology
morphology	syntax	semantics
	communicative functions	

CHAPTER 2

PHONETICS: THE SOUNDS
OF LANGUAGE

All human languages (except those produced by the deaf) are transmitted via sound, and we begin our scientific study of language by investigating this module of the grammar of all languages.

Linguists divide the world of sound into two major fields: Phonetics studies the individual sounds of speech, that is, those sounds which are used by humans to transmit their language. Phonology, in contrast, studies how sounds pattern together in entire systems of sounds, both within a given language and across a range of languages. We move to the world of Phonology proper in Chapter 3, after laying some groundwork in Phonetics here.

The field of phonetics is further sub-divided: Acoustic phonetics studies the physics of speech sounds by concentrating on the physical properties of speech, as sound is transmitted from one individual's mouth to another individual's ears. Auditory phonetics studies the physiological and computational processes involved as an individual's brain turns the results of the acoustic transmission into meaningful mental representations. Articulatory phonetics studies the physiological mechanisms that are related to the production of speech sounds. While both acoustic and auditory phonetics comprise extremely interesting areas of research, reasons of time and space limit our focus in this text to articulatory phonetics only.

Due to various anatomic constraints, we humans can generate only a comparatively small number of speech sounds. If we were to add up all the consonants and all the vowels produced by all the languages of the world, we'd find each would total some seven or eight dozen. These numbers may seem large to you, but they pale in comparison with the number of words in a given language. For example, while speakers of (most varieties of) English produce only about twenty-five consonants and fifteen vowels, the average high school graduate in the United States likely has a vocabulary in excess of sixty thousand words.

One way languages differ from each other is in the inventories of consonants and vowels each contains. Concomitantly, languages can differ from each other based on the sizes of these inventories. For example, some varieties of Slave (an Athabaskan language spoken in the Northwest Territories of Canada) have forty-three consonant sounds, and some varieties of

Cambodian (Mon-Khmer family) have as many as thirty vowels. In contrast, Samoan (Austronesian family) has only nine consonants and five vowels.

One way to think of the sounds of human speech is this: There is one fairly small set of sound segments available to all languages. Out of this set of universally-available sounds, each language selects a subset for its own use. As a result, many languages share speech sounds, though a particular language may have more sounds, or less sounds, or different sounds than some other language.

This state of affairs is represented very schematically in Figure 1, where the square box is meant to represent the universal set of human speech sounds and each circle is meant to represent a separate language (e.g., English, Swahili, and Cantonese). As you can see, the three circles overlap in one area, denoting that all three share at least some speech sounds. Additionally, two of the circles overlap in some areas, to the exclusion of the third circle, denoting sounds shared by two languages. Finally, each circle contains areas of non-overlap, denoting sounds which occur in that language, but not in the others.

Figure 1:   *Inventories of Speech Sounds*

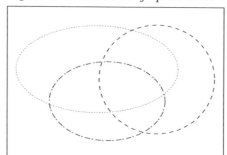

In this chapter, we focus on the sounds which occur in most varieties of American English. The material presented here may appear quite detailed and rather complex. However, this level of complex detail is necessary in order to establish a foundation in basic phonetics that is solid enough to allow you to grasp the types of phonological systems discussed in Chapter 3. We begin our phonetics discussion by considering some details of the human speech production system.

A. The Human Speech Production System

The speech production system comprises the lungs, the larynx, the pharynx, the oral cavity, and the nasal cavity, as schematized in Figure 2:

Figure 2:   *The Speech Production System*

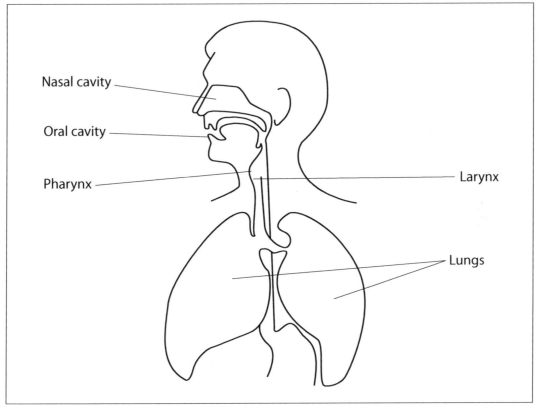

The lungs are necessary for producing speech sounds for one reason: All sound—regardless of whether it is a sound of speech or the sound of a car back-firing—consists of nothing other than a series of pressure changes or vibrations in the ambient air (i.e., the surrounding air) which occur between the source of the sound and the listener. These pressure changes in the ambient air are driven by moving air. When the sound is a car back-firing, the source of the moving air is some malfunction within the car's combustion system. When the sound is a speech sound, the moving air comes from our lungs. That is, as we produce speech sounds, we force air out of our lungs into the ambient air, thereby causing pressure changes in the ambient air.

Above the lungs lies the larynx. The larynx is composed most crucially of complexes or sets of muscles and cartilages which lie horizontally in the throat area. Informally, the larynx is sometimes referred to as the "voice box" or the "Adam's apple" (as it tends to protrude on the front of men's necks). As we speak, we constantly move the muscles and cartilages in the larynx to adjust and adapt the flow of air coming from the lungs and to assist in setting the air in motion.

Above the larynx are the pharynx (a technical term for throat), the oral cavity, and the nasal cavity, all of which operate to modify the flow of air in various ways to produce a variety of speech sounds, both consonants and vowels. The pharynx does not play a large role in the production of speech sounds in English (though it does in languages such as Arabic and Hebrew); since we are focusing on English here, we abstract away from details of the pharynx. In the following section, we consider the larynx and the oral and nasal cavities, all of which play significant roles in the production of the sounds of English.

B. Consonants

Our discussion of consonants begins with details of the functions of the larynx, followed by details of the roles of the oral and nasal cavities.

B1 The Larynx and Laryngeal States

The complexes of muscles inside the larynx are called the vocal folds (sometimes, vocal cords). You're likely quite unaware of the fact that you continuously adjust and shape your vocal folds as you speak. We can adjust our vocal folds into various shapes or positions, and two of these positions are especially significant in English.

One position used in English entails placing the vocal folds fairly close together and holding them fairly loosely, leaving only a narrow passage between them. When the air from the lungs passes through this narrow passage, it causes the lax vocal folds to vibrate. Consonants made with this laryngeal state include those which begin *vie, thy,* and *zoo.* We call such consonants voiced consonants, whose label refers to the vibration of the vocal folds.

The second position important in English entails keeping the vocal folds fairly wide apart and fairly stiff, so that the airflow from the lungs is unimpeded as it passes through a relatively wide passage. The first consonants of words such as *fie, thigh,* and *sue* are produced with this laryngeal state. Such consonants are called voiceless consonants, whose label denotes the lack of vibration of the vocal folds.

Figure 3 schematizes these two laryngeal states. These stylized drawings view the larynx from the top down, with the front of the throat at the top. The shaded areas represent the vocal folds, and the white space between them is called the glottis. The white, triangular-shaped areas at the bottom are the arytenoid cartilages, which help to spread or close the vocal folds.

Figure 3: *Laryngeal States of English*

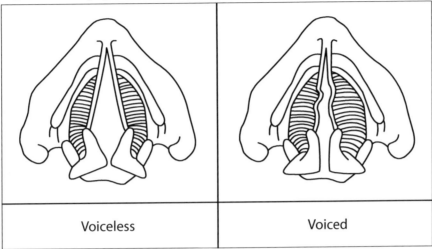

| Voiceless | Voiced |

Of course, it's quite possible to whisper when speaking English. In this event, the volume of the sound is lowered, and the vocal folds assume a third position that is neither exactly voiceless nor voiced. In so-called "whisper voice" the bands of vocal folds are held very tightly together in the front, with no space in between, but spread slightly at the back.

There is no single and simple method for students new to phonetics to learn to distinguish voiceless consonants from their voiced counterparts. Some find it helpful to hold their finger tips lightly against their throats and in this way to feel the vibrations caused by the production of voiced consonants. Other students find it helpful to close their ears with their fingers and then to repeat the given consonant sound several times. With this method, you may be able to sense the vibration caused when you produce a voiced consonant. Still other students report that they find voiced consonants to be somewhat lower in pitch than their voiceless counterparts.

There is a significant problem with the methods just mentioned: It is generally quite difficult to produce a consonant without producing a vowel at the same time. Since all vowels of English are voiced, it is easy to mistake the voicing of the vowel with that of the consonant. The only foolproof way to determine laryngeal state is to first learn a set of words which contain the relevant sounds—and to then compare the sounds in the words you know to the sounds of other words. This process obviously entails a fair amount of practice.

Whichever method you choose, keep in mind that you must pronounce the consonants you practice with out loud. If you whisper those sounds, you will be producing consonants that are neither voiceless nor voiced, and your test cannot lead to conclusive results.

Here are some further examples of voiceless and voiced consonants in English:

1.

Voiceless	Voiced
<u>p</u>all, <u>t</u>all, <u>c</u>all	<u>b</u>all, <u>d</u>oll, <u>g</u>all
<u>f</u>ace, <u>th</u>in, <u>s</u>ue, da<u>sh</u>er	<u>v</u>ase, <u>th</u>en, <u>z</u>oo, a<u>z</u>ure
<u>ch</u>ug	<u>j</u>ug
<u>h</u>ug	ba<u>m</u>, ba<u>n</u>, ba<u>ng</u>
uh<u>-</u>uh	<u>l</u>aw, <u>r</u>aw
<u>wh</u>ich	<u>w</u>itch

In all these examples, concentrate on the underlined letters, which are the focus of this discussion. Note that the hyphen between the two syllables in the word *uh-uh* (meaning 'no') is underlined. This is because the voiceless consonant which is produced here has no orthographic counterpart in English. This same sound occurs in some varieties of British English in words such as *bottle*, pronounced as *bot'l*.

Now observe that, in many varieties of English (particularly Mid-western and Eastern), *which* is pronounced with a voiceless consonant in initial position and so differs from *witch*, which begins with a voiced consonant. However, if you speak the variety of English that is most common in Southern California, you may well pronounce *which* and *witch* identically, both with voiced consonants in initial position.

Laryngeal state—the voiceless vs. voiced distinction—is one way in which consonants may differ from each other. But clearly laryngeal state is not the only way consonants may differ from each other. We easily recognize that *pall, tall,* and *call* represent three entirely different words of English, which begin with three different consonants; the fact that all three begin with voiceless consonants does not help us to differentiate them. To understand these kinds of differences in consonant sounds, we need to move above the larynx to the oral and nasal cavities. (As mentioned above, we ignore the pharynx here, as it does not play a role in the production of consonants of English.) The oral cavity contains what are sometimes referred to as organs of articulation.

B2 Organs of Articulation

To account for the differences among the voiceless consonants that begin *pall, tall,* and *call*, we need to focus on the organs of articulation inside the oral cavity. As you say these words, you should notice that producing the initial consonant of *pall* requires you to close your lips; producing the initial consonant of *tall* requires you to place the tip of your tongue against the hard, bony ridge just behind your upper front teeth; and producing the initial consonant of *call* requires you to position the back of your tongue up high in the back of the roof of your mouth.

In the sagittal (i.e., cut-away side) view of the head in Figure 4, the labels for the organs of articulation that are significant in English are circled:

Figure 4:   *Organs of Articulation*

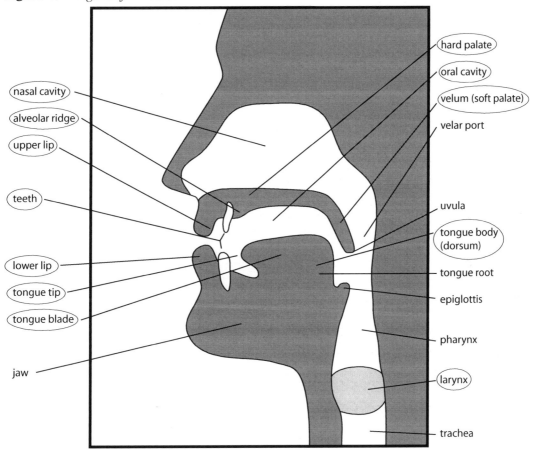

Observe that both the upper and lower lips are involved in the production of (some) speech sounds, as are the front teeth. Now, if you put your tongue against your (upper) front teeth and then draw it back a little, you'll encounter the hard, bony area known as the alveolar ridge. The word *alveolar* comes from the Latin word *alveolus* 'socket'. The alveolar ridge functions as the socket which holds your upper front teeth in place.

If you continue drawing your tongue back across the roof of your mouth, you should notice that at some point the roof of your mouth begins to feel softer, wetter, and warmer. The area between your alveolar ridge and this softer, wetter, warmer part of the roof of your mouth is the (hard) palate; and the softer, wetter, warmer part is the velum (traditionally called the soft palate).

At the very back of the velar area is the uvula; if you look at yourself in a mirror, you can see your uvula hanging down in the back of your mouth. The uvula does not play a role in the production of English sounds (though it does play a role in many languages, including French and German).

Finally, we divide the tongue into three major sections: the tip, the blade, and the dorsum (or body), all of which play important roles in the production of English consonants.

With this bit of physiology behind us, we are in position to consider what linguists refer to as the places of articulation of the consonants of English.

B3 Places of Articulation

Consonants in English are produced in one of eight places of articulation. The most common order of presentation is from the front of the oral cavity to the back, as follows:

Table 1:   *Places of Articulation in English Consonants*

Place	Produced with	Examples
Bilabial	the lower and upper lips touching each other	*pit, bit, mitt*
Labio-dental	the lower lip contacting the upper (front) teeth	*fairy, very*
Dental	the tip of the tongue contacting the bottom of the upper (front) teeth	*thought, though*
Alveolar	the tip of the tongue touching or approaching the alveolar ridge	*tip, dip, sip, zip, nip, lip, rip*
Post-alveolar	the tongue blade touching or approaching the soft palate just behind the alveolar ridge	*mission, vision, chip, gyp*
Palatal	the back of the tongue blade approaching the palate	*you*
Velar	the tongue dorsum touching the velum	*hack, hag, hang*
Glottal	only the vocal folds	*uh-uh, hat*

In other texts, you will sometimes find the labels inter-dental instead of dental and either palato-alveolar or alveo-palatal instead of post-alveolar. These terms in general represent differences in nomenclature, not differences in place of articulation.

In addition to the eight places of articulation listed above, all speakers of English have at least one consonant which is produced at two places of articulation simultaneously—the initial consonant in a word like *witch*. (If you distinguish between *witch* and *which*, then you have two consonants produced this way.) This sound is produced with the tongue dorsum approaching the velum, while the lips are rounded at the same time. This consonant sound is thus described as having a <u>labio-velar</u> place of articulation.

The eight places of articulation are schematized in Figure 5, where those places relevant to English are encircled, though labio-velar is omitted:

Figure 5:   *Places of Articulation*

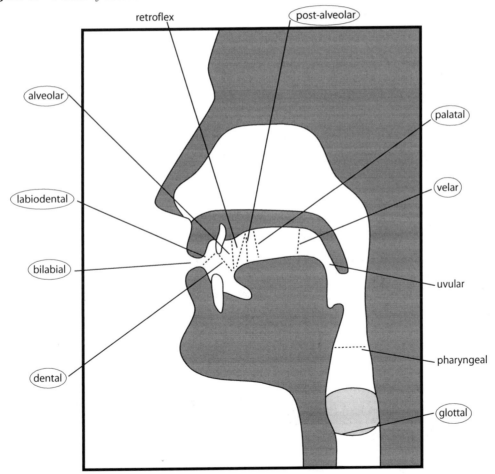

Our discussion of places of articulation has thus far focused on what are called the passive articulators. In general, passive articulators do not themselves move during the production of speech sounds. Instead, the passive articulators are those areas which the active articulators move to or toward:

- The <u>active</u> articulators include the tongue, the lower lip, and the vocal folds.
- The <u>passive</u> articulators include the upper lip, the alveolar ridge, the palate, and the velum.

A moment's reflection should suffice to clarify the difference between these two sets of articulators. For example, it's easy to move your tongue independently into quite a few positions, even though some of these positions are not used to produce speech sounds. Now try to move your alveolar ridge or your palate while holding the rest of your articulators in place; such feats are likely not attested by anyone except cartoon characters.

In terms of the active articulators, we need refer to only four categories of articulation in English: <u>Labial</u> (from the Latin word for 'lip'), in which the lower lip functions as the active articulator; <u>Coronal</u>, in which either the tip or the blade of the tongue is the active articulator; <u>Dorsal</u>, in which the tongue dorsum serves as the active articulator; and <u>Laryngeal</u>, in which only the vocal folds are classified as the active articulators. Observe that some of the active places of articulation subsume more than a single passive place of articulation, as follows:

Table 2:   *Places of Articulation: Active vs. Passive*

Active place label	Subsumes passive place label(s)
Labial	bilabial, labio-dental
Coronal	dental, alveolar, post-alveolar
Dorsal	palatal, velar
Laryngeal	glottal

(The labio-velar consonants in <u>witch</u> and <u>which</u>, as doubly-articulated consonants, are excluded from this table.)

In phonetics, we most frequently describe place of articulation in terms of the passive articulators, leading to the eight places of articulation described in Table 1. When we enter the world of phonology in Chapter 3, we will occasionally find it convenient to describe place of articulation in terms of the active articulators, as outlined in Table 2.

So far, we've discussed two dimensions through which consonants may vary: laryngeal states and places of articulation. But we need to enlarge our discussion in order to distinguish, for example, *to* from *sue* and *do* from *zoo*. The consonants of *to* and *sue* are both voiceless alveolars, and those of *do* and *zoo* are both voiced alveolars. Yet we have no difficulty in recognizing that the consonants of *to* and *sue* are very different from each other, as are those in *do* and *zoo*. The members of each of these pairs differ in what is called manner of articulation.

B4 Manner of Articulation

Manner of articulation refers to the amount or degree of closure required to produce a given consonant. This degree of closure ranges from complete closure (as in *do*), to partial closure (as in *zoo*), to approximating a closure (as in *you*). The five manners of articulation pertinent to English are detailed below.

Stops

To produce the type of consonant called a stop (technically, a plosive) requires making a complete closure of the articulators involved so that the airstream cannot escape through the mouth. The closure is often quite brief and generally followed by a rapid release of the articulators. Stops occur word-initially in *pi, buy, tie, dye, kye,* and *guy* and in the middle of the word *uh-uh*. These stops are illustrated in (2), arranged by place of articulation (from front to back).

2.

	Bilabial	*Alveolar*	*Velar*	*Glottal*
voiceless	pi	tie	kye	uh-uh
voiced	buy	dye	guy	

Observe that we find pairs of voiceless and voiced consonants in the bilabial, alveolar, and velar places of articulation: The consonants of *pi* and *buy* are both bilabial stops, produced by closing the upper and lower lips firmly together; while the vocal folds do not vibrate in *pi*, they do in *buy*. Likewise, the consonants of *tie* and *dye* are alveolar stops produced by holding the tip of the tongue firmly against the alveolar ridge; the vocal folds do not vibrate in *tie* but they do in *dye*. Similarly, the consonants of *kye* and *guy* are velar stops, produced by holding the body of the tongue against the velum; the vocal folds do not vibrate in *kye*, but they do in *guy*.

Finally, the stop in the middle of the word *uh-uh* is called the glottal stop. It is produced by drawing the vocal folds firmly together for a brief moment. Because no air can pass through the glottis, the vocal folds cannot be set in motion, and glottal stops are always voiceless.

Fricatives

Fricatives are produced by placing two articulators close enough together so that the airstream is obstructed but not completely blocked. Because the closure is partial, the airflow is continuous; thus we can describe fricatives as having a slow or delayed release (compared to the rapid release of stops). Because the partial closure leaves only a narrow space, the escaping air causes audible turbulence or friction, though the resulting noise is more obvious with some fricatives than with others.

The fricatives of English are illustrated (primarily word-initially) in (3). Note that all but the glottal fricative occur in voiceless and voiced pairs.

3.

	Labio-dental	*Dental*	*Alveolar*	*Post-alveolar*	*Glottal*
voiceless	fat	thin	sip	dasher	high
voiced	vat	then	zip	azure	

Like many languages, English has more fricatives than stops, and the fricatives occur at more places of articulation than do the stops.

Affricates

Affricates are produced as a combination of [stop + fricative]. That is, affricates are single consonants whose production begins like that of a stop but then releases into (or 'slackens' into) a fricative. As such, affricates require a complete closure followed by a slow or delayed release. English has only the two affricates shown in (4):

4.

	Post-alveolar
voiceless	chin
voiced	gin

Consonants produced with the three manners of articulation discussed above (stops, fricatives, and affricates) are grouped together as the obstruent class of consonants; the label arises since production of any of these consonants requires the vocal tract to be obstructed in some fashion.

The other class of consonants, counterparts to the obstruents, are the sonorants (nasals and approximants, detailed below). These two classes differ in three particular ways: (a) We've just seen that most of the obstruents occur in voiceless and voiced pairs; however, sonorants are most generally voiced. (b) While the obstruents always require some obstruction within the vocal tract, many of the sonorants tend to be relatively free of such obstruction. (c) As we soon see, most speakers of English allow some of the sonorant consonants—but none of the obstruent consonants—to occur in syllables with no vowel present. Thus, from both articulatory and acoustic points of view, the sonorant consonants are much more 'vowel-like' than are the obstruents.

Nasals

When we produce an oral consonant—whether voiced or voiceless and regardless of its place of articulation—we simultaneously raise the velum. In contrast, we lower the velum when we produce a <u>nasal</u> consonant. These two possibilities are schematized in Figure (6a-b) for the bilabial consonants in *buy* and *my;* the arrows point to the (raised or lowered) velum:

Figure 6:   *Production of Oral vs. Nasal Consonants*

(a)   oral consonant of *buy*   **(b)**   nasal consonant of *my*

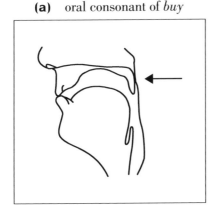 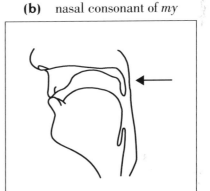

Raising the velum, as in (a), has the automatic effect of blocking off the entrance into the nasal cavity, thereby allowing the air supply to enter the oral cavity only. When the closure at the lips is released, the air supply exits through the mouth, and we recognize the consonant produced as that in *buy.*

In contrast, in (b), the velum is lowered and the entrance into the nasal cavity is opened. Thus, even without releasing the closure at the lips, air can exit through the nostrils; we recognize the resulting *hmmm* as being nasal, but we may have some difficulty in specifically identifying which nasal is being produced. If the closure at the lips is released while air is exiting through the nostrils, we easily recognize the consonant being produced as the nasal consonant in *my.*

Observe that while the nasal consonants include a continuous flow of air through the nasal cavity, they also require a simultaneous complete closure somewhere inside the oral cavity. It's the different places of closure inside the oral cavity which allow us to distinguish the three nasals of English. These nasal consonants of English are illustrated word-finally in (5). Note the nasals occur in the same places of articulation as some oral consonants, but while their oral counterparts are obstruents, the nasals are sonorants:

5.

	Bilabial	Alveolar	Velar
voiced	ta<u>m</u>	ta<u>n</u>	ta<u>ng</u>

Because nasal consonants require a complete closure within the oral cavity, we could refer to them as "nasal stops." If we did so, we would be obliged to refer to the other stops as "oral stops." Common practice is to delete one word in each of these phrases. Thus, ~~oral~~ *stop* is shortened to *stop* and *nasal* ~~stop~~ is shortened to *nasal*. In this way, the label *stop* implies that the consonant in question is produced only in the oral cavity, and the label *nasal* implies that the consonant in question is a stop.

Approximants

The second type of sonorant consonants are the approximants. With approximants, a partial closure is made within the oral tract, but this partial closure is large enough so that no friction or turbulence ever results. The approximants are split into two smaller sub-classes, the liquids and the glides.

English has two liquids, as in *law* and *raw*. Both liquids of English are voiced and both share the alveolar place of articulation. The consonant in *law* is called a lateral liquid. To produce a lateral sound, we raise the center of the tongue to create an obstruction in the center of the oral tract, and we concomitantly lower the sides of the tongue. We then release air over one side (or both sides) of the tongue, rather than along the center of the tongue, as a result of the obstruction of the airstream in the center of the oral tract. It is this lateral release (of air) that particularly distinguishes the consonant in *law*. In contrast, all other sounds of English are produced with a central release (of air).

The consonant in *raw* is called a rhotic liquid, named after the Greek letter <P> 'rho'. The production of this sound is extremely complex and may vary from speaker to speaker. We'll ignore much of this complexity here and describe this sound as a voiced alveolar rhotic liquid approximant, which (unlike its counterpart liquid in *law*) has a central release.

Glides are produced with a partial closure within the vocal tract but are articulated very rapidly and never result in any turbulence or friction. The palatal glide in *you* is produced with the tongue dorsum approaching the palate. The glide which begins *we* is more complex, as it requires having the back part of the tongue approach the velum accompanied by the simultaneous rounding of the lips. As mentioned before, this glide is doubly-articulated, and its place of articulation is labio-velar.

6.

voiced	Liquid		Glide	
	Alveolar		Palatal	Labio-velar
	lateral release	central release	you	we
	law	raw		

Some speakers (notably those who speak a Mid-western or Eastern variety of American English) also have a voiceless labio-velar glide, as in *whee*.

This concludes our discussion of the production of the consonants of English, each of which can be described uniquely through a combination of three dimensions: or features its laryngeal state (voiceless or voiced), its place of articulation (bilabial, labio-dental, dental, alveolar, post-alveolar, palatal, velar, or glottal), and its manner of articulation (stop, fricative, affricate, nasal, or approximant).

Now we need a system of symbols to work with, a system which will guarantee us a one-to-one correspondence between a given sound and the symbol we use to represent that sound. A moment's reflection shows that the orthographic system of English is incapable of achieving this goal.

Consider, for example, the word *tack,* noting that *tack* contains exactly the same sounds as do the words *act* and *cat* (though in a different order). *Tack* differs orthographically from both *act* and *cat,* as it includes the letter <k>. But clearly, the existence of this letter has no particular effect on the sound of this word; thus we also find words like *Mac* and *sac,* which end with precisely the same sound that *tack* does. This single example offers a glimpse into what can be a stumbling block for many students as they begin the scientific study of language: We all have spent many years being very carefully trained in the spelling system of English. As expert readers, we have come to believe our eyes, rather than our ears, when we think of what a given word sounds like. As a student of linguistics, you must strive to consciously remember that the words produced in human speech are in fact sequences of sounds made up of individual sound segments, regardless of what our writing system tells us.

If we consider further examples from English, our orthographic problems become even clearer. For example, a given sound may be represented by various letters; thus, the <ti> in *nation* sounds like the <s> in *sugar* and like the <ss> in *assure.* Further, a given letter may represent more than one sound. Thus, the letter <c> in *city* sounds like the letter <s> in *sit;* but the letter <c> in *cat* sounds like the letter <k> in *kit.*

To further complicate matters, a single sound is sometimes represented by a sequence of letters; consider the <th> in *thin* or the <ch> in *chin* or the <sh> in *shin*—not to mention the various sounds, all of which are single sounds, represented by the string of letters <ough> in *though, through,* and *thought.*

With a set of symbols which guarantees a one-to-one correspondence between sound and symbol, we can overcome the idiosyncrasies of English spelling, 'see' the sounds of languages whose orthographic systems differ from that of English (e.g., Chinese, Russian, and Arabic), and even represent the sounds of languages which have no writing system at all. Fortunately, an appropriate set of symbols has already been created for us.

C. The International Phonetic Alphabet

The International Phonetic Alphabet (IPA) was first developed at the end of the nineteenth century and has been revised on various occasions to add, delete, or modify symbols. It is widely used by linguists throughout the world today.

The discussion here focuses on consonant symbols for those sounds which occur in most varieties of American English and is organized by manner of articulation. The IPA symbols for the stops of English are presented below, inside square brackets:

7.

Place	*IPA*	*as in . . .*
bilabial	[p b]	pop, bob
alveolar	[t d]	tat, dad
velar	[k g]	kick, gig
glottal	[ʔ]	uh-uh, bot'l

The first thing you should notice about the symbols in (7) is that most of them look like letters of the English alphabet. But don't let this superficial appearance deceive you. While letters of the alphabet may represent more than a single sound, as does <g> in *gal* and *gel,* each IPA symbol represents only a single sound. The sound of the word-initial consonant in *gal* is the voiced velar stop represented by the IPA symbol [g]—a symbol which clearly does not represent the sound of the word-initial voiced post-alveolar affricate of *gel.*

The second thing you should notice about the symbols in (7) is that which represents the glottal stop. This symbol, [ʔ], is rather like a question mark which lacks the dot underneath.

The IPA symbols for the fricatives of English are presented in (8):

8.

Place	IPA	as in . . .
labio-dental	[f v]	fife, valve
dental	[θ ð]	bath, bathe; ether, either
alveolar	[s z]	saps, zags
post-alveolar	[ʃ ʒ]	mission, vision
glottal	[h]	hat

Again, some of the symbols resemble letters of the English alphabet; some of the other symbols have been borrowed from the writing systems of other languages. The symbol for the dental fricative [θ] was borrowed from the Greek letter <θ> 'theta'. The symbol [ð] was borrowed from the Old English alphabet; this character goes by several names, with 'eth' being among the most frequently used. The IPA symbols for the post-alveolar fricatives [ʃ] and [ʒ] are called 'elongated s' and 'elongated z', respectively.

The IPA symbols for the affricates of English are shown in (9):

9.

Place	IPA	as in . . .
post-alveolar	[tʃ ʤ]	church, judge

The affricates [tʃ, ʤ] appear as complex symbols made up of two parts: [stop + fricative], a representation which denotes their manner of articulation. But do not let this representation lead you astray, as the symbol for each affricate denotes only a single sound.

Those who have been paying close attention will notice that, when consonants appear in pairs, the one on the left is always voiceless. This convention has been widely adopted by linguists throughout the world and is employed throughout this text.

The symbols in (7), (8), and (9) above, comprise the set of IPA symbols for the obstruents of English. Those for the sonorant consonants follow, with symbols for nasals and approximants presented in (10) and (11), respectively.

10.

Place	IPA	as in . . .
bilabial	[m]	mom
alveolar	[n]	none
velar	[ŋ]	King Kong

11.

Liquids			Glides		
Place	IPA	as in . . .	Place	IPA	as in . . .
alveolar	[l]	lull	palatal	[j]	yoyo
alveolar	[ɹ]	roar	labio-velar	[w̥ w]	whether, weather

Three symbols in these tables may seem unusual to you: First, the velar nasal [ŋ], called 'engma', is often <ng> orthographically. The IPA symbol can be thought of as combining these two letters into a single character.

Second, the rhotic liquid [ɹ] looks like an upside-down letter <r>, but it must not be confused with [r], which is the IPA symbol for a trill. Trills (often heard in varieties of English spoken in Scotland, as well as in Spanish words such as *perro* 'dog') are produced by vibrating the tip of the tongue against the alveolar ridge, an action which does not produce the rhotic liquid symbolized as [ɹ].

Third, the open circle under the voiceless labio-velar glide is one type of <u>diacritic</u>, a small symbol added to an existing IPA symbol to alter or narrow the features it represents. The open circle diacritic denotes that the ordinarily voiced glide is voiceless.

Finally, observe carefully that the IPA symbol for the palatal glide looks like letter <j>; don't let this confuse you, as letter <j> in English rarely, if ever, sounds like IPA [j].

We can pull all of the IPA symbols presented in this section into a single consonant chart, as shown below, where brackets and some labels are omitted for convenience:

Table 3: *The Consonant Chart of English* (passive articulators)

	bilabial	labiodental	dental	alveolar	post-alveolar	palatal	velar	glottal
stop	p b			t d			k g	ʔ
fricative		f v	θ ð	s z	ʃ ʒ			h
affricate					tʃ ʤ			
nasal	m			n			ŋ	
liquid				l , ɹ				
glide	(w̥ w)					j	w̥ w	

This consonant chart observes various conventions which all linguists follow:

- The <u>columns</u> depict the places of articulation (in terms of passive articulators), from front to back.
- The <u>rows</u> depict the obstruents (stops, fricatives, and affricates) and then the sonorants (nasals, liquids, and glides).
- When pairs of consonants appear in a single <u>cell</u> and are not separated by a comma, the one on the left is voiceless.
- The liquids [l] and [ɹ] appear in the same cell, but the comma separating them denotes that the two do not differ in laryngeal status (both are voiced); the comma is simply a typographic convenience that allows us to collapse the lateral and the rhotic into a single cell (instead of taking up two entire rows).
- Finally, the labio-velar glides [w̥, w] are entered in both the velar and bilabial columns to denote their double articulation.

If we were to present the same consonants in a chart which focused on the active articulators instead of the passive articulators, we'd find the somewhat simpler chart presented below:

this is the table you look for phonology

Table 4: *English Consonant Chart; Active Articulators*

	Labial (lower lip)	Coronal (tongue tip, blade)	Dorsal (tongue body)	Laryngeal (vocal folds)
stop	p b	t d	k g	ʔ
fricative	f v	θ ð s z ʃ ʒ		h
affricate		tʃ ʤ		
nasal	m	n	ŋ	
liquid		l, ɹ		
glide	(w̥ w)		j w̥ w	

While phonetics most commonly relies on consonant charts expressed in terms of the passive articulators, the world of phonology more often relies on charts expressed in terms of the active articulators. In passing, note that English has more sounds produced in the Coronal area than in any other place of articulation, a fact also true of many of the world's languages.

Before leaving this discussion, we consider two further facts about consonants in English. First, many speakers of English sometimes allow certain consonants to function like a vowel by serving as the nucleus of a syllable. In such instances, there is no discernible vowel produced. However, the consonants which are so privileged are restricted to the liquids and two of the nasals. Consider these words, where the syllabic consonants are indicated by adding a diacritic (a short straight line) underneath the regular IPA symbol:

12.

funnel	bird	button	rhythm
funn[l̩]	b[ɹ̩]d	butt[n̩]	rhyth[m̩]

A second interesting point about English consonants is that, sometimes, the voiceless stops are produced with aspiration. Informally, aspiration is often defined as a noticeable puff of air that exits from the oral cavity. Technically, aspiration results from the brief delay in voicing between the release of the voiceless stop and the onset of voicing on the immediately following voiced vowel. To denote an aspirated consonant, we add a superscript [^{h}] to the regular IPA symbol.

The phenomenon of aspiration in English is restricted to only those voiceless stops which occur at the beginning of stressed syllables, as illustrated in these examples for each of [p, t, k]:

13.

a	[p^h]ill	s[p]ill	*s[p^h]ill	[p^h]aper	*pa[p^h]er
b	[t^h]ill	s[t]ill	*s[t^h]ill	[t^h]otal	*to[t^h]al
c	[k^h]ill	s[k]ill	*s[k^h]ill	[k^h]ookie	*coo[k^h]ie

We consider the details of such rule-governed behavior in the Phonology chapter.

D. The Vowels of English

Unlike consonants, all vowels are characterized by being produced with a free flow of air through the oral cavity. Vowels in English, and in most other languages, are generally voiced and are the most sonorous of all human speech sounds.

Three major features are used to describe vowels: (a) the height of the body of the tongue; (b) the backness of the tongue within the oral cavity; and (c) the roundness of the lips. To begin to understand the importance of these features, say the words *heat, hate,* and *hat* slowly, focusing on the vowels. You should notice that your tongue is high and close to your palate when you say *heat,* that it moves down some when you say *hate,* and that it moves even further down when you say *hat.* You'll likely also notice that your jaw becomes progressively lower and lower as you say these words. This follows naturally, since your tongue is directly connected to your jaw. We call the vowel in *heat* a high vowel, the vowel in *hate* a mid vowel, and the vowel in *hat* a low vowel.

Now say *hat* and *hot,* again focusing on the vowels in each. You should notice that, while your tongue may feel like it's bunched up in the front of your mouth when you say *hat,* this 'front-bunchiness' is missing when you say *hot,* and instead it feels like your tongue moves to the back of your mouth. We call the vowel in *hat* a front vowel and the vowel in *hot* a back vowel.

Finally, say the words *heat* and *hoot.* You should immediately notice that your lips are spread when you say *heat* but quite rounded when you say *hoot.* We call the vowel in *heat* unround and the vowel in *hoot* round.

Figure 7 illustrates the different positions of the tongue for the three different vowels of English that occur in the words *he, hah,* and *who;* the IPA symbols for these vowels ([i], [ɑ], and [u], respectively) are also shown here.

Figure 7: *The vowels [i], [a], and [u]*

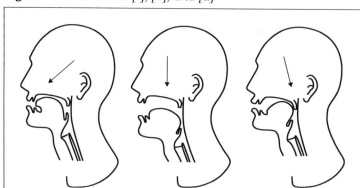

In the vowel [i], as in *he,* the tongue is high in the oral cavity and approaches the hard palate; hence, we describe the vowel in *he* as a high, front vowel. In the vowel [a] of *hah,* the tongue is very low in the oral cavity and approaches the pharyngeal wall. We describe the vowel in *hah* as a low, back vowel. In the vowel [u], as in *who,* the tongue is quite high in the oral cavity and approaches the velar area. Note that the lips protrude slightly when saying *who;* this is the direct effect of lip rounding. Hence, we describe the vowel in *who* as a high, back, round vowel. For completeness, we should also add the feature 'unround' to both the high front vowel in *he* and the low back vowel in *hah.*

English of course has more vowels than just those already mentioned. We'll consider first the five front vowels of the language, and then add the five back vowels and two central vowels. The front vowels, along with their IPA symbols and some sample words, are shown below:

14.

	IPA	*as in . . .*
high	i	heed, heat, mete
	ɪ	hid, hit, myth
mid	e	hayed, hate, save, paid
	ɛ	head, bed, said, epsilon
low	æ	had, hat, have, ash

Several example words in each row have been included to reinforce the difference between English orthography, which is inconsistent when it comes to representing sound, and IPA symbols, which always guarantee a one-to-one correspondence between sound and symbol.

Several of the symbols in (14) are familiar to you; if you are literate in Spanish, the sounds of some of these symbols will also be familiar to you. If you are a native speaker of English, you must be sure to remember that the IPA symbol which looks like letter <i> sounds like the vowel in *heat*. Likewise, the IPA symbol which looks like letter <e> sounds like the vowel in *hate*.

Other symbols in (14) are less familiar. What looks rather like an upper-case <I> (but is really a small cap), is the IPA symbol for the vowel in *hit*. What looks like the Greek letter <ε> is in fact a lower-case 'epsilon'; and it represents the sound in the first vowel in the word *epsilon*. Finally, the IPA symbol [æ] comes from the Old English alphabet; its name is 'ash' and it represents the vowel sound in the word *ash*.

Here are IPA symbols for the five back vowels of (many varieties of) English:

15.

	IPA	*as in . . .*
high	u	hoot, booed, jute
	ʊ	hood, book, put
mid	o	hope, boat, hoed, bowl
	ɔ	hawk, caught, bawdy
low	ɑ	hock, cot, body

The IPA symbol for the high back vowel in *hoot* looks like the English letter <u> and is always produced with a great deal of lip rounding. The IPA symbol [ʊ] also represents a high back vowel, but one produced with somewhat less lip rounding than required of [u]. IPA [o] sounds much like the letter <o> is often (but not invariantly) pronounced in English.

The mid back vowel symbolized [ɔ], which looks like a backward letter <c>, is called 'open-o'. Most speakers of the Southern California variety of English have collapsed this mid back vowel with the low back vowel [ɑ]. If you have the same pronunciation for pairs of words such as *hawk* and *hock,* or *caught* and *cot,* or *bawdy* and *body,* then you have lost [ɔ] and replaced it with [ɑ]. Those who speak Mid-western or Eastern varieties of English tend to retain both vowels.

While none of the front vowels of English is round (produced with rounding the lips), all of the back vowels are round—except for the low back vowel [ɑ]. Thus, we can make a generalization about the vowels of English in the form of an implicational statement: If a vowel is round, it must be back. Our generalization is only a one-way implicational statement, as its opposite (If a vowel is back, it must be round) is false.

English also has two central vowels, that is, vowels which are produced neither very far in the front nor very far in the back:

16.

	IPA	*as in . . .*
mid	ʌ	jump, <u>o</u>ven, h<u>u</u>bba
	ə	sof<u>a</u>, ov<u>e</u>n, hubb<u>a</u>

These two vowels—[ʌ] 'wedge' and [ə] 'schwa'—sound the same. The difference between them relates to the stress system of English: Wedge occurs in stressed syllables (including one-syllable words pronounced in isolation; e.g., *jump*). In contrast, schwa occurs only in stressless syllables; you'll find that every vowel-letter of the English alphabet may sometimes be pronounced as schwa (e.g., sof<u>a</u>, ov<u>e</u>n, Phil<u>i</u>p, catastr<u>o</u>phe, fill-<u>u</u>p (noun), and sometimes s<u>y</u>llabic).

We can pull all the vowels discussed so far into one vowel chart, as follows:

Table 5:   *English Vowel Chart*

	front	central	back
high	i		u
	ɪ		ʊ
mid	e		o
	ɛ	ʌ, ə	ɔ
low	æ		ɑ

While we have sufficient features to distinguish between the two mid central vowels (based on stress patterns), and between the two low vowels (based on backness), we do not have features sufficient to distinguish four pairs of vowels: the two high front, the two mid front, the two high back, and the two mid back. Since we differentiate the vowels of *beat* and *bit*, and those of *bait* and *bet*, for example, we need to add another feature to our set in order to describe the differences between these pairs.

The feature most frequently used classifies each of the non-low, non-central vowels of English as being either <u>tense</u> or <u>lax</u>:

- The tense vowels are [i, e, u, o].
- The lax vowels are [ɪ, ɛ, ʊ, ɔ].

One way these two sets of vowels differ is that the tense vowels take a longer amount of time to produce than do the lax vowels; that is, the vowels in *beat* [bit], *bait* [bet], *boot* [but], and *boat* [bot] are longer (in time) than are the vowels in *bit* [bɪt], *bet* [bɛt], *book* [bʊk], and *bought* [bɔt], respectively.

Additionally, some linguists have argued that the tense vowels are produced with a 'stiffening' of the tongue, which may cause the tip of the tongue to be pushed against the back of the bottom front teeth. The lax vowels, in contrast, are produced with a relaxation of the tongue (compared to the tense vowels). If you practice saying these pairs of vowels in tense-lax order (e.g., [e] vs. [ɛ]), you may feel your tongue moving back from your front teeth as you produce the lax vowel; and if you practice saying pairs of words such as *bait* and *bet,* you may notice that the (tense) vowel in the first word takes more time to say than does the (lax) vowel in the second word.

We could modify our vowel chart to add the tense/lax labels. However, we adopt a simpler convention here: When (non-low, non-central) vowels appear in pairs, the one on the top is tense.

The vowels illustrated in Table 3 are all 'simplex' vowels (technically referred to as <u>monophthongs</u>). English also has a series of <u>diphthongs</u>, complex vowels which consist of two vowels, produced one after the other but in a very rapid sequence. These are exemplified below:

17.

IPA	*as in . . .*
aɪ	high, hi, aisle, my
aʊ	how, now, brown, cow
ɔɪ	hoist, joy

Because diphthongs by definition involve movement (from the position of one vowel to that of another), they are usually omitted from vowel charts, as vowel charts serve to relate position rather than movement.

Although the diphthong [aɪ] is disappearing from the inventory of some speakers of Southern English, the diphthongs in (17) do occur in most varieties of American English. It's also the case that many speakers of American English often diphthongize the mid tense vowels; in such varieties, [e] may be diphthongized to [eɪ] and [o] may be diphthongized to [oʊ].

We have now developed two different sets of features—one set for consonants, the other set for vowels—so that we can uniquely describe the sounds of most varieties of English. We have also adopted a set of symbols—those of the International Phonetic Alphabet—to guarantee a one-to-one correspondence between sound and symbol. If we were to extend our discussion beyond English, we would need to extend our set of IPA symbols. We will be extending our discussion in just this way in the next chapter as we consider the distribution of sounds in various languages, and we will introduce additional IPA symbols as necessary. The full set of IPA symbols used for the world's languages is presented in Table 6 below:

Table 6:   *The International Phonetic Alphabet*
(updated 1996; adapted from Ladefoged 2001)

	Consonants										
	Labial		Coronal				Dorsal			Laryngeal	
	bilabial	labio-dental	dental	alveolar	post-alveolar	retro-flex	palatal	velar	uvular	pharyn-geal	glottal
plosive	p b			t d		ʈ ɖ	c ɟ	k g	q ɢ		ʔ
implosive	ɓ			ɗ			ʄ	ɠ	ʛ		
ejective	p'			t'			k'				
trill	ʙ			r					ʀ		
tap or flap				ɾ		ɽ					
fricative	ɸ β	f v	θ ð	s z	ʃ ʒ	ʂ ʐ	ç ʝ	x ɣ	χ ʁ	ħ ʕ	h ɦ
lateral fricative				ɬ ɮ							
affricate	pf			ts dz	tʃ dʒ		tɕ dʑ				
nasal	m			n		ɳ	ɲ	ŋ	N		
central approximant		ʋ		ɹ		ɻ	j	ɰ			
lateral approximant				l		ɭ	ʎ	L			
labio-velar approximant	(ʍ w)							ʍ w			

When symbols appear in pairs, the one on the left is voiceless.

Vowels					
Front		Central		Back	
unround	round	unround	round	unround	round

	Front unround	Front round	Central unround	Central round	Back unround	Back round
High	i	y	ɨ	ʉ	ɯ	u
	ɪ	Y				ʊ
Mid	e	ø	ə , ʌ		ɤ	o
	ɛ	œ				ɔ
Low	æ		a		ɑ	ɒ

When symbols appear in pairs, the one on the top is tense;
when symbols are separated by a comma, the one on the left is stressless.

E. Suprasegmentals

The term "suprasegmental" refers to phenomena whose affect is deemed to be above the level of individual sound segments. A variety of suprasegmental phenomena show up in the world's languages, though not all occur in every language. In this section, we briefly discuss length (of vowels and/or consonants) and various prosody effects that show up in different languages.

E1 Length

One phenomenon that frequently occurs cross-linguistically involves the length of individual segments, either consonants or vowels, as each may show up as short or long in time. As a rule of thumb, long vowels and long consonants take about twice as much time to pronounce as do their short counterparts.

In some languages, the difference between long and short vowels can create meaning distinctions between words. For example, consider the following sentence of Cambodian, noting that the difference between the verb 'catch' and the noun 'bird' is only the length of the vowel [a].

18. tʃmaa   tʃap   tʃaap.
     cat   catch   bird
     'The cat caught a bird.'

Here, I've indicated the long vowel in *ʧaap* 'bird' by showing the vowel twice; alternatively, sometimes colons are used to show length: [ʧaːp]. English has no words equivalent to Cambodian's *ʧap* and *ʧaap*, which differ from each other only by the length of the vowel.

However, most native speakers of English sense that the vowels in the words in (19a) take a longer amount of time to say than do the vowels in the words in (19b):

19.

a	cab	bead	rag	leave	his	edge
b	cap	beat	rack	leaf	hiss	etch

The difference in vowel duration here relates to the fact that the vowels in (19a) are followed by voiced obstruents, but those in (19b) are followed by voiceless obstruents. It is the case that most speakers of English routinely produce long vowels, whether tense or lax, when those vowels occur before voiced obstruents, as in the examples in (19a). As a result, we feel that the vowel in *cab* is longer than the vowel in *cap* and the vowel in *bead* is longer than the vowel in *beat*. It turns out that for most speakers the vowel in *bee* (with no following consonant of any sort) is roughly the same length as the vowel in *bead*. Thus it appears that what is reflected in (19b) is in fact shortening of the vowels when they precede a voiceless obstruent, rather than lengthening of the vowels when they precede a voiced obstruent, as in (19a).

Some languages have both short and long consonants, so that the length of a given consonant can create meaning distinctions between words in the language. In a word which has a long consonant, the same consonant occurs at the end of one syllable and at the beginning of the immediately following syllable and so is pronounced twice. Such long consonants are called geminates (from the Latin word for 'twin'). Geminate consonants are exemplified below in Italian, Arabic, and Japanese:

20.

a	Italian	[nono] 'ninth'	[nonno] 'grandfather'
b	Arabic	[darasa] 'studied'	[darrasa] 'taught'
c	Japanese	[saka] 'slope'	[sakka] 'author'

English apparently lacks geminates inside simple words; certainly English lacks pairs of words which differ only by the length of a given consonant, thus differing from the languages cited in (20). But in conversation, we produce strings of words. As a result a given consonant may occur at the end of one word and also at the beginning of the following word. In such instances, we speakers of English, particularly in rapid speech, tend to delete one of the identical consonants in series, a process known as <u>degemination</u>:

21.

		careful speech	*rapid speech*
a	rat tail	[ɹæt tel]	[ɹætel]
b	milkcrate	[mɪlk kɹet]	[mɪlkɹet]
c	house sale	[haʊs sel]	[haʊsel]

While we can produce what would amount to geminate consonants in such examples, we usually don't. Instead, we degeminate the consonant, producing a single sound instead of two.

E2 Prosody

Several phenomena can be grouped under the general rubric of <u>prosody</u>, a term which denotes what are traditionally referred to as variations in loudness and pitch (at either the word level or the sentence level). We'll consider each phenomenon separately.

Stress

The perceptual term "loudness" relates to what linguists call <u>stress</u>. English is a so-called stress language, meaning that we assign varying degrees of stress to individual syllables within a given word. The amount of stress assigned to a given syllable is always relative (to that assigned to other syllables), and is never absolute. One result is that we can stress individual syllables when we are screaming as well as when we are whispering. Speakers of English make very good use of stress assignment to distinguish both syntactic categories and certain constructions in the language.

Consider, for example, words such as *subject, permit, record,* and *increase* and try to determine their syntactic category (i.e., their part of speech, in traditional terms). This task is in fact impossible to carry out when such words are presented in isolation in their written forms. But if their stress patterns are marked in some way, the task becomes straightforward. In (22), the stressed syllables are underlined:

22.

a	<u>sub</u>ject	<u>per</u>mit	<u>rec</u>ord	<u>in</u>crease
b	sub<u>ject</u>	per<u>mit</u>	re<u>cord</u>	in<u>crease</u>

Given the stress assignment shown in (22), it's easy to see that the words in (a) are nouns while those in (b) are verbs. In the sentences below, the first italicized word is a verb and the second a noun. You can see just how crucial stress assignment is in the language if you try to say these sentences out loud while stressing the wrong syllable in the italicized words (the appropriately-stressed syllable is underlined):

23. a. The king always *subjects* his *subjects* to excessive taxes.
     b. As a game warden, I will *permit* you to have a fishing *permit*.

The English stress system also helps us to distinguish compound words from phrases. A compound word has two parts, each of which can be an independent word; the meaning of the compound is often greater or more complex than the simple sum of its parts. For example, a *highchair* is a seat generally restricted for use by infants, rather than simply a chair that is high in some way. In contrast, the meaning of most phrases is strictly compositional, such that the meaning of the phrase is equivalent to the sum of its parts.

Now consider the following examples, where the stress assigned to those in (24a) identifies them as compound words, while the stress assigned to those in (24b) identifies them as phrases:

24.

a	hot dog	green house	wet suit	dark room
b	hot dog	green house	wet suit	dark room

The examples in (24b) can be paraphrased as 'a dog that is hot', ' a house that is green', 'a suit that is wet', and 'a room that is dark', respectively. That is, each consists of a noun plus a modifier of that noun, and the meaning of each is equivalent to the sum of its parts. But those in (24a) have more complex, often idiosyncratic meanings: a sausage, a building designed for growing plants, a special piece of clothing worn by those who swim in cold waters, and an area for developing film, respectively.

You likely had no trouble at all in determining that *subject* is a noun while *subject* is a verb, or that you'd rather have a *hot dog* for lunch than a *hot dog*. Consequently, these examples clearly demonstrate not only that stress is crucial in English but also that you have a great deal of tacit knowledge of the language's sound system.

Tone

While English is a stress language, other languages are tonal languages. Tone is perceptually related to relative pitch (at the word level). The term "relative pitch" here entails the fact that different speakers have different ranges of pitch available to them; for example, the pitch range of young children is generally much higher than that of older adults, particularly men. Consequently, tones are 'relative' to a given speaker, rather than absolute in a given language.

Many languages of Southeast Asia, Africa, and the Americas are tonal languages, though as we soon discover, the effects of tone may vary rather significantly across languages.

Mandarin Chinese has four tones, described as high level, high rising, falling-rising, and high-falling, as demonstrated, respectively, in the data below. Diacritics have been added above the vowels to reflect the various tones:

25. [mā] 'mother' [má] 'hemp' [mǎ] 'horse' [mà] 'scold'

The important point here is that each of these four words contains precisely the same segments of sound: [m] and [a], but the tonal differences produce four different words. If you are interested in hearing these words, you can investigate this link to the UCLA Phonetics Lab:

http://hctv.humnet.ucla.edu/departments/linguistics/VowelsandConsonants/vowels/chapter2/chinese/recording2.1.html

While many people assume that 'Chinese' is a single language with several (geographic) dialects, tonal systems can be used to show that, in fact, the differences between two varieties may be quite significant. For example, while Mandarin has the four tones outlined above, Cantonese has the nine tones schematized below. Because of the complexity of the Cantonese system, diacritics are usually eschewed in favor of simple descriptions. Observe that all of the words in (26a) consist of the same segments ([s] and [i]), but differ in tone; the tones exemplified in (26b) are the so-called 'checked' tones, which occur in syllables with short vowels and a following consonant, which may be one of the three voiceless stops [p, t, k]:

26.

	high falling	[si] 'poetry'	low falling	[si] 'time'			
a	high rising	[si] 'send'	low rising	[si] 'market'			
	high level	[si] 'try'	low level	[si] 'affairs'			
b	high	[sɪk] 'know'	mid	[sɛk] 'lead'	low	[sɪk] 'eat'	

Many tonal languages spoken in Africa exhibit a phenomenon known as <u>downdrift</u> (or tone downstepping). Most of these languages have only two tones: high (e.g., [á]) and low (e.g., [à]). When downdrift occurs, low tones remain at the same pitch throughout an utterance, but high tones become progressively lower, syllable-by-syllable. Downdrift is demonstrated below with a sentence from Akan (a Niger-Congo language spoken primarily in Ghana). While the sentence in (27) was undoubtedly contrived specifically to show the effect of downdrift, it is still a perfectly good sentence in Akan. You can see the high tones becoming progressively lower in

Figure 8, where the term "citation tone" refers to the tone that would show up if the word were produced in isolation.

27. pàpá kòfí rìfré nì bá kwàbìná
     father Kofi calls his son Kwabena
     'Father Kofi is calling his son Kwabena.'

Figure 8:   *Schematization of Downdrift in Akan*

syllable	pà	pá	kò	fí	rì	fré	nì	bá	kwà	bì	ná
		—									
				—							
						—					
								—			
											—
	—		—		—		—		—	—	
citation tone	L	H¹	L	H²	L	H³	L	H⁴	L	L	H⁵

In isolation, all high tones would be produced at the same pitch (by a given individual); but in context, the effects of downdrift cause the high tones to become successively lower, as schematized in Figure 8.

Intonation

While tone is the use of pitch to convey meaning at the level of the word, <u>intonation</u> is the use of pitch to convey meaning at the sentence or discourse level. The speakers of all languages can employ different patterns of intonation for expressing a whole range of information, including emphasis, surprise, emotion (e.g., empathy vs. loathing), irony, humor, and so forth.

Consider for instance the difference in emphasis in these sentences, both of which contain the same words in the same order:

28. a. That │child│ stole an apple.

     b. That child stole an │ap│ple.

In (28a), the highest pitch in the utterance is on the word *child,* thereby putting emphasis on that word; but in (28b), the highest pitch occurs on the first syllable of the word *apple.* Even though both utterances contain the same words, the different patterns of intonation lead us to feel that the speaker of (a) intends to convey something different than does the speaker of (b): The speaker of (a) is emphasizing (or talking about) the child, while the speaker of (b) is emphasizing (or talking about) the apple.

It's also the case that many languages (including English) use different patterns of intonation to signal the statement-question distinction. For example, intonation tends to go down at the end of declarative sentences in English, denoted below by the downward pointing arrows:

29. a. I stepped in a mud puddle. ↓
     b. That child stole an apple. ↓

With such falling pitch, these sentences are invariantly interpreted as simple statements (of fact). Now consider what happens when the pitch raises dramatically at the end of each:

30. a. You stepped in what? ↺
     b. That child stole what? ↺

Even though the utterances in (30) have the form of statements, they are interpreted as a certain kind of question, called an <u>echo question</u>. Echo questions are not simple requests for information; instead, they frequently repeat in part a previous speaker's statement. In this way, (30a-b) could be felicitously uttered by a second speaker immediately after a first speaker had uttered (29a-b), respectively.

In contrast, questions which are requests for content generally have downward intonation patterns in English, thus patterning with statements of fact:

31. a. What did you step in? ↓
     b. What did that child steal? ↓

But questions which request a "yes" or "no" answer generally end with rising intonation, though the rise is not as dramatic as in the echo questions in (30) above:

32. a. Did you step in a mud puddle? ↑
     b. Did that child steal an apple? ↑

One of the more interesting intonational patterns employed by many speakers of English (and of a range of other languages also) has been called <u>motherese</u>. Motherese is often spoken to babies and infants and is notable for both its use of short, simple words and its "cooing" intonation pattern. This "cooing" pattern is characterized by an overall high pitch that is frequently punctuated with pronounced variations in pitch. If you can picture a happy mother bending over her baby while saying, "Oh, what a good boy you are!", then you have an idea of what motherese sounds like.

Some adults extend the use of motherese and employ the "cooing" pattern when talking to their pets or to other adults; these instances are usually seen as a form of affection or intimacy. But some adults may employ the motherese pattern when talking to other adults in order to bully, patronize, or insult the other. Consider what the sentence cited in the previous paragraph might convey when spoken by an angry woman to her husband, who had once again failed in his promise to take out the trash. In Chapter 6, we discuss further cases where the meaning we intend to convey extends well beyond the sum of the words we use.

This ends our technical discussion of the phonetics of English. You may well find it necessary to return to some of the details presented here when we delve into phonology proper in the next chapter. Before we move into phonology, we consider a few key facts about the child's ability to perceive the sounds of her native language.

F.   A Note on Language Acquisition

One of the most amazing things about language acquisition is how early the process begins. In the early 1970s, researchers (e.g., Eimas, Siqueland, Jusczyk, and Vigorito 1971) demonstrated that four-week old infants perceive the difference between the consonants in the syllables [pɑ] and [bɑ], even though these sounds differ only in their laryngeal status.

The earliest experimental paradigm used to test infant perception of human speech sounds is called high amplitude sucking, a paradigm which avails itself of a well-attested attribute of infants: When infants are interested in something, their rate of sucking on a pacifier increases; but infants who are bored suck less frequently.

To test sucking rate, Eimas et al. connected a pacifier to a sound-generating mechanism, so that a particular syllable—say [pɑ]—was produced every time the infant sucked. When the infants first heard this particular syllable, they sucked on their pacifiers frequently, in the process generating more repetitions of the syllable. After a period of time, however, the infants became bored with the repetition, and their sucking rates decreased. But as soon as the syllable changed from [pɑ] to [bɑ], sucking rates increased rather dramatically—until of course the infants became bored with the repetition of [bɑ].

The most reasonable account of the change in the rates of sucking is simply that the infants in fact perceived the difference between [pɑ] and [bɑ].

So the interesting question now becomes whether infants have a hard-wired, built-in language faculty which allows them to discriminate between such sounds or whether they have attained this knowledge through exposure to their native language.

The former hypothesis can be tested by using sounds which do not occur in the language of the infants in a given study. To this end, Werker, Gilbert, Humphrey, and Tees (1981) tested infants growing up in monolingual English environments against sounds of Hindi (an Indo-European language of India) and Thompson (a Salish language of British Columbia). In all instances, the sounds used consisted of a consonant plus a vowel (i.e., CV syllables).

Two pairs of sounds from Hindi were used: retroflex [ʈɑ] vs. alveolar [tɑ] and voiced aspirated [dʰɑ] vs. voiceless aspirated [tʰɑ]; neither the retroflex not the voiced aspirated stop occurs in English. (Retroflex sounds are produced by curling the tip of the tongue up and back so that the underside touches or approaches the back part of the alveolar ridge.)

The sounds from Thompson were a pair of voiceless ejectives, velar [k'i] vs. uvular [q'i]. Ejectives are a type of stop produced by holding the vocal folds tightly together while making a simultaneous closure within the vocal tract; then pulling the larynx upward, thereby compressing the air in the pharynx; and finally forcefully ejecting the air trapped within the oral cavity. Ejective sounds are produced only irregularly in English (those speakers who do produce them tend to do so in word-final position when speaking very emphatically, as in *definitely not!*)

The infants in these (high amplitude sucking) experiments had no trouble discriminating between the sounds in any of these sets, even though at least one sound in each pair never occurred in their language-learning environment. Werker et al. concluded that their results confirm the hypothesis that we humans are born fully-equipped with the ability to acquire language; that is, it is our brains—not our experience(s)—which are responsible for our language-learning abilities.

While very young infants consistently excel at discriminating sounds from non-native languages, adults do not have this same advantage. Any of you who have studied a foreign language in college appreciate just how difficult such discrimination between unfamiliar sounds can be.

It turns out that this extraordinary ability dissipates rapidly: While four-week old infants are quite good at such cross-language discrimination, Werker et al. found that most infants lose this ability by the time they reach twelve months of age. That is, by the time infants are a year old, they behave like the adult speakers of their language; while they are perfectly able to discriminate among the sounds of the language spoken around them, they can no longer discriminate non-native contrasts.

On many accounts, this loss is characterized as "active forgetting." Active forgetting entails that we somehow reorganize our brains so that we can block out those sounds which do not occur in our native language. Apparently, "forgetting" allows us to focus our attention on precisely those sounds which have value in our own language—but on no other sounds. It also seems apparent that the sounds which have been "forgotten" in this way are difficult for many of us to recover.

KEY TERMS AND CONCEPTS

Consonant Features
Laryngeal states: voiced, voiceless
Active articulators: lower lip, tongue, vocal folds
Passive articulators: upper lip, upper teeth, alveolar ridge, palate, velum
Places of articulation: (Labial) bilabial, labio-dental; (Coronal) dental, alveolar,
    post-alveolar; (Dorsal) palatal, velar; (Laryngeal) glottal; and labio-velar
Manners of articulation: (obstruent) stop, fricative, affricate; and (sonorant) nasal,
    approximant (lateral and rhotic liquids, glide)

Vowel Features

height of tongue	backness of tongue	roundness of lips
stressed vs. stressless	tense vs. lax	monophthong
	diphthong	

Prosody Terms

length	stress	intonation	tone	downdrift

PRACTICE PROBLEMS

1. For each pair of words, select the one which <u>ends</u> in a *voiceless* consonant sound:

    a. his/hiss   b. fuss/fuzz   c. bath/bathe   d. edge/etch
    e. beds/bets   f. walked/jogged   g. light/lied   i. wick/wig

2. For each set, select the words which <u>begin</u> with the *manner of articulation* noted:

    a. fricative   race/breath/bush/bring/breathe/tough/though/rave/hate
    b. nasal   pant/range/rang/dumb/dump/knee/deaf /gnu/pneumonia
    c. stop   pill/lip/lit/graph/crab/dog/hide/laugh/back/hike
    d. lateral   nut/lone/ball/bar/rob/one/run/bare/bale
    e. approximant   we/you/were/lone/one/run/yell/roll/your

3. For each set, select the words which <u>end</u> with the *manner of articulation* noted:

    a. fricative   race/breath/bush/bring/breathe/tough/though/rave/hate
    b. nasal   pant/range/rang/dumb/dump/knee/deaf /gnu/pneumonia
    c. stop   pill/lip/lit/graph/crab/dog/hide/laugh/back/hike
    d. affricate   much/back/edge/ooze/chews/touch/tough/just/push
    e. rhotic   nut/lone/ball/bar/rob/one/run/bare/bale

4. For each set, select the words which <u>begin</u> with the *place of articulation* noted:

    a. velar   knot/got/lot/cot/hot/pot/gnat/lack/tug/ghost/tough
    b. labiodental   fat/cat/that/mat/chat/vat/wife/live/with/by/width
    c. alveolar   zip/nip/lip/sip/tip/dip/pill/pat/pad/par/hiss/his
    d. post-alveolar   lurch/lush/cough/lunge/touch/choose/huge/juice/sugar

5. For each set, select the words which <u>end</u> with the *place of articulation* noted:

    a. bilabial   mat/gnat/sat/bat/rat/pat/map/nab/dad/tam/tar
    b. alveolar   zip/nip/lip/sip/tip/dip/pill/pat/pad/par/hiss/his
    c. dental   pie/guy/shy/thigh/thy/high/with/width/height/length
    d. post-alveolar   lurch/lush/cough/lunge/touch/choose/huge/juice/sugar

6. Give the complete phonetic symbol for the <u>first</u> sound in each of these words.

    a. Thomas   b. hired   c. knee
    d. committee   e. choice   f. psychic

47

7. Give the complete phonetic symbol for the last sound in each of these words.

    a. use (verb)   b. lamb   c. laugh
    d. use (noun)   e. walked f. jogged

8. Give the IPA symbol for each of the following descriptions of sounds.

    a. voiceless laryngeal stop   b. voiced alveolar fricative
    c. voiced velar stop   d. voiceless post-alveolar affricate
    e. voiced palatal glide   f. voiceless alveolar stop
    g. voiced velar nasal   h. voiceless laryngeal fricative
    i. voiced dental fricative   j. voiced labiodental fricative

9. Give a complete phonetic description of the sounds represented by the following IPA symbols. Include laryngeal state and place and manner of articulation.

    [z] [v] [ʤ] [k] [m] [pʰ] [θ] [w̥]

10. Say the following words aloud; then check those whose voiceless stops are produced with aspiration.

    a. later   b. tag   c. segments d. pending
    e. appall f. careful g. apple   h. bookie   i. hitting

11. Find the errors in the transcription of the consonant sounds in each of these words; each error represents an impossible pronunciation of that word for a native speaker of (any variety of) English. Identify both the error(s) and the correct symbol(s).

    a. strong   [stɹɔng]   b. crime   [cɹɑɪm]
    c. wishing [wɪshɪŋ]   d. wives   [wɑɪvs]
    e. these   [θiz]   f. jacket [jækɪt]
    g. sixty   [sɪxti]   h. thesis [ðisɪs]

12. Decide which of these words contain a schwa ([ə]) and which contain a wedge ([ʌ]).

    a. sludge b. appall c. hung   d. quality
    e. sofa   f. oven   g. funny h. nation

13. For each set, select the words which contain the *vowel sounds* with the dimension noted. Exclude consideration of diphthongs in your responses to (b) through (g):

    a. diphthong   sat/sot/set/soy/seat/soot/sate/sit/sight/sought/sew/suit/souse
    b. front   sat/sot/set/soy/seat/soot/sate/sit/sight/sought/sew/suit/souse
    c. back   sat/sot/set/soy/seat/soot/sate/sit/sight/sought/sew/suit/souse
    d. high   sat/sot/set/soy/seat/soot/sate/sit/sight/sought/sew/suit/souse
    e. low   sat/sot/set/soy/seat/soot/sate/sit/sight/sought/sew/suit/souse
    f. round   sat/sot/set/soy/seat/soot/sate/sit/sight/sought/sew/suit/souse
    g. tense   sat/sot/set/soy/seat/soot/sate/sit/sight/sought/sew/suit/souse

14. Transcribe the vowels (or diphthongs) in these words, ignoring the consonants.

    a. key   b. cheese   c. heat   d. shield
    e. through   f. clue   g. shoe   h. too
    i. straw   j. talk   k. fought   l. lost
    m. good   n. food   o. should   p. sound

15. Using IPA symbols, transcribe these English words as you pronounce them in casual speech. Don't base your transcription on overly slow, precise pronunciation; be careful not to confuse the sounds of a word with its spelling.

    a. easy   b. judge   c. pack   d. gnome   e. weather
    f. coughs   g. bicycle   h. whether   i. often   j. through
    k. filed   l. field

16. The following transcriptions represent the normal pronunciation, in casual speech, of a speaker from Ohio. Write the word(s) represented by each transcription. Indicate the differences, if any, between this dialect and your own pronunciation.

    a. [dɔg]   b. [θæŋk]   c. [ho]   d. [ɔt]   e. [amənz]
    f. [ʤɑli]   g. [ðɛm]   h. [ʃæk]   i. [kwin]   j. [mjul]

17. Each of the following words contains a single error; because of differences in varieties of English, there may sometimes be alternative possible corrections. Identify the errors in the transcriptions and the correct IPA symbol.

    a. man-made   [mɑnmed]   b. football   [fʊtbol]   c. chest   [ʧest]
    d. tomcat   [tʰomkæt]   e. tiptoe   [tʰipto]   f. avoid   [ævɔɪd]

CHAPTER 3

PHONOLOGY: PATTERNS OF SOUNDS

Phonologists study how sounds pattern together within a given language and across languages. Our purpose in this chapter is to discover some of the general principles which underlie those patterns of sounds. To achieve this purpose, we investigate how and why linguists classify individual speech sounds in individual languages as representing either contrastive sounds or as rule-governed, context-driven sounds, a classification which many consider the core of phonological analysis. We explore various phonological processes which occur in many, but not all, languages; we discover natural classes, sets of sounds which share one or more features and which undergo the same phonological processes; and we consider how best to represent the phonological knowledge that an individual speaker has of her native language.

But the first part of our discussion here introduces how languages organize individual segments of sound into syllables. Syllables comprise the building blocks of words, and syllable structure serves as a bridge between the world of phonetics (which we have just left) and the world of phonology proper (which we are about to enter).

We extend the range of languages considered, to include a number of languages besides English. But we discuss sufficient data from English to convince you that you possess a great deal of tacit knowledge of the principles of the sound patterns of the language as well as of the distribution of individual sound segments, as do all speakers of their native languages.

A. Syllable Structure

All languages organize their words into syllables. Each syllable forms a rhythmic unit (often described as a pulse of energy), and the total number of rhythmic units (pulses) in a given word is approximately equal to the number of vowels (that are pronounced) in that word.

Intuitively, it's easy to count the number of syllables in any word. You can verify this by counting the number of syllables in each of the animal names in the following list, which range from one to six: *ox, giraffe, crocodile, alligator, hippopotamus, tyrannosaurus-rex*. In fact, this task is so easy that pre-schoolers master it straightforwardly.

What may not be so intuitive is the internal structure of syllables, as every syllable consists of up to four constituents, through which linearly-produced sounds are organized hierarchically. The four constituents which may comprise a syllable are the nucleus, the onset, the coda, and the rime; each is detailed below.

Every syllable contains a <u>nucleus</u>; in this respect, syllables are like atoms, as neither can exist without a nucleus. Most generally, the nucleus of any syllable is a vowel. In fact, syllables which consist of nothing other than a nucleus are not all that rare; consider, for example, the indefinite article *a* or the first person singular personal pronoun *I* in English.

The <u>onset</u> of a syllable consists of any consonant (or consonants) which precedes the nucleus. For example, the onset of the word *ray* consists of a single consonant, while that of *tray* consists of two consonants, and that of *stray* consists of three consonants.

The <u>coda</u> of a syllable consists of any consonant (or consonants) which follows the nucleus. Thus, *at* has a single consonant in coda position, *act* has two, and *acts* has three.

The <u>rime</u> of a syllable consists of the nucleus plus the coda. The reason this particular constituent is called the rime is because words with identical rimes in fact rhyme: *at, fat, rat, frat, mat, gnat, cat, scat, splat,* and so forth. Notice that the onset plays no role in rhyming; this fact is automatically captured in syllable structure, as onset consonants comprise a constituent separate from the constituent that comprises the rime.

The structure of a syllable is illustrated below for the word *seat*, transcribed into IPA symbols. The labels for the various constituents are abbreviated: σ (lower case Greek sigma) for syllable, O for onset, R for rhyme, N for nucleus, and Cd for coda.

1.

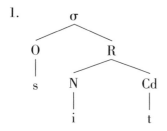

This syllable tree provides a range of information: It tells us the syllable consists of the sound segments [s i t], in that linear order. Thus this tree does not represent the structure of other words with the same sounds (e.g., *east* or *eats*), as it identifies the nucleus of the syllable as the vowel [i], its onset as the consonant [s], its coda as the consonant [t], and its rime as the sequence [i t].

Each constituent—nucleus, onset, coda, rime, and syllable—may form a simple or a branching constituent. Simple constituents are filled with a single element; branching constituents are filled with two or more elements. The indefinite article *a* has a simple nucleus, a simple rime, and a simple syllable (neither coda nor onset occurs). But *sprouts* has a branching nucleus (the diphthong), a three-way branching onset, and two-way branching coda, rime, and syllable constituents.

Syllable trees for *eat* (which lacks an onset), for *tea* (which lacks a coda) and for *sprouts* (which has both onset and coda and has only branching constituents) are presented below:

2.
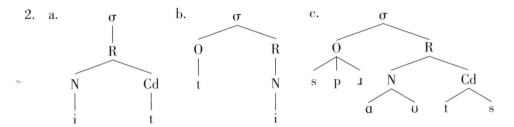

The trees in (2a-b) clarify two very important generalizations about syllables in English. First, nothing in the grammar of English forces any syllable to have either an onset or a coda. In fact, a great many words of the language are vowel-initial and every one lacks on onset in (at least) its first syllable (e.g., *oven*). Second, a great many words end in vowel sounds. But such syllables do not lack rimes; instead, their non-branching rimes consist of a single constituent, the nucleus (e.g., *sofa*).

But there is no syllable of English which lacks a nucleus. In fact, the very strong claim is that the existence of a nucleus is a *universal restriction* on syllable structure. That is, there is no language in the world known to linguists which can form a syllable which lacks a nucleus. We capture this fact through the <u>Nucleus Rule</u>, which states that every syllable must have a nucleus—even if that nucleus ends up being filled with a segment generally considered a 'consonant'. This is what happens for those speakers of English who allow one of the sonorant consonants to be realized as the nucleus of a syllable, in words such as *funnel, button, bird,* and *rhythm,* as discussed in Chapter 2 (see (12) in the text).

Syllable Typology

We begin our exploration into types of syllables with two definitions: An <u>open syllable</u> is any syllable which lacks a coda; e.g., *pay, pray, spray.* In contrast, a closed syllable is any syllable in which a coda is present; e.g., *an, ant, ants.*

It turns out that a number of languages allow only open syllables. Many languages of the Austronesian family—including most notably Hawaiian and Samoan—are languages of this type. And many words of English consist of nothing other than a series of open syllables; for example, the word *relativity* consists of a series of five open syllables. In addition, open syllables are allowed in every language (though a given language may also allow closed syllables also). For these reasons, a syllable of the form CV (a single consonant onset preceding the vocalic nucleus) is sometimes called the <u>core syllable</u>.

As noted above, many languages also allow closed syllables, syllables with one or more consonants following the nucleus. But no language has been shown to allow only closed syllables. Thus, we find an asymmetry between syllables of the form CV (which may be the only syllable form allowed in a given language) and those of the form VC (which may occur in a language, but not as the only syllable form allowed).

Quite a few languages allow branching onsets, but fewer languages allow branching codas. For example, Cambodian allows some eighty-five different pairs of consonants in onset position, but the language never allows any syllable to end in more than a single consonant. So we could say that the maximum syllable in Cambodian consists of CCVC. English is fairly rare among the world's languages in allowing syllables of the form CCCVCCCC, as in the word *strengths* [stɹɛŋkθs] (though in some varieties of English this word is reduced to [stɹɛŋθs]).

Phonotactics

So far, we've encountered one universal restriction on syllable structure (the Nucleus Rule) and some language-specific restrictions on syllable typology (whether codas are allowed, whether branching onsets are allowed, and so forth). There are a great many more restrictions that a given language can impose on its onsets and codas; these restrictions are generally grouped together under the rubric phonotactics—restrictions which refer to the sequences of sounds which are allowed to be adjacent to each other. ("Phonotactics" was coined by combining *phōnē*, the Greek word for 'sound' with *tactitus,* the Latin word for 'touch'.) While complete discussion of the phonotactics of any language requires consideration of all allowable sequences of consonants and vowels, we limit the discussion here to the sequences of consonants which are allowed in either onset or coda position. We've seen that each language has its own set of sounds; likewise, each language has its own set of phonotactic principles governing licit onsets and codas.

For example, English allows sequences such as [ps], [pt], and [pk] to occur across syllable boundaries; cf. *gypsy, helicopter,* and *napkin.* However, English does not allow these sequences in onset position; **psaa, *ptuk,* and **pkaa* are all impossible words of English. But while these sequences are restricted in English, they need not be so in some other language. In fact, these same sequences form perfectly good onsets in Cambodian, where *psaa, ptuk,* and *pkaa* are the words for 'market', 'to load', and 'flower', respectively.

Even though Cambodian allows some eighty-five pairs of consonants to occur in onset position, including those discussed in the preceding paragraph, not all possibilities are attested in the language. For example, sequences including [pn], [tl], and [kj] all occur as onsets, as in *pnum* 'mountain', *tlaɪ* 'to cost', and *kjal* 'wind'. But the sequences **[np], *[lt],* and **[jk]* never occur in this position. In fact, the latter set of onset sequences turns out to be impossible in all languages of the world, a fact which arises based on the relative sonority of the consonants in such sequences.

The *Sonority Hierarchy*

<u>Sonority</u> involves the relative openness of the vocal tract and/or the relative loudness of various speech sounds. Vowels are the most sonorous of all speech sounds; then come nasals, approximants, and fricatives, with stops being the least sonorous of all. In general, a syllable builds up to a peak of sonority and then tapers down. This statement entails that a more sonorous consonant needs to be closer to the nucleus than a less sonorant consonant. The word *plump* is schematized below; here the lengths of the straight lines above the segments are meant to denote relative sonority and the dotted lines the building up to and subsequent tapering down from a peak of sonority:

3.

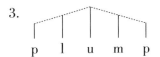

p   l   u   m   p

Each of our licit onset sequences above ([pn], [tl], and [kj]) has a stop on the outside and a liquid or nasal or glide (all sonorants) on the inside, closer to the nucleus. These sequences are reversed in our illicit onsets, *[np], *[lt], and *[jk], in which the more sonorant consonant is farther from the nucleus.

In particular, each of the latter sequences violates the <u>Sonority Hierarchy</u>, schematized for onsets in (4a) below, where the left-ward pointing arrowheads denote that sonority increases as you move through the segments to the right. Of course, the Sonority Hierarchy also restricts sequences of consonants in coda positions, but in the opposite order from those in onset positions. The ordering by sonority for coda consonants is given in (4b), where the right-ward pointing arrowheads denote that sonority decreases as you move to the right.

4.

	Sonority Hierarchy for Onsets (from least to most sonorous)							
a	stop	<	fricative	<	approximant	<	nasal	<	(vowel)

	Sonority Hierarchy for Codas (from most to least sonorous)							
b	(vowel)	>	nasal	>	approximant	>	fricative	>	stop

The Sonority Hierarchy ensures that, while a given language might have a word such as *plump,* no language will ever have a (one-syllable) word such as **lpupm,* as the sequences of consonants in both onset and coda positions violate this Hierarchy.

We've now encountered two universal principles of syllable structure: The Nucleus Rule requires every syllable to have a nucleus, and the Sonority Hierarchy governs the distributions of consonants in onset and coda positions in all syllables. We've also seen that, subject to these two universal principles, every language may choose its own set of phonotactics to restrict sequences of consonants in onsets and/or codas.

How to Syllabify Words of English

We can combine our knowledge of these universal principles and the phonotactics of English to help us syllabify words of more than one syllable in the language. Let's start with the two-syllable word *onset*, transcribed here as [ɔnsɛt] (though you may have a different vowel in the first syllable). Our intuitions tell us that this word should be syllabified as [.ɔn . sɛt.], where the periods indicate the syllable boundaries. To understand why this is the correct way to syllabify this word, we must consider the other two possibilities: *[.ɔ . nsɛt.] and *[.ɔns . ɛt.].

The first possibility, *[.ɔ . nsɛt.], violates the Sonority Hierarchy, as the onset of the second syllable consists of a [nasal + stop] sequence. The second possibility, *[.ɔns . ɛt.] does not in fact violate the Sonority Hierarchy, as the sequence [nasal + stop] is perfectly good in coda position. Yet we somehow sense that this syllabification is not quite right.

The problem lies in yet another universal restriction on syllable structure. This restriction—Maximize Onset—requires every onset in every syllable of every language to be as large as the phonotactics of that language allow. Before we proceed, you should know that there is no such principle as 'Maximize Coda'; this lack follows naturally from the asymmetry noted previously in connection with our discussion of syllable typology. While all languages allow CV syllables, and some languages allow only CV syllables, there is no known language which allows only VC syllables. This asymmetry between onsets and codas is encoded in Maximize Onset.

In our second possibility, *[.ɔns . ɛt.], the second syllable has no onset at all. Since [s] alone forms a perfectly legal onset in English, this second possibility violates Maximize Onset. But our third possibility, [.ɔn . sɛt.], violates no universal principle (nor the phonotactics of English), thereby assuring us that our original intuition was correct.

We can thus set up a simple algorithm for syllabification in English; this algorithm works for any language, and is the algorithm which was used to produce the syllable trees in (1) and (2) above. There are five basic steps in this algorithm, after first transcribing a word of English into IPA symbols.

Table 1:   *Syllabification Algorithm*

Step 1	Project nuclei (for all syllables in the word)
Step 2	Project onsets (making them as large as the language allows)
Step 3	Project codas (incorporate all non-onset consonants)
Step 4	Project rimes (connect nucleus and coda)
Step 5	Project syllables (connect onset and rime)

Project is an operation used to produce the sorts of (linguistic) trees which, when complete, show both the linear order of elements and their hierarchical order. When creating syllable trees, project entails identifying a particular element as comprising a particular constituent (e.g., a vowel as a nucleus or a consonant as an onset), labeling that constituent (e.g., N or O), and, when appropriate, connecting constituents (e.g., connecting N and Cd to create R).

To see how the algorithm in Table 1 operates, we detail below the steps required for the syllabification of two examples, beginning with the word *apply,* [əplaɪ]. Step 1, which enforces the Nucleus Rule, produces this partial syllable tree, where only the two nuclei (one for each syllable) are projected:

5.   N   N
     | ╱╲
     ə   p   l   ɑ   ɪ

Step 2 projects onsets; so now we must consider the sequence [pl]. Since this sequence satisfies the Sonority Hierarchy, and since it's a licit sequence in English (cf., *play, plow, ply*), these two consonants must—based on Maximize Onset—form a branching onset in the second syllable, as schematized below:

6.   N   O   N
     | ╱╲   ╱╲
     ə   p   l   ɑ   ɪ

Since we have no more consonants to incorporate into syllable structure, we can project two (non-branching) rimes (Step 4) and two syllables (Step 5), completing our syllabification of this word ([.ə . plaɪ.]):

7.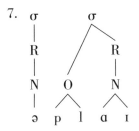

Notice carefully that the syllabification of words in linguistic analysis is only tangentially related to how words are hyphenated in dictionaries. Hyphenation in dictionaries is based on the spelling system of the language. Syllabification in linguistic analysis is based on a particular language's set of phonotactic principles, operating in concert with universal principles.

Our second syllabification example is of the word *explain*. Transcription into IPA yields [ɛksplen]. Like *apply*, *explain* is a two-syllable word, but now we have a sequence of four consonants in the middle of the word. Thus our possibilities are *[.ɛkspl . en.], *[.ɛksp. len.], *[.ɛks. plen.], and [. ɛk. splen.].

It's easy to see that *[.ɛkspl . en.] must be incorrect, as the second syllable lacks an onset (though more than one consonant is available to fill this position) and so violates Maximize Onset. Our second possibility, *[.ɛksp . len.], fares a little better, as the second syllable has an onset. But it still violates Maximize Onset: [l] is not the largest onset English allows, as [pl] makes a perfectly good onset. So this brings us to our third possibility, *[.ɛks . plen.]; this possibility is better yet—but still not good enough, as English allows the sequence [spl] in onset position (cf., *splint, splay, spleen*). As a result, our fourth possibility, [.ɛk . splen.], is the correct syllabification of this word.

In Table 2, *explain* is syllabified following the five steps of the algorithm presented in Table 1:

Table 2:   *Syllabification Algorithm Exemplified*

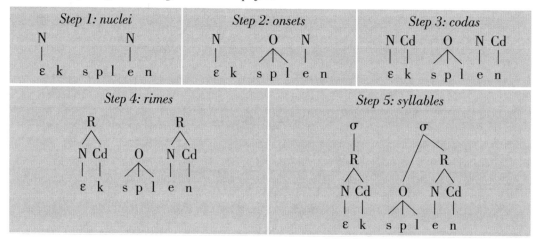

(Careful readers may well wonder how English allows the sequence [spl] in onset position, as this sequence, in which the stop is closer to the nucleus than the fricative, appears to violate the Sonority Hierarchy in (4). You might also notice that stops can appear inside fricatives in coda position, in words such as *stops* for example, and so appear to represent further violations of the Sonority Hierarchy. Full explication of these facts is beyond the scope of this text; here we simply note that English is like a range of other languages in allowing [s] (and [z]) to serve as an appendix to a syllable, rather than inside either onset or coda. As an appendix, the [s] in [ɛksplen] would be attached directly to the syllable node of the second syllable, rather than to its onset node. We abstract away from this process here and continue to incorporate potential appendices into either onset or coda position.)

With the algorithm given in Table 1, you should be able to syllabify any word of English (as long as you can transcribe that word into symbols of the IPA!).

In the next section, we discover how linguists classify individual sound segments within a given language as representing either contrastive sounds or rule-governed, context-driven sounds. In the process, we extend the range of languages considered well beyond English.

B. Phonemes and Allophones

We saw in the preceding chapter that one way languages differ from each other is in their inventories of individual speech sounds. Consider for example the various rhotic sounds that occur in different languages: While English contains the alveolar approximant [ɹ], French contains the uvular fricative [ʁ], Hindi the retroflex tap [ɽ], and Cambodian the alveolar trill [r].

More interestingly, two languages may contain the same sound, but that sound may pattern differently in the two languages: In one language, the distribution of this sound might be (relatively) free, and the sound is easily recognized by native speakers as being a contrastive or distinctive sound segment in the language. But in another language, the distribution of this same sound might be quite restricted, occurring only in certain phonetic environments; native speakers are often completely unaware that such a sound even occurs in their language.

Understanding how a particular sound patterns differently in two languages forms an integral part of phonological analysis and is best accomplished through illustration. This section focuses on two problems in phonological analysis: The first considers the distribution of [k] and [g] in English and Swampy Cree; the second considers the distribution of plain and aspirated voiceless stops in English and Cambodian.

B1 English and Swampy Cree

This problem focuses on the sounds [k] and [g]. These sounds share place of articulation (velar) and manner of articulation (stops); they differ from each other only in laryngeal status: [k] is voiceless while [g] is voiced. We know both of these are sounds of English, and that each can occur word-initially, word-medially, and word-finally:

8.

	word-initial	*word-medial*	*word-final*
a	code [kod]	hackle [hækəl]	pick [pɪk]
b	goad [god]	haggle [hægəl]	pig [pɪg]

Pairs of words such as *code/goad, hackle/haggle,* and *pick/pig* in English are called <u>minimal pairs</u>. A minimal pair is defined as two words of the same language which have different meanings and which differ from each other by only a single segment which occurs in the same phonetic context or environment in each word.

The reference to "different meanings" in the preceding definition entails that we would not consider alternate pronunciations of a single word as evidence of distinctive sounds in a given language. So whether we pronounce *tomato* as [təmeto] or [təmɑto] tells us nothing about the distribution of the sounds [e] and [ɑ] in English. (However, *gate* [get] and *got* [gɑt] form a minimal pair which do provide evidence that [e] and [ɑ] are distinctive sounds of English.)

The reference to "same phonetic context or environment" in the definition entails that two words with different numbers of segments cannot form a minimal pair, as the sounds in question cannot by definition occur in the "same" phonetic context. Thus, while *seep* [sip] and *sip* [sɪp] form a minimal pair in English, *seep* [sip] and *sleep* [slip] do not. And of course *sip* [sɪp] and *seat* [sit] do not form a minimal pair, as they differ in two segments.

Whenever you find a minimal pair (in English or in any language of the world), what you have found are <u>distinctive</u> sounds in that language, that is, sounds which <u>contrast</u> with each other. If, in a given language, you were to substitute one contrastive sound for another, you would quite likely change the meaning of the word. For instance, if we were to substitute [g] for [k] in the word *code*, we would have an entirely different word of English, *goad*.

Such distinctive or contrastive sounds are <u>phonemes</u> of a given language. It's the phonemes of a language which show up in consonant and vowel charts. As a native speaker, you have tacit knowledge of the phonemes of your language as part of your linguistic competence. In terms of our current example, it's fair to say that native English speakers straightforwardly and unerringly differentiate between *code* and *goad* and so know the sounds [k] and [g] contrast in the language. Here is a working definition of phonemes:

■   <u>Phonemes</u> are sounds within a given language which may or may not be phonetically similar to each other, which have contrastive (i.e., the same) distribution, and which occur in minimal pairs.

Now consider the distribution of the sounds [k] and [g] in Swampy Cree (an Algonquian language spoken in Ontario, Manitoba, and Saskatchewan), as illustrated in (9) below. Vowel length is omitted here, as such is not relevant to this problem.

9.

[tɑhki] 'all the time'	[niskɑ] 'goose'
[ospwagan] 'pipe'	[kogos] 'pig'
[kodɑk] 'another'	[waskow] 'cloud'
[ogik] 'these'	[nigi] 'my house'

Inspection of the Swampy Cree data in (9) reveals no minimal pairs. By definition, then, the sounds [k] and [g] must not be distinctive, contrastive sounds in Swampy Cree. So we expect the two sounds should have different distributions in the language. We can begin to test this expectation by re-arranging the data, as in (10) below, where all the words in which [k] occurs are listed in (a), and all the words in which [g] occurs are listed in (b). Note that words in which both [k] and [g] occur are listed in both rows.

| 10. | a | [k] *occurs in* | [tahki] | [niska] | [kogos] | [kodak] | [waskow] | [ogik] |
| | b | [g] *occurs in* | [ospwagan] | [kogos] | [ogik] | [nigi] | | |

Our next step is to carefully delineate the distribution of each sound, by notating the phonetic context in which each occurs. "Phonetic context" refers to the position in a word in which a sound occurs (word-initial, word-medial, or word-final) and/or to the sounds which surround that sound. When the relevant context is word-initial, linguists use the shorthand notation "#_", where the symbol "#" denotes a word boundary and the underline denotes the position of the sound relative to that boundary. Analogously, the notation "_#" represents word-final position. When the sound under consideration occurs word-medially, it's often crucial to notate the surrounding sounds. The contexts in which each of [k] and [g] occur in Swampy Cree are delineated in (11):

11.		[k] *occurs in*	[tahki]	[niska]	[kogos]	[kodak]	[waskow]	[ogik]
	a	[k] *contexts*	h_i	s_a	#_	#_ _#	s_o	_#
	b	[g] *occurs in*	[ospwagan]	[kogos]	[ogik]	[nigi]		
		[g] *contexts*	a_a	o_o	o_i	i_i		

With the information provided in (11), we can now straightforwardly generalize over the data, as follows: [g] occurs only between vowels; this is a position in which [k] never occurs. Instead, [k] occurs in word-initial position, in word-final position, and in word-medial position between a consonant and a vowel; these are positions in which [g] never occurs.

In Swampy Cree, the phonetically-similar sounds [k] and [g] occur in <u>complementary distribution</u> and are <u>allophones</u> of a single phoneme. This statement entails that one allophone occurs in one phonetic context while the other allophone occurs in another phonetic context; in this way, the contexts of the two allophones together <u>complete</u> the distribution of the phoneme. Here is a working definition of allophones:

- ■ <u>Allophones</u> are sounds which are phonetically similar to each other and which have complementary (i.e., different) distributions.

The existence of complementary distribution entails a systematic, predictable variation in a segment that is conditioned by the phonetic context in which it occurs. Therefore, once we have ascertained (from a given data set) the context in which each allophone occurs, then we can make predictions about where each allophone occurs throughout the language. Based on what we now know of the phonological system of Swampy Cree, we can straightforwardly fill in [k] and [g] correctly in the blanks in the string [tɑ __ i __], to make the hypothetical word [tɑgik].

Observe that we are unable to make such predictions about the distribution of these same two sounds in English. In the hypothetical word [tɑ __ i __], either [k] or [g] could occur in either blank; thus both [tɑkig] and [tɑgik] would be possible words of English. This situation arises because [k] and [g] are both phonemes of English; that is, both are distinctive sounds with the same (i.e., contrastive) distribution in English.

If you take a moment to ponder what our ability to make predictions about the distribution of these two sounds in Swampy Cree entails, you might become aware of two points: First, speakers of Swampy Cree must have some sort of 'rule' in mind, a rule which requires [k] to become voiced [g] when it is surrounded by vowels. Second, we ascertained that 'mental rule' by observing its application, that is, by observing from the data in (9) how speakers of Swampy Cree actually pronounce this sound in different phonetic contexts.

Significantly, while we as phonologists may be aware of the allophonic differences between between [k] and [g] in Swampy Cree, native speakers may not have this level of awareness of the language, even though the allophonic differences are present in the utterances of all speakers. But they are still likely to find that words pronounced differently (e.g., [niki] instead of [nigi]) sound 'funny' or are simply not recognized as words of the language.

To recap our discussion so far: The sounds [k] and [g] occur in both English and Swampy Cree. But the distributions of these sounds differ: In English, both occur in the same context, are in contrastive distribution, and are phonemes of the language. But in Swampy Cree, the two occur in different contexts, are in rule-governed complementary distribution, and are allophones of a single phoneme in the language.

B2 English and Cambodian

As mentioned in Chapter 2, the voiceless stops of English, [p, t, k], are aspirated at the beginning of stressed syllables, as in (12a). The examples in (12b) show that aspiration does not occur when a voiceless stop is preceded by [s], and the examples in (12c) show aspiration does not occur when a voiceless stop comes in word final position. The examples in (13) show the relationship between aspiration and stress. Taken together, these examples entail that speakers of English can produce voiceless stops either with or without aspiration.

12.

a	[pʰ]ill	[tʰ]ill	[kʰ]ill
b	s[p]ill	s[t]ill	s[k]ill
c	*pi[pʰ]	*pi[tʰ]	*pi[kʰ]

13.

a	a[p]le	*a[pʰ]le	a[pʰ]all
b	[tʰ]otal	*to[tʰ]al	to[tʰ]ality
c	[kʰ]ookie	*coo[kʰ]ie	ca[kʰ]ophony

Now consider these examples from Cambodian (a Mon-Khmer language) and note the voiceless stops are sometimes aspirated but sometimes not. (The vowel [ɒ] is a low back round vowel.)

14.

a	[pɒɒŋ]	'to intend'	[tɑɑ]	'uncle'	[kae]	'to correct'
b	[pʰɒɒŋ]	'too, also'	[tʰɑɑ]	'to say'	[kʰae]	'month, moon'

The data in (14) show that Cambodian shares sounds with English; both languages have the same voiceless stops, [p, t, k], and in both languages these may be pronounced with or without aspiration.

But notice that these sounds pattern differently in the two languages: In English, we can make predictions about where aspirated voiceless stops show up: all and only at the beginning of stressed syllables. But we cannot make such predictions about the distribution of aspirated voiceless stops in Cambodian, as the minimal pairs in (14) show that they have precisely the same distribution as do the plain voiceless stops in the language: All are allowed to occur word-initially, at the beginning of stressed syllables.

Thus, in Cambodian, the plain voiceless stops [p, t, k] and their aspirated counterparts [pʰ, tʰ, kʰ] all function as phonemes of the language. If we change a plain voiceless stop into an aspirated voiceless stop, the result is a different word in the language.

In English, the plain and aspirated voiceless stops function as allophones. If we change one into the other, we judge the result as 'funny-sounding' or 'non-English'.

Intuitively, our knowledge of English tells us that, although each of these sounds has variants at the phonetic level of representation (as each is only sometimes produced with aspiration), still at some other level, English has only one voiceless bilabial stop, one voiceless alveolar stop, and one voiceless velar stop.

We call this other level, in which the plain and aspirated voiceless stops are mentally represented as a single sound, the phonemic level of representation. We can schematize each of the voiceless stops of English as shown below, where by convention the phonemic level is represented in slashes (i.e., "/ . . . /") and the phonetic level in square brackets (i.e., "[. . .]"):

15. a.

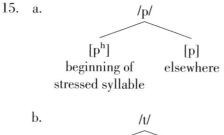

b.

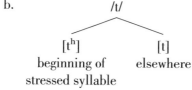

c.

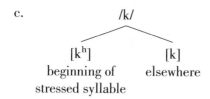

These schematizations entail, for English, that the phonemes /p, t, k/ each have two allophonic variants and are pronounced as [pʰ, tʰ, kʰ] when they occur at the beginning of stressed syllables, but as [p, t, k] in every other phonetic environment in which they occur. In other words, these schematizations illustrate three separate but closely related 'mental rules' which all speakers of English share.

The representation of these same sounds in Cambodian differs, however, as in this language all six of these sounds are distinctive, contrastive sounds. Thus, we have six separate phonemes, each of which has a single allophone:

16. a. /p/   b. /t/   c. /k/   d. /pʰ/   e. /tʰ/   f. /kʰ/
         | | | | | |
        [p]   [t]   [k]   [pʰ]   [tʰ]   [kʰ]

If we compare the representations in (15) and (16), we find the same physical, phonetic reality in both languages. But native speakers of Cambodian have different rule systems (equivalent to different mental grammars) in their minds than do native speakers of English. Where

Cambodian has six distinctive phonemes, each with a single allophone, English has only three distinctive phonemes, each with two allophones.

The phenomenon of allophonic variation is universal, as a given sound in any language may have variants based on the context in which it occurs. But the patterning of phonemes and allophones is always specific to a particular language.

We have now identified five differences between phonemes and allophones; these differences are summarized below:

Table 3: *Phonemes vs. Allophones*

	separate phonemes	*allophones of a single phoneme*
1	contrastive, distinctive sounds	non-contrastive, rule-governed sounds
2	distribution is unpredictable	distribution is predictable
3	perceived as different	not easily perceived as different
4	not necessarily phonetically similar	always phonetically similar
5	test: minimal pairs	test: complementary distribution

Before we leave this section, there are two significant points to be made, one about allophones and one about phonemes. First, we can find the concept of "allophones" outside the world of phonology. Since allophones are simply variants that occur predictably in certain environments, we could imagine that H_2O is the equivalent of a "phoneme" which has the three "allophones" schematized below:

17.

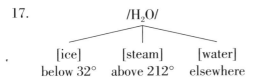

/H_2O/

[ice]   [steam]   [water]
below 32°   above 212°   elsewhere

As this example from the physical world demonstrates, we can predict where the "allophones" of H_2O occur, based on the environment: When the temperature is 32° or lower, we find the "allophone" we call *ice;* when the temperature is 212° or higher, we find the "allophone" *steam.* In all other environments (above 32° but below 212°), we find the "allophone" *water.*

Second, sounds in a given language may appear to be in complementary distribution with each other but still cannot be considered allophones of the same phoneme. The classic example involves the sounds /ŋ/ and /h/ in English. Both sounds have restricted distribution in English: The former occurs only at the end of syllables while the latter occurs only at the beginning of syllables. Thus we have words such as *singing* [sɪŋɪŋ] and *high-hat* [hɑɪ-hæt] but no words such as *[ŋɪsŋɪ] or *[ɑɪh-tæh]. But we cannot use such apparent complementary distribution to argue these sounds are allophones of a single phoneme, since they are not phonetically similar. In fact, they share no features at all: /ŋ/ is a voiced velar nasal while /h/ is a voiceless glottal fricative.

In summary, the significance of the phoneme/allophone distinction stems from the combination of two facts: On one hand, we all have tacit knowledge of the phonemes of our native language, regardless of what that language is. On the other hand, it's quite likely we are completely unaware of the existence of the allophones of our native language. As phonologists, we want to account for what a native speaker knows about her language, and ascertaining the phoneme/allophone distinction within a given language forms an important part of that analysis.

Ascertaining the phoneme/allophone distinction from a given data set in a particular language is an analytic endeavor which requires a certain level of expertise in phonology. Practicing with a range of problems can certainly improve your proficiency in this area. And such practice on your part is clearly worth the effort, as solving such problems provides you with conscious knowledge of what native speakers know only tacitly.

Before we return to our discussion of the phoneme/allophone distinction in Section D, we pause to consider some phonological processes which occur in various languages.

C. Some Phonological Processes

A phonological process is an operation which causes an articulatory adjustment or alternation in a given sound segment during speech production. Six of these processes are outlined in this section.

C1 Assimilation

When <u>assimilation</u> occurs, a given sound becomes similar to another sound by picking up or sharing a feature of that other sound. When the two sounds are adjacent (i.e., immediately next to each other), we refer to the process as <u>local assimilation</u>.

Local assimilation is a very common process, some form of which operates in most (if not all) of the world's languages. As we'll see in the examples in this section, local assimilation may occur between two adjacent consonants, as the two come to share voicing, place, or manner features; or between a consonant and an adjacent vowel, when one picks up a feature of the other.

Local Assimilation

Local assimilation occurs quite frequently in English and is often, but not always, the result of coarticulation. Coarticulation occurs when the production of one sound is physiologically influenced by the production of another sound.

Consider the words *ban* and *bad;* each consists of a sequence of the voiced bilabial stop /b/, the low front vowel /æ/, and a final voiced alveolar stop, either nasal /n/ or oral /d/. If you say each word with a lengthened vowel, while omitting but anticipating the final consonant, you may well notice that the vowel /æ/ doesn't sound exactly the same in each word. If you repeat this exercise several times, you may sense the vowel is somewhat higher in pitch in *ba(d)* than it is in *ba(n)* and you may even notice that your velum is higher when you pronounce *ba(d)* than when you pronounce *ba(n)*.

The reason the vowel sounds different is because the vowel *is* different: Native speakers routinely nasalize the vowel in *ban,* but never in *bad*. The <u>vowel nasalization</u> occurs as you lower your velum to produce the nasal while you are still producing the vowel. As a result, the vowel picks up a feature—nasal—from the /n/ which immediately follows it; in the process, the vowel becomes somewhat like its neighbor, as both share a feature. Of course, such nasal assimilation never occurs when an oral consonant such as /d/ follows the vowel, as an oral consonant has no nasal feature to share. We represent nasalized vowels by placing a tilde as a diacritic over the IPA symbol: [bæ̃n].

Now consider the word *bank*. Here the vowel is nasalized, as it is in *ban*. But most speakers also find a second assimilatory process in this word, as the nasal takes on the place of articulation of the following stop. Thus this word is generally pronounced [bæ̃ŋk], rather than [bæ̃nk]. In fact, it is very difficult for native speakers of English to produce the alveolar nasal here.

Nasal consonants in English (and in many of the world's languages) quite frequently undergo <u>nasal place assimilation</u>, by taking on the place of articulation of an adjacent stop. In English, this process occurs quite regularly within simple words, as exemplified in (18), and inside complex words, as in (19), where the examples are all adjectives which begin with the prefix *in-* 'not'. When the adjectives begin with vowels or alveolar stops, the nasal in the prefix surfaces as [n]. But when the adjectives begin with a bilabial stop, the nasal surfaces as [m], a fact often reflected orthographically; when the adjectives begin with a velar stop, the nasal surfaces as [ŋ], a fact never reflected orthographically:

18.   ca[m]p, li[m]bo   te[n]t, te[n]d   thi[ŋ]k, thi[ŋ]g

19.   i[n]audible, i[n]operable   i[n]tolerant, i[n]destructible
      i[m]possible, i[m]bred   i[ŋ]conceivable, i[ŋ]grown

The examples in (20) show precisely this same process occurring across word boundaries, when the words are in the same syntactic phrase. Here, the phrases all contain the preposition *in.* The nasal in the preposition surfaces as [n] when it precedes a word which begins with a vowel or an alveolar stop; but it surfaces as [m] when it precedes a word beginning with a bilabial stop and as [ŋ] when it precedes a word beginning with a velar stop:

20.	i[n] Omaha, i[n] Eastwick	i[n] Torrance, i[n] Downey
	i[m] Paris, i[m] Bakersfield	i[ŋ] Kalamazoo, i[ŋ] Gardena

We can, of course, speak very slowly and distinctly and, in the process, actually produce alveolar [n] in every instance. But nasal place assimilation frequently occurs in conversational speech.

Nasal place assimilation occurs in many of the world's languages, though not always across word boundaries, as it does in English.

When one sound influences the sound which precedes it, we refer to the process as anticipatory assimilation, as it results from our anticipating the positions of our organs of articulation in one sound when producing the preceding sound. In English, nasal place assimilation is an instance of anticipatory assimilation, as is the vowel nasalization in a word such as *ban,* discussed above.

Under perseverative assimilation, one sound influences the sound which follows it. This results when we 'persevere' in the production of one sound into the production of the following sound. This perseverance shows up in several places in English, including in the formation of (regular) plural nouns. Consider the examples below, and observe that the plural marker is sometimes pronounced as [z] and sometimes as [s]:

21.	a	cab[z]	cad[z]	gag[z]	tree[z]
	b	cap[s]	cat[s]	joke[s]	

When the singular form ends in a voiced sound (either consonant or vowel), the plural marker is pronounced as voiced [z]; but when the singular form ends in a voiceless sound, the plural marker is pronounced as voiceless [s]. That is, the plural marker assimilates to the voicing status of the sound which precedes it, a phenomenon known as voicing assimilation.

Here is a further example of voicing assimilation in English. We know that the approximants are routinely voiced sounds. When an approximant occurs alone in onset position or when it follows a voiced consonant, it is voiced, as shown in (22a-b). However, an approximant regularly becomes voiceless when it immediately follows a voiceless consonant, as shown in (22c). Such devoiced approximants are denoted by adding a small open circle under the regular IPA symbol:

22.	a	[ɹ]ye	[l]ight	[j]ou	[w]e
	b	d[ɹ]y	b[l]ight	b[j]eauty	d[w]eeb
	c	t[ɹ̥]y	p[l̥]ight	p[j̥]ew	tweeze

One result of the devoicing of English approximants is this: Even those of you who lack the voiceless labio-velar glide at the beginning of a word like *wheeze* can still pronounce this sound, as you routinely produce it in a word like *tweeze*.

A further instance of assimilation occurs in most varieties of American English; this particular type of assimilation is sometimes described as being simultaneously anticipatory and perseverative, as the alternation that occurs is dependent on both surrounding contexts (i.e., the immediately preceding and the following contexts). This instance of assimilation is often referred to as flapping assimilation, and it occurs in words such as *butter, writer,* and *city:*

23.	butter [bʌɾəɹ]	writer [ɹɑɪɾəɹ]	city [sɪɾi]

The IPA symbol [ɾ] denotes a voiced alveolar flap. A flap is a stop, but one which is produced extraordinarily rapidly. Various acoustic studies have found the mean closure time (the amount of time the tip of the tongue is in contact with the alveolar ridge) varies among the alveolar stops of English, as follows: For [tʰ], the mean closure time is up to 129 ms; for [d], the time is reduced to some 75 ms. In contrast, the mean closure time for [ɾ] is a mere 26 ms. (The abbreviation "ms" is shorthand for "millisecond," a unit of time equal to one-thousandth of a second.)

Flapping assimilation requires a very specific context in which to occur: First, as shown in (24a), the syllable following the flap must be stressless. Second, as shown in (24b), the flap must be surrounded by vowels. That is, both the context which precedes the flap and the context which follows it must meet certain conditions; as a result, the assimilation has been described as being both anticipatory and perseverative at the same time.

24.	a	satin [sæɾən]	catty [kʰæɾi]
	b	sateen [sætʰin]	hasty [hesti]

For most speakers of English, the presence of [t] instead of [ɾ] in words like *satin* and *catty* sounds funny, 'prissy', or affected. But native speakers find it almost impossible to produce [ɾ] instead of [t] in words like *sateen* and *hasty.*

We know that the phoneme in such examples must be /t/, rather than /d/, based on pairs of words in which one is simple and the other complex, but which have different stress patterns. In the simple words *atom* and *total*, the second syllable is stressless—and a flap occurs in the middle of the words. But in the complex words *atomic* and *totality*, the stress shifts onto the second syllable; and in place of the flaps which occurred in the simple words, we now find voiceless, aspirated alveolar stops:

25.

a	atom [æɾəm]	atomic [ətʰɑmɪk]
b	total [tʰoɾəl]	totality [tətʰælɪɾi]

All of the examples we've considered so far represent instances of local assimilation, where the assimilation that occurs is between adjacent sounds. In some languages (but not in English) assimilation may be 'long distance', where the assimilating sounds are not adjacent to each other.

Long Distance Assimilation

The most important type of long distance assimilation is called vowel harmony, in which a vowel in one syllable becomes similar to a vowel in another syllable, with one or more consonants intervening between the vowels. While this process does not occur in English, it does in Turkish. In Turkish, all vowels in a given word must be either all front or all back; and the high vowels must be either all round or all non-round. One result is that the genitive (i.e., possessive) suffix has four phonetic realizations. This suffix is abbreviated as "gen" in (26):

26.

Turkish	ev-in	gøz-yn	akʃam-in	kol-un
gloss	house-gen	eye-gen	evening-gen	arm-gen
translation	'of the house'	'of the eye'	'of the evening'	'of the arm'

Observe that Turkish has vowels which do not occur in English. You can glean the features of each from the following vowel chart, which has been laid out specifically to accommodate the eight vowels of Turkish:

Table 4: *Turkish Vowel Chart*

	front		back	
	unround	round	unround	round
high	i	y	ɨ	u
low	e	ø	ɑ	o

The Turkish vowels in Table 4 form a symmetrical set, with four front and four back vowels, four high and four low vowels, and four unround and four round vowels. Linguists often prefer to develop symmetrical charts, when the distribution of sounds in a given language allows such.

With this vowel chart, it's easy to see that the vowels in the possessive suffix are in 'harmony' with the vowels in the root of the word, as in every instance these vowels share features: Both vowels in [ev-in] are front and unround; both vowels in [gøz-yn] are front and round; both vowels in [ɑkʃam-in] are back and unround; and both vowels in [kol-un] are back and round. In each instance, there are no other vowels of Turkish which share the same two backness/roundness features.

C2 Dissimilation

The process of <u>dissimilation</u>—under which two sounds become less like each other—can be considered the opposite of the process of assimilation. Following are several examples of dissimilation.

In the Middle English period (the form of the language spoken between the eleventh and the fourteenth centuries), a rather extensive set of words changed /n/ into [m], but only when the alveolar nasal was preceded by another Coronal consonant somewhere in the word. As a result, we now have words such as *seldo<u>m</u>, rando<u>m</u>,* and *veno<u>m</u>,* which were *seldo<u>n</u>, rando<u>n</u>,* and *veno<u>n</u>* in the earlier stage of the language.

Today, many speakers of both American and British English tend to delete the first of two [ɹ] sounds in a given word. For these speakers, *berserk* becomes [bəzɹ̩k] (with a syllabic [ɹ]), *surprise* turns into [səpɹaɪz], and *governor* becomes [gʌvənəɹ]. (Of course, the single [ɹ] in *government* is exempt here.)

Additionally, many speakers of English (who may or may not be from the same set of speakers mentioned above) find the sequence of fricatives at the end of the word *fifths* difficult to pronounce. One way to overcome this difficulty is to change one of the fricatives into a stop, so that one sound in the sequence becomes less like the others in the sequence. For these speakers, /fɪfθs/ is pronounced as [fɪfts].

Rather similarly, the word in Classical Greek for 'school' was pronounced [sxolio] (IPA [x] represents a voiceless velar fricative). But in Modern Greek, the second fricative dissimilated to become a stop. The Modern Greek pronunciation of this word may sound somewhat familiar to you: [skolio].

C3 Deletion

<u>Deletion</u> is the phonological process through which a segment (sometimes, more than a single segment) is omitted. This process occurs in most varieties of English, particularly in informal

and/or rapid speech. Quite frequently, this deletion attacks the stressless vowel [ə], as in these examples:

27.

	careful	rapid		careful	rapid
parade	[pɔɹed]	[pɹed]	suppose	[səpʰoz]	[spoz]
family	[fæməli]	[fæmli]	general	[ʤʌnəɹəl]	[ʤʌnɹəl]

Some speakers may delete consonants in certain contexts; for example, another way to repair a sequence of fricatives that is difficult to pronounce is simply to delete one of them. For such speakers, *fifths* may be pronounced as [fɪfs].

French has a phonological operation through which word-final consonants get deleted when the following word begins with an obstruent or the lateral liquid [l], illustrated in (28), but not when the following word begins with a vowel or the labio-velar glide [w], illustrated in (29). (Recall IPA [ʁ] represents a voiced uvular fricative.)

28.

deletion	
petit cadeau [pəti kado] 'small gift'	nos cadeaux [no kado] 'our gifts'
petit livre [pəti livʁ] 'small book'	nos livres [no livʁ] 'our books'

29.

no deletion	
petit ami [pətit ami] 'small friend'	nos amis [noz ami] 'our friends'
petit oiseau [pətit wazo] 'small bird'	nos oiseaux [noz wazo] 'our birds'

Lardil (an Aboriginal language of Australia) has two rules of deletion, which can operate together on the same word. *Rule 1* requires the deletion of a word-final vowel in all words which consist of three or more syllables. *Rule 2* requires words to end with only a single consonant, and that consonant must be made with the tip of the tongue. We can see these two rules in operation in the word for 'dragonfly', exemplified in (30). Here, the original word-final /u/ is deleted by Rule 1, and then the newly-word-final /p/ is deleted by Rule 2. Because the word still ends with a consonant that is not made with the tip of the tongue, Rule 2 operates again to delete the now word-final /m/:

30.

	a	original input	ʧumpuʧumpu
	b	Rule 1 applies	ʧumpuʧump
	c	Rule 2 applies	ʧumpuʧum
	d	Rule 2 re-applies	ʧumpuʧu

If you're wondering how we know what the original input for the Lardil word 'dragonfly' is, those details are provided in Section C6 below.

C4 Epenthesis

Epenthesis (sometimes called insertion) is the opposite of deletion as it entails creating something out of nothing.

In English, the epenthetic segment may be a consonant, particularly given the sequence [nasal + fricative] inside a word. For example, most speakers epenthesize stops in words like *length, tenth,* and *something:* [lɛŋk̲θ], [tɛnt̲θ], [sʌmpθɪŋ]. Note that the epenthetic stop which shows up has the same place of articulation as the nasal which precedes it; this is the result of nasal place assimilation as discussed in Section C1.

It is also the case that some speakers (primarily sportscasters, in my experience) pronounce *length* without epenthesis: [lɛŋθ]. But very few speakers leave out the epenthetic consonant in *tenth. Something* is interesting, as this particular word contrasts with the phrase *some thing;* while epenthesis occurs for most speakers in the word, such is almost non-existent when the phrase is pronounced.

All speakers of English epenthesize vowels in certain contexts; in most varieties of American English, [ə] is the epenthetic vowel of choice. One context in which such epenthesis occurs is in the formation of (regular) plural nouns—but only when the singular forms end with either an affricate or a particular subset of the fricatives. (Here, *garage* is meant to be pronounced with a word-final [ʒ] rather than with [ʤ], in order to give the full range of sounds which trigger epenthesis.)

31.   dress[əz]   fez[əz]   dish[əz]   garage[əz]   witch[əz]   judg[əz]

The six sounds which force vowel epenthesis—[s, z, ʃ, ʒ, ʧ, ʤ]—are the so-called <u>sibilants</u>. Sibilants are distinguished by the high-frequency, hissing noise each results in. Note that the plural marker is also a sibilant; so in this instance, we can say the epenthesis serves to break up a sequence of sibilants.

Our final examples of epenthesis demonstrate what may occur when one language borrows words from another language. We have already discovered that many languages prefer CV syllables, so that all or most syllables consist of nothing other than a simple onset plus a vowel. But "CV-languages" may well borrow words from another language which has more flexible syllable structure. As a result, epenthetic vowels are sure to crop up in the borrowing language, as it works to maintain its own rules of syllable structure.

With this in mind, consider the English words in (32); those in (a) have been borrowed into Japanese, while those in (b) have been borrowed into Hawaiian:

32.					
	a	*English*	bat	strike	baseball
		Japanese	[bɑt.to]	[su.to.ɹɑɪ.ku]	[be.su.bu.ɹo]
	b	*English*	Merry Christmas		
		Hawaiian	[me.li kɑ.li.ki.mɑ.ke]		

As an automatic consequence of the process, vowel epenthesis increases the number of syllables in a given word; English *strike* is a single syllable while the Japanese version is four syllables, and two-syllable *Christmas* becomes a five syllable word in Hawaiian.

Note in passing that further phonological changes occur in the loanwords in (32), as Japanese changes the [l] of *baseball* into an [ɹ] (a voiced alveolar lateral flap) while Hawaiian changes the [ɹ]s of *Merry Christmas* into [l]s and the [s] into [k]. Such changes show that borrowing languages alter loanwords to fit their inventory of sounds, as well as to fit their syllable structure requirements.

C5 Metathesis

Metathesis is sometimes referred to as the 'typo' effect, through which two segments are transposed in position. Metathesis is familiar to many of us from 'child' English, where *spaghetti* may be pronounced as [pəskɛti] and *animal* may be pronounced as [æmɪnəl].

But metathesis is not restricted to child language. In fact, the words *bird, horse,* and *third* came to be pronounced this way only in the Middle English period; in Old English (the form of the language spoken before the eleventh century), the words were *brid, hros* and *thrid*.

Here is a more complicated instance of metathesis that occurs in complex verbs in Hebrew (a Semitic language spoken primarily in Israel). The data in (33) and (34) exemplify the infinitive forms (those in the left-hand columns; translated into English as 'to V') and the so-called 'reflexive' forms (those in the right-hand columns, prefixed with [lehit] and translated in various ways). The interesting point here is that metathesis occurs in the reflexive form <u>only</u> if the infinitive form begins with either a fricative or an affricate. As a result, the prefix is sometimes pronounced [lehit], as in (33); but it is sometimes pronounced [lehits] or [lehiʃ] or [lehis], as in (34). (IPA [ts] represents a voiceless alveolar affricate.)

33.

	no metathesis
[kɑbel] 'to accept'	[lehit-kɑbel] 'to be accepted'
[pɑter] 'to fire'	[lehit-pɑter] 'to resign'
[bɑjeʃ] 'to shame'	[lehit-bɑjeʃ] 'to be ashamed'

34.

	metathesis
[tsɑdek] 'to justify'	[lehits-tɑdek] 'to apologize'
[ʃɑmeʃ] 'to use for'	[lehiʃ-tɑmeʃ] 'to use'
[sɑder] 'to arrange'	[lehis-tɑder] 'to arrange oneself'

Observe that if metathesis fails to operate in the three forms in (34), the results are ungrammatical in the language: *[lehit-tsɑdek], *[lehit-ʃɑmeʃ], *[lehit-sɑder].

C6 Reduplication

Reduplication is a phonological process through which an entire word or part of a word is repeated. The details of reduplication may vary considerably from language to language.

Although reduplication is not a particularly productive process in English, still it's possible to claim that forms such as *helter-skelter, hodge-podge, itsy-bitsy,* and *teeny-weeny* are the results of reduplication. Since only parts of the words are repeated, these all exemplify partial reduplication. In other languages, reduplication is a very productive process—one which occurs so frequently in the language that native speakers are fully familiar with it. Some examples of total reduplication, in which an entire word is repeated, follow.

The Lardil word for *dragonfly* is the result of total reduplication and consists of two pieces: /tʃumpu + tʃumpu/. Of course, as we saw above, deletion rules operate so that what speakers of Lardil actually pronounce gets reduced to [tʃumputʃu].

In many languages, the effect of reduplication is to add an 'intensive' type of meaning to the un-reduplicated original. Thus while the Cambodian word [pseɪŋ] means 'thing', its reduplicated counterpart [pseɪŋ-pseɪŋ] means 'all kinds of things'. Similarly, Mandarin [hóŋ] means 'red', but reduplicated [hóŋ-hoŋ] means 'intensively, vividly red'.

Here are two more examples of total reduplication, one from Maidu (a Maiduan language spoken in Northern California) and one from Karuk (likely a language isolate, also spoken in Northern California); in each instance, the semantic effect of reduplication is intensification of meaning. (IPA [y] denotes a high front round vowel):

35.	a	Maidu	'to wave' [jenesysy]	→	[jenesysy-jenesysy] 'to wave back and forth'
	b	Karuk	'to cough' [ʔaxuh]	→	[ʔaxuh-ʔaxuh] 'to have tuberculosis'

Partial reduplication—in which only part of a word is repeated—can have a similar semantic effect in intensifying a word's meaning. Patterns of partial reduplication can be quite interesting. As the examples in (36) show, in Dakota (a Siouan language spoken primarily in the Northern Plains States), the pattern requires reduplicating the last syllable of the root and attaching the result at the end of the original root. (The final [a] in [xap-a] 'to rustle' is not part of the verbal root; it has been epenthesized in order to create an open syllable at the end of the word.)

36.		'to cut' [ksa]	→	[ksa-ksa]
	Dakota	'to be tall' [haska]	→	[haska-ska]
		'to rustle' [xap-a]	→	[xap-xap-a]

In contrast, Koasati (a Muskogean language spoken in Louisiana) reduplicates the second CV sequence in the word, and attaches the result in the middle of the word. (IPA [c] represents a voiceless palatal stop):

37.		'to glitter' [cikaplin]	→	[cika-ka-plin]
	Koasati	'to clabber' [watoplin]	→	[wato-to-plin]
		'to feel a stabbing pain' [waciplin]	→	[waci-ci-plin]

We discuss reduplication further in Chapter 4, as quite a few languages of the world use this phonological process in order to derive new words from old.

D. Natural Classes

A <u>natural class</u> is a set of sounds which share one or more features. The significance of natural classes arises because all members of a natural class undergo the same kinds of phonological processes.

We've already encountered several natural classes in English, though we did not describe them as such. One of these natural classes is the set of voiceless stops in the language, all of which are aspirated only at the beginning of stressed syllables. But only the voiceless stops of English undergo the process of aspiration. This privilege is not available to any voiced stop or to any voiceless fricative or to any other consonant of the language. Instead, aspiration in English is a process open to only the voiceless stops.

The concept of natural classes is a powerful concept, one which allows us to make significant generalizations about a given language. For example, (15) schematized the phonemes of the three voiceless stops of English separately, as each has both a plain and an aspirated allophone. But we can collapse these three representations into the single representation in (38):

38.

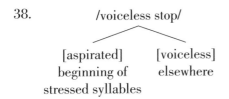

The representation in (38) reads as follows: In English, the voiceless stops are produced with aspiration when they occur at the beginning of stressed syllables; otherwise, they are produced as plain voiceless stops, with no aspiration.

This representation makes a strong claim from the perspective of language acquisition, as it entails that a child must learn only two things: the set of voiceless stops in the language, and the fact that each of them undergoes aspiration at the beginning of stressed syllables. Significantly, the child is not forced to learn three separate instances of aspiration, one for the phoneme /p/, another for the phoneme /t/, and a third for the phoneme /k/. Given that the acquisition process appears to be simple to those undergoing it, achieving simplicity in phonological representation (i.e., one representation instead of three) is a worthy goal.

A second natural class of English that we've already encountered is the set of approximants in the language. As shown in (22), each of /l, ɹ, j, w/ is devoiced when it immediately follows a voiceless stop, though each is voiced elsewhere. We can parsimoniously represent this devoicing process as shown below:

39.

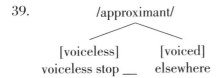

Now recall we previously found (see (9) above) that [k] and [g] are not separate phonemes of Swampy Cree, as the two sounds are in complementary (rather than contrastive) distribution. We found the distribution of [g] was restricted to inter-vocalic position; [k] on the other hand, has (relatively) free distribution—except it never occurs between vowels. Since these two sounds are phonetically similar (differing only in voicing status), we could represent the phoneme as follows:

40.

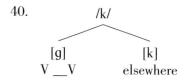

The notation "V __ V" is shorthand for "inter-vocalic position." This schematization entails that the phoneme /k/ is realized as allophone [g] when it occurs between vowels and as allophone [k] every where else.

Now consider these further data from Swampy Cree; the data in the left-hand column focus on the distribution of [t] and [d], while those in the right-hand column focus on the distribution of [p] and [b]:

41.

[t] vs. [d]		*[p] vs. [b]*	
[tɑhki]	'often'	[asɑbɑp]	'thread'
[nisto]	'three'	[nɑbew]	'man'
[ɑdim]	'dog'	[pimi]	'lard'
[mide]	'heart'	[wɑbos]	'rabbit'
[mibit]	'tooth'	[pɑskwɑw]	'prairie'

You should notice rather immediately that the distributions of the voiced stops [b, d] are restricted just as the distribution of [g] is: None of the voiced stops occurs unless it is surrounded by vowels. Elsewhere—preceding a vowel in word-initial position, following a vowel in word-final position, or between a consonant and a vowel in word-medial position—only voiceless stops occur. We could thus schematize the bilabial and alveolar stops of Swampy Cree as follows:

42. a.   b.

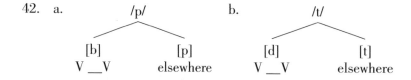

But we can put forward a much stronger analysis. In Swampy Cree, the voiceless stops are always realized as their voiced allophonic variants when they occur inter-vocalically, as schematized below:

43. /voiceless stop/

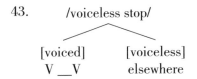

[voiced]   [voiceless]
V __V   elsewhere

So far, we've relied on natural classes to account for the distribution of allophones in a given language. We can also use the concept of natural classes to distinguish between two varieties of the same language.

The data in (44) compare the pronunciations of a set of words in British English and in American English. The puzzle here is that sometimes consonants are produced with a following palatal sound, but sometimes the palatal sound is not allowed in American English. The palatal sound is denoted through the addition of [j] following the relevant consonant. (There are also assuredly vocalic differences between these two varieties of English, which we can safely ignore here.) Notice that many of these words are pronounced the same in both varieties of English; more interestingly, some are pronounced differently:

44.

British	[pj]ure	[nj]ew	[kj]ute	pre[zj]ume	[tj]une
American	[pj]ure	[n]ew	[kj]ute	pre[z]ume	[t]une
British	a[bj]use	[vj]iew	[dj]ues	ar[gj]ue	[mj]use
American	a[bj]use	[vj]iew	[d]ues	ar[gj]ue	[mj]use
British	[sj]uit	[hj]ue	[lj]ewd	en[θj]use	[fj]ew
American	[s]uit	[hj]ue	[l]ewd	en[θ]use	[fj]ew

We could of course simply conclude that these two varieties are different for some mysterious reason and leave the difference unexplored. Or we could scrutinize the data carefully and strive to determine a principled reason for the difference. We take the latter approach here.

As always when solving phonology puzzles, we begin by making lists. The words in (45) represent the 'same' list, as a palatal sound occurs in both British and American English. The words in (46) represent the 'different' list, as these are pronounced with palatal sounds in British English but not in American English.

45. | *same* | [pj]ure | [kj]ute | a[bj]use | [vj]iew | ar[gj]ue | [mj]use | [hj]ue | [fj]ew |

46.

Brit.	[nj]ew	pre[zj]ume	[tj]une	[dj]ues	[sj]uit	[lj]ewd	en[θj]use
Amer.	[n]ew	pre[z]ume	[t]une	[d]ues	[s]uit	[l]ewd	en[θ]use

Generalizing over the list in (45) shows the set [p, k, b, v, g, m, h, f] can be followed by a palatal sound in both varieties, while the lists in (46) show the set [n, z, t, d, s, l, θ] can be followed by a palatal sound only in British English. Now we must determine how these two sets differ from each other.

Clearly, laryngeal status is not the key to our solution, as both sets contain voiceless and voiced sounds. Manner of articulation must not be the key, as both sets contain stops, fricatives, and nasals. The only possibility left is place of articulation—which turns out to lead directly to a straightforward account of the difference between these varieties of English. The relevant consonants from the data in (44) are displayed below in a somewhat stylized consonant chart; those consonants which are allowed to precede a palatal sound only in British English, as shown in (46), are in the encircled area:

47.

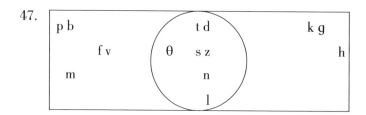

As displayed quite strikingly in this chart, the encircled consonants are all and only the set of Coronal consonants (produced with either the tip or the blade of the tongue as the active articulator). Those outside the encircled area are either the Labials or the Dorsals.

We can now easily describe the differences here: Speakers of American English do not allow palatal [j] to follow a Coronal consonant, but speakers of British English are not subject to this same constraint. There is nothing mysterious about the difference; instead, we have a principled account for the difference, one that is based solely on place of articulation.

To sum up the significance of natural classes: Neither phonological processes (e.g., the inter-vocalic voicing of otherwise voiceless stops of Plains Cree) nor phonological constraints (e.g., lack of a following palatal based on place of articulation in American English) target random collections of sounds. Instead, such processes and constraints operate on groups of sounds which share one or more features—that is, on natural classes of sounds. Recognizing and making use of natural classes allows phonologists to make important generalizations over the patterning of classes of sounds in a given language. More significantly, the existence of natural classes greatly reduces the task of language acquisition, as the child needs to learn quite broad patterns of the distributions of classes of sounds rather than the distribution of each sound individually.

E.   Representing Speaker Knowledge

The notation we have developed here to represent phonemes in a given language provides a great deal of information about the phoneme/allophone distinction, but its format is rather cumbersome. There is a simpler way to denote this part of a speaker's knowledge, through a notation specifically designed for illuminating <u>phonological rules</u>.

Phonological rules are computational statements which function to encode a speaker's knowledge of a particular phonological process which occurs in her native language. Rules provide much the same information as do the representations of phonemes developed previously, but their format is much more concise.

To make this point concrete, consider the inter-vocalic voicing of voiceless stops in Swampy Cree discussed above. The representation in (48a) can be converted into the sentence of English in (48b) and into the phonological rule in (48c):

48.   For Swampy Cree

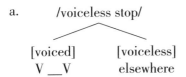

   b.   Voiceless stops are voiced when they occur inter-vocalically; in all other environments, they remain voiceless.

   c.   Inter-vocalic Voicing: /stops/ → [voiced] / V __ V

The arrow in (48c) can be read as "become" or "are pronounced as;" the slash is shorthand for "in the environment of" or "in the context defined as follows."

Phonological rules are computational statements which describe alternations in sounds by <u>deriving</u> one sound from another in a particular phonetic environment. In this way, phonological rules mediate between the phonemic level and the phonetic level.

We can appreciate these points further by recalling the devoicing of approximants in English discussed around (22); we provided a generalized representation for these sounds in

(39). This representation is repeated below in (49a) to show how it can be converted into the sentence in (49b) and into the phonological rule in (49c):

49. For English

    a.   /approximant/

         [voiceless]   [voiced]
    voiceless stop ___   elsewhere

    b.   Approximants are devoiced when they immediately follow a voiceless stop; otherwise, they remain voiced.

    c.   Approximant Devoicing: /approximant/ → [voiceless] / voiceless stop ___

The rule in (49c) clearly provides a more convenient format for expressing the devoicing of approximants in English than either the schematic representation in (49a) or the sentence in (49b).

    Now recall that the stressless vowel [ə] is frequently deleted in rapidly-spoken English; the data presented in (27) are repeated in (50):

50.

	careful	*rapid*		*careful*	*rapid*
parade	[pɚɹed]	[pɹed]	suppose	[səpʰoz]	[spoz]
family	[fæməli]	[fæmli]	general	[ʤʌnəɹəl]	[ʤʌnɹəl]

We can propose the rule in (51a) to account for this vowel deletion, where "Ø" is the null sign; the English-language counterpart to the rule is given in (51b):

51. a.   Schwa Deletion: /ə/ → [Ø] / C ___ CV

    b.   Schwa becomes nothing (i.e., gets deleted) word-medially, when it occurs between consonants and is not the last vowel in the word.

The phonetic context for Schwa Deletion shown in (51a) is somewhat complex, to ensure that only certain schwas can be targeted for deletion. Thus, this rule entails that for a schwa to be deletable, it must be surrounded by consonants; in this way, our rule will not delete either the initial schwa of *apply* nor the final schwa of *sofa*. Further, schwa is not deletable if the consonant which follows schwa is not itself followed by another vowel; in this way, our rule will not delete the second schwa in *general.*

Now observe that in rapid speech, the [ɹ] of *parade* becomes voiceless, as indicated in (50). That a voiceless approximant shows up here entails that two phonological rules of the language interact with each other, and they must do so in a certain way. In particular, the Schwa Deletion rule must operate before the Approximant Devoicing rule does, as shown in the following <u>derivation</u> of the phonetic output, [pɹ̥ed], from the phonemic input /pəɹed/:

52.	a	Phonemic Input	/ pəɹed /
	b	Schwa Deletion	pɹed
	c	Approximant Devoicing	pɹ̥ed
	d	Phonetic Output	[pɹ̥ed]

The phonemic input in (52a) is our mental representation for this word, that is, what we have memorized and stored. The Schwa Deletion rule operates on this input, yielding (that is, deriving) the output in (52b). Now our Approximant Devoicing rule operates on the output in (52b), deriving the output in (52c). There are no more rules to apply, so the phonetic output is that in (52d).

If these two rules were to apply in the opposite order, we would derive an incorrect phonetic output, as shown in the derivation in (53):

53.	a	Phonemic Input	/ pəɹed /
	b	Approximant Devoicing	-----
	c	Schwa Deletion	pɹed
	d	Phonetic Output	*[pɹed]

The dashed lines in (53b) indicate that Approximant Devoicing does not apply here; in fact, it can not apply, as the context it requires does not exist. That context (in which the approximant immediately follows a voiceless stop) does not exist until the schwa has been deleted. But in (53), we have delayed Schwa Deletion, forcing it to operate after Approximant Devoicing. Because the rules have applied in an incorrect order, the output that is derived is incorrect, as indicated by the asterisk in (53d).

Phonological rules such as those discussed above are <u>generative</u> rules, whose operation on a given input generates an appropriate output. As the immediately preceding discussion entails, sometimes more than one rule can operate on an input; when such occurs, the rules operate in a certain order to ensure a correct output.

Relying on a phonological rule clearly provides a much more convenient way for phonologists to account for a native speaker's knowledge than does relying on a simple schematization of the phoneme. Just as significant, however, is the conceptual difference between the two representations: Schematizations are fundamentally static, but rules encode computational processes. That is, while schematizations tell us (part of) what a speaker knows about her language, rules tell us (part of) what that speaker actually <u>does</u> with her language. In this way, phonological rules are powerful tools for anyone interested in accounting for the patterning of sounds within a given language.

This Chapter presented a series of steps crucial to solving phonology problems; these steps are summarized in the flowchart which follows.

Table 5:   *Flowchart for Solving Phonology Problems*

	For the sounds in question, is there a MINImal PAIR in the data?	
	(NO) ◄	► (YES)
Step 1	The distribution is <u>complementary</u>.	The distribution is <u>contrastive</u>.
	The sounds are <u>allophones of one phoneme</u>.	The sounds are <u>separate phonemes</u>.
		Proceed directly to Step 4.
Step 2	Make two lists, one for each sound.	
	Identify the context in which each sound occurs.	
	Generalize over those contexts.	
Step 3	Use your generalizations to identify both the restricted-context and the elsewhere allophones.	
Step 4	Schematize the phoneme.	Schematize the phonemes.
Step 5	Write a phonological rule to derive the restricted-context allophone from the elsewhere allophone.	

F.   A Note on Language Acquisition

We discovered in the last chapter that children begin to perceive different sounds as early as a few weeks of age. Production of speech sounds is generally delayed until around six months of age, primarily as a result of the delay in the maturation of the vocal track. The vocal track begins to approximate the adult shape at around four months, but the process is not complete until the child reaches almost three years of age.

Around six months of age, children enter a milestone in speech production referred to as the babbling stage. Here are three amazing facts about babbling:

- All children start babbling at approximately the same age.
- Babbling has syllabic organization, almost always consisting of strings of reduplicated CV syllables (e.g., *bababa* or *badaba*), which are not related to meaning.
- Most children produce about the same range of consonants (most frequently stops and nasals) and vowels (most frequently low vowels such as [ɑ] and [æ]), regardless of the language spoken in their individual environments.

The latter findings are arguably linked to the lack of maturation of the vocal tract: Making a complete closure for stops and nasals takes less control than modulating the degrees of closure required of fricatives and approximants. Similarly, lowering the jaw to produce low vowels requires less control than raising the body of the tongue to produce high vowels.

When children reach the age of eight to ten months, however, both consonants and vowels begin to become modulated by the ambient language. Boysson-Bardies and Vihman (1991), investigating children whose ambient languages were French, British English, Cantonese, Arabic, Swedish, or Yoruba, found that the quality of the vowels and the types of consonants produced by these infants varied, based on those of their linguistic communities. For example, adult French has front round vowels which are lacking in British English; these vowels were produced by the French infants, but not by the British infants. Analogously, labial consonants occur in more French words than in English words, and infant French learners produce more labials than do their (about-to-be) English-speaking counterparts.

At around ten to twelve months of age, most children begin producing their first understandable words. At this one-word stage, a "word" is defined as a sequence of sound segments with which the child has associated a specific meaning and which the child uses fairly consistently to denote that meaning.

However, many children adopt a series of phonological rules when producing such words; most of these rules relate to simplifying the speech stream and, as such, likely relate closely to lack of full maturation of the vocal track. Among the most common rules adopted by English learners are simplification of consonant clusters, substitution of one sound for another, and assimilation; each is outlined below. (The data presented here, adapted from O'Grady,

Archibald, Aronoff, and Rees-Miller (2005, 367–369), are not from any one child; they are intended to exemplify the range of phonological rules various children may adopt.)

The simplification of consonant clusters is illustrated below, where one consonant in either onset position (the (a) examples) or coda position (the (b) examples) is deleted:

54.

a	stop [tɑp]	try [tɑɪ]	sleep [sip]
b	desk [dɛk]	bump [bʌp]	tent [dɛt]

Observe that fricatives are deleted (cf. *stop, desk*), liquids are deleted (cf. *try, sleep*), and nasals are deleted (cf. *bump, tent*). But stops are saved in all the data. As already noted, stops are considered easier to produce than other consonants, so we might expect infants to preserve stops, when possible, and delete other types of consonants.

The second process—substitution of one sound for another—is illustrated below:

55.

		child	*adult*		*child*	*adult*
a	sing	[tɪŋ]	[sɪŋ]	zebra	[dibɹə]	[zibɹə]
b	spoon	[bud]	[spun]	room	[wub]	[ɹum]
c	laughing	[jæfɪŋ]	[læfɪŋ]	look	[wʊk]	[lʊk]

Once again, the pre-eminence of stops in infants' production shows up. In both (55a) and (55b), stops are substituted for the fricatives and (most) nasals which occur in adult speech (the child version retains [ŋ]). Observe that in both instances the new stops have the same place of articulation and the same laryngeal status as the sounds they substitute for. In (55c) liquids are replaced with glides; note that the glide [j] occurs here preceding a front vowel, while the glide [w] occurs preceding a back vowel; it's likely that these co-occurrences are not random, but are closely related to the third phonological rule: assimilation.

The most common instances of assimilation that occur in one-year olds involve the voicing of onset consonants which are voiceless in the adult language. The claim is that such voiceless consonants assimilate to the voicing of the immediately following vowel:

56.   tell [dɛl]   pig [bɪg]   push [bʊs]   soup [zup]

Similar assimilation has also occurred in the child versions of *tent* in (54a) and *spoon* in (55b).

Some children extend the process of assimilation so that all consonants in a given word end up with the same place of articulation, a process called consonant harmony. Consonant harmony does occur in adult languages (e.g., Navajo), but it is a fairly rare process cross-linguistically.

57.   doggy [ɡɑɡi]   table [bebu]   nipple [mibu]   knife [maɪp]

Observe that it is the second consonant which determines the place of articulation of the first. Thus, it's fair to say that the voicing rule outlined in (56) and consonant harmony rule outlined in (57) both exemplify anticipatory assimilation.

KEY TERMS AND CONCEPTS

syllabic constituents: nucleus, onset, coda, rime

core syllable	open / closed syllables	phonotactics
The Nucleus Rule	The Sonority Hierarchy	Maximize Onset

phoneme	allophone	contrastive distribution
complementary distribution	minimal pair	phonetic level
phonemic level	assimilation	local assimilation
nasal place assimilation	anticipatory assimilation	perseverative assimilation
voicing assimilation	vowel nasalization	flapping
long distance assimilation	vowel harmony	dissimilation
deletion	epenthesis	metathesis
reduplication	natural classes	phonological rules
derive / derivation	babbling stage	one-word stage
	consonant harmony	

PRACTICE PROBLEMS

1. Use the algorithm given in Table 1 of the text to draw complete syllable trees for these words of English:

   a. trees   b. breathless   c. path   d. eggs   e. fox
   f. highball   g. minefield   h. aisle   i. eye   j. width

2. The following sets of minimal pairs show that English /p/ and /b/ contrast in initial and final position: (initial) p̲it / b̲it; and (final) cap̲ / cab̲. Find similar sets of minimal pairs, for both initial and final positions, for each of the consonant pairs below. Remember phonetic transcription, rather than spelling, is the key.

   a. /l/ vs. /m/   b. /d/ vs. /s/   c. /p/ vs. /z/   d. /g/ vs. /f/

3. These data are from Arabic (Afro-Asiatic family; throughout the Middle East and Africa). Consider the sounds [h] and [ʔ]; determine if they are separate phonemes in Arabic or if they are allophones of a single phoneme. Provide evidence to support your conclusion (if phonemes, show the contrast by citing a minimal pair; if allophones, describe the complementary distribution); and provide a representation of the phoneme(s).

[ʔuru:b]	'wars'	[huru:b]	'flight'	[fahm]	'understanding'
[faʔm]	'coal'	[ha:l]	'cardamon'	[habba]	'gust, squall'
[ʔa:l]	'condition'	[ʔabba]	'grain, seed'		

4. Consider these data from Russian and determine if the sounds [l] and [lʲ] are separate phonemes or allophones of a single phoneme. Provide evidence to support your conclusion and provide a representation of the phoneme(s).

[lʲat]	'demon'	[polka]	'shelf'	[lat]	'agreement'
[polʲka]	'polka'	[mel]	'chalk'	[milʲ]	'of miles'

5. Consider the sounds [s] and [ʃ] in the following data from Bemba (a Bantu language of Zambia) and determine if they are separate phonemes or if they are allophones of a single phoneme. Provide evidence to support your conclusion and provide a representation of the phoneme(s).

[ukuʃika]	'to be deep'	[insa]	'clock, hour'	[amakalaʃi]	'glasses'
[fuse:ke]	'go away!'	[isabi]	'fish'	[ame:nʃi]	'water'
[ukusela]	'to move'	[nʃi]	'what'	[akasuba]	'sun'
[inso:koʃi]	'socks'	[soma]	'read!'	[paso:po]	'beware!'

88

6. These data are from Brazilian Portuguese; IPA [ɲ] symbolizes a palatal nasal. Determine if [d] and[ʤ] represent two different phonemes in the language or if they are allophones of the same phoneme. Provide evidence to support your conclusion and provide a representation of the phoneme(s).

[dadu]	'given'	[madriɲa]	'godmother'	[modernu]	'modern'
[unidu]	'united'	[gwarda]	'guard'	[ʤiɲeiru]	'money'
[verʤi]	'green'	[verdaʤi]	'truth'	[grãʤi]	'big'

7. In some dialects of English, there is a predictable variant [ʌɪ] of the diphthong [aɪ], often called 'Canadian raising.' What phonetic segments condition this change? What feature(s) can be used to characterize the class of conditioning segments?

[bʌɪt]	'bite'	[ɹaɪz]	'rise'	[taɪm]	'time'	[taɪ]	'tie'
[baɪ]	'buy'	[tʌɪp]	'type'	[ɹaɪd]	'ride'	[ɹʌɪs]	'rice'
[naɪnθ]	'ninth'	[ɹʌɪt]	'write'	[lʌɪf]	'life'	[bʌɪk]	'bike'

8. These data are from Tamil (Dravidian family; spoken in Southern India and Sri Lanka). The symbols [ṭ, ḷ, ẓ] are retroflexes, in which the tongue tip is curled up and back, touching or approaching the back of the alveolar ridge; [t̪, n̪] represent dental sounds; [ɯ] is a high back non-round vowel. In Tamil, the vowels [ɯ] and [ʊ] are allophones of the phoneme /ʊ/. Determine the context in which [ɯ] occurs, and state that context. Hint: You must look beyond the segments which are immediately adjacent to the vowels under discussion.

[ʊppʊ]	'salt'	[ʊmi]	'husk'	[mʊrɔ]	'winnowing fair'
[puẓʊ]	'worm'	[paẓɯ]	'waste'	[t̪erɯ]	'street'
[urʊ]	'village'	[aðɯ]	'it'	[puṭṭʊ]	'lock'
[t̪olʊ]	'leather'	[t̪oḷʊ]	'shoulder'	[net̪t̪ɯ]	'yesterday'
[min̪ɯ]	'fish'	[neɲʤɯ]	'heart'		

9. a. Which consonants are aspirated syllable-initially in English?
    b. If we ignore the 'ordinal' suffix [θ] (as in *sixth*), which consonants can appear word-finally (and in the same syllable) after [s] in English?
    c. Which consonants can occur between [s] and [ɹ] in onsets of English words?
    d. What is the significance of the fact that the three questions in (a), (b), and (c) have the same answer?

10. In Old English, the members of the pairs [f] and [v], [h] and [x], [n] and [ŋ] were in complementary distribution. Based on the following data, what was the distribution of each of these sounds? Answering this question fully requires considering each of the three pairs of sounds. The symbol [y] represents a high front round vowel; the symbol [x] denotes a voiceless velar fricative.

[briŋgan]	'to bring'	[luvu]	'to love'	[driŋkan]	'to drink'
[mannes]	'man's'	[fæst]	'fast'	[mo:na]	'moon'
[fi:fta]	'fifth'	[ni:xsta]	'next'	[fɔlk]	'folk'
[no:n]	'noon'	[fɔnt]	'font'	[ɔffrian]	'to offer'
[hɑt]	'hot'	[ɔvnas]	'ovens'	[hlo:θ]	'troop'
[ru:x]	'rough'	[hlyxxan]	'to laugh'	[ləŋgan]	'to lengthen'
[θuŋgɛn]	'full grown'	[hrævn̩]	'raven'	[nixt]	'night'

11. The following data are from Gascon (Romance language; southwest France). The segments [b], [β], [d], [ð], [g] and [ɣ] all surface in the language. The symbols [β] and [ɣ] represent voiced bilabial and velar fricatives, respectively; nasalized vowels are not shown.

[bux]	'you'	[aβe]	'to have'	[bako]	'cow'
[alaβets]	'then, well'	[umbro]	'shadow'	[saliβo]	'saliva'
[breɲ]	'endanger'	[noβi]	'husband'	[dilus]	'Monday'
[buðet]	'gut'	[diŋko]	'until'	[eʃaðo]	'hoe'
[duso]	'sweet'	[biɣar]	'mosquito'	[gat]	'cat'
[riɣut]	'he laughed'	[guteʒa]	'flow'	[dariɣa]	'pull out'
		[eŋgwan]	'last'		

a. Which pairs among the segments [b], [β], [d], [ð], [g] and [ɣ] are the most phonetically similar? (Given the six segments, you should come up with three sets of pairs.) Support your claim with phonetic descriptions of the similar pairs.
b. List the environments in which each of the six segments is found.
c. Do your responses in (a) and (b) provide evidence for grouping these pairs of sounds into phonemes? If so, explain that evidence for each pair.
d. Provide schematic representations of each of the phonemes you found in (c).
e. What are the phonemes of the medial consonants, circled in the following forms?

    i. [p u ⓨ o]   ii. [d e ⓓ a t]   iii. [g u ⓑ a r]   iv. [a m ⓑ u d]

12. Consider the problems in (3) through (6) again. If you found that the sounds in question in any of these problems were allophones of the same phoneme, write the phonological rule that would generate the relevant allophone (the one whose distribution is easily stated).

13. Consider the following data sets and name the phonological process(es) exemplified in each; your choices are assimilation, dissimilation, epenthesis, or deletion.

a.
English	*careful speech*	*more natural articulation*
love to go	[lʌvtəgo]	[lʌftəgo]
as well as can be	[əzwɛləzkənbi]	[əzwɛləskənbi]
has to go	[hæztəgo]	[hæstəgo]
loathe to go	[loðtəgo]	[loθtəgo]

b.
Greek	'cheap'	'seven'	'eight'
Classical Greek	[fθinos]	[epta]	[okto]
Modern Greek	[ftinos]	[efta]	[oxto]

c. Japanese
simple words
'fold' [ori]   'paper' [kami]   'shelf' [tana]   'make' [tsukuri]

compound words
'paper folding'	/ori-kami/	→	[origami]
'origami shelf'	/origami-tana/	→	[origamidana]
'origami shelf making'	/origamidana-tsukuri/	→	[origamidanadzukuri]

d. Russian
simple words
'place'	[mest-o]
'star'	[zvjozd-ɪ]
'Ireland'	[irland-ija]
'giant'	[gigant]

complex words
'local'	/mest-nɪj/	→	[mesnɪj]
'stellar'	/zvjozd-nɪj/	→	[zvjoznɪj]
'Irish'	/irland-skij/	→	[irlanskij]
'gigantic'	/gigant-skij/	→	[giganskij]

e. <u>English</u>   *regular past tense verb forms*
Develop two different responses here; first contrast the data in (i) and (ii), and then consider only the data in (iii):
  i.   grab / slam / seethe / please / plan / fog / hang / enjoy / chew
  ii. peep / fix / flush / pack
  iii. fit / knit / fade / blend

CHAPTER 4

MORPHOLOGY: INSIDE WORDS

This chapter explores the internal structure of words. One of our initial tasks, therefore, is to define precisely what a 'word' is. As we soon discover, such a definition can prove somewhat elusive. Nevertheless, it's easy to see that we have a great deal of knowledge—albeit tacit knowledge—about a very large number of words in our native language: We know how to pronounce many words and what those words mean; additionally, we know the syntactic category (i.e., 'part of speech') of those words, we know something about their idiosyncratic properties, and we know something about their internal structure.

A. What Is a 'Word'?

Before we can define 'word' very precisely, it's useful to consider what words are not. First, words are not phonemes. While phonemes consist of sound, words have meaning in addition to sound. Moreover, in all languages, the difference between the number of sounds and the number of words is enormous. As mentioned in Chapter 2, most varieties of English contain some forty sounds, but high school graduates in the United States control some sixty thousand words—fifteen hundred times the number of sounds they use.

Second, words are not syllables. Although many languages contain mono-syllabic words, almost every language also contains a multitude of multi-syllabic words. For instance, the very last sentence contains sixteen words; of these, four have only one syllable but the other twelve contain two or more syllables. The word *syllable* in fact contains three syllables.

One intuitive way for determining what is a word (and what is not) might be to rely on the written language, so that a word is whatever can occur between spaces. But this method cannot apply to languages such as Cambodian or the Chinese languages which do not separate words in their written forms. Nor can it account for pre-literate children; even young children who can neither read nor write have conceptualized *mommy* and *daddy* as separate words. Nor does it necessarily apply to literate adults, a fact illustrated with the following sentence:

1.   Every surfer appreciates a wet suit on a cold, wintry day.

If we used nothing other than typographic spacing to determine word-hood, we would be forced to conclude that this sentence contains eleven separate words. But certainly, within the mini-context established in this sentence, the only plausible meaning of *wet suit* is "a tight-fitting garment made of foam neoprene rubber or similar material, which traps a thin insulating layer of water near the skin and helps keep the wearer warm." That is, *wet suit* here must be a single, compound word. Consequently, the sentence in (1) contains only ten words.

We found in Chapter 2 that native speakers of English use the stress system of the language to tease apart compound words from simple phrases. While the meanings of compound words are often idiosyncratic, the meanings of phrases are generally equivalent to the sum of their parts. We know that *wet suit* in (1) cannot reasonably refer simply to a suit (of clothing) that is wet, as such would surely not be appreciated by any surfer. And it is the stress system of the language, not its orthographic conventions, which leads us to this conclusion. What this entails is that we can rely (at least in part) on the phonological system to help us determine what is (and what is not) a word.

A second test for word-hood is this: A word is an element that can be pronounced meaningfully in isolation. We can demonstrate this test with the following mini-discourse:

2.   a.   Speaker #1:   Mikey'll eat anything!
     b.   Speaker #2:   Who'll eat anything?
     c.   Speaker #1:   { Mikey / *Mikey'll / *'ll }

We know of course that *Mikey'll* in Speaker #1's exclamation in (2a) consists of the string [*Mikey will*], but *will* has been reduced through contraction, a phenomenon that occurs frequently in conversational speech in English. We also know that Speaker #2's question in (2b) is asking for clarification of Speaker #1's exclamation, in seeking repetition of the identification of the 'anything eater'. Now notice how Speaker #1's clarification in (2c) is restricted: Speaker #1 can respond with *Mikey;* but not with either *Mikey'll* or with *'ll*. Even though *Mikey'll* is orthographically 'one word', it is not a 'word' that can be produced in isolation. And while *'ll* has meaning in context (when it occurs within a given sentence and is phonologically attached to something), it has no meaning when pronounced in isolation; therefore, it cannot be a 'word'. The name *Mikey,* in contrast, is a word which has meaning when pronounced in isolation.

These two tests are not fool-proof, and they do not work for every human language, as not every language is a stress language and not every language allows contraction in the way that English does. But these tests can be helpful for dealing with the facts of English. As a working definition, we can say a 'word' is a single, pronounceable unit of sound-meaning.

Even though defining 'word' is not an easy task, it's still fair to say that we have a great deal of tacit knowledge of the words of our native language. For one thing, we realize that, in the vast majority of instances, the connection between the sound of a given word and the meaning of that word is completely arbitrary. Thus, there is no connection between the sequence of sounds /dɛsk/ and the meaning "a table specially designed for convenience in reading and/or writing."

Moreover, we have the ability to straightforwardly distinguish possible words in our native language from impossible words. Some words which are possible though non-existent words of English are given in (3a); those in (3b) are impossible in the language:

3.

a	blick	strale	pask	wung
b	*bnick	*ztrale	*pafk	*wumg

The impossible words in (3b) do not violate any universal restriction on syllable structure; but they do violate the phonotactics of English. The possible words in (3a) all satisfy both universal and language-specific restrictions. These two sets taken together demonstrate one way in which the phonological and the morphological components of the grammar of English interact with each other.

But our tacit knowledge of words of English goes much farther. Given a possible word used in a sentence, we have the ability to ascertain its syntactic category. For example, in (4) below, we unerringly judge *blick* to be a verb, the type of word which denotes an activity or event:

4.   Sam always wants to <u>blick</u> his new car.

Given that *blick* is a verb, we have no trouble at all in creating its past tense and progressive forms: *blicked* and *blicking,* respectively. We can also derive various nouns from this verb: *blicker, blickation,* and *blickant,* for example. Moreover, we can derive adjectives from the verb *blick,* including *blickative, blickish,* and *blicky;* from these adjectives we can derive the adverbs *blickatively, blickishly,* and *blickily.* Finally, given the adjective *blicky,* we can also derive another noun, *blickiness.* In other words, we know how to string certain pieces of meaning together to make other words; ergo, we must know that words can have internal structure.

Excursus on Syntactic Categories

So far, we have rather blithely assumed that words fall into different <u>syntactic categories</u> (traditionally referred to as 'parts of speech'), and that we can easily distinguish among these categories. Here, we begin to formalize these concepts in linguistic terms.

Linguists find it convenient to split the words of all languages into two major classes: the <u>content categories</u> and the <u>functional categories</u> (these classes are sometimes referred to as lexical and grammatical categories, respectively).

Included in the content categories are nouns, verbs, adjectives, and (sometimes) prepositions. These are also referred to as the <u>open categories</u> because it is always easy to make up a new member, as demonstrated above for the hypothetical word *blick.* (While it may be difficult to make up a new preposition, it's straightforward to make up complex prepositions in English: *up back behind, over beyond, down around,* and so forth.)

The functional categories include pronouns (e.g., *I, me, my*), articles and demonstratives (e.g., *a* and *those*), modal auxiliaries (e.g., *will, would, can, could*), and so forth. These categories are called closed categories as it is virtually impossible—in English or in any other language—to add new members to these classes of words.

Knowing a language consists in part of having knowledge of a great many words in that language. To a large extent, this type of knowledge must be memorized, as the connection between the sound of a word and the meaning of that word is arbitrary, as already noted. Linguists represent this static part of our knowledge through entries in the mental lexicon, a giant dictionary in our brains which serves as the repository of the words of our language.

Each word has its own separate entry in the mental lexicon, and each entry contains a range of information about that word. For example, the entry for *steal* contains its sound (/stil/), its meaning ("to take dishonestly or wrongly"), its syntactic category (verb), as well as the facts that it is a transitive verb (i.e., requires a direct object following it) and has an irregular past tense form (/stol/).

We explore lexical entries in greater detail in Chapter 5, and we discuss what we know of word meaning in Chapter 6. Right now, we explore what we know of the internal structure of words.

B. Our Knowledge of Words

As demonstrated above with the hypothetical word *blick,* we have a great deal of tacit knowledge of the internal structure of words of English. Let's consider what we know about some actual words of the language; for concreteness, consider the words in (5):

5.

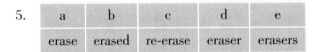

a	b	c	d	e
erase	erased	re-erase	eraser	erasers

We know that the words in (5a-c) are all verbs, while those in (5d-e) are nouns. We can easily tell that the root (the smallest part of the form which has meaning, and from which other forms may be derived) in all instances is the same, *erase* "rub or scrape out; delete." And we know that (5b-e) are complex words: *erased* consists of the root *erase* plus *-ed* (past tense); *re-erase* consists of the root plus *re-* (which means 'again'); *eraser* consists of the root plus *-er* ('one who or thing which verbs'); and *erasers* consists of the root plus *-er* and *-s* (plural).

We identified five pieces of words in the previous paragraph, and we associated each piece with a meaning: the root *erase*, *-ed*; *re-*, *-er*, and *-s*. Each of these pieces of meaning is a morpheme, by definition the smallest piece of a word that is meaningful.

While meaning plays a limited role in phonology, it plays a primary role in morphology. For a given string to be identified as a morpheme, it must have meaning and it must retain that meaning inside a given word. As a result, -er is a morpheme in *writer,* 'one who writes', and in *warmer,* 'more warm'. But -er cannot be a morpheme in *weather,* as *weather* means neither 'one who weaths' nor 'more weath'; that is, in *weather,* the string -er represents a phonological string (with sound) but not a morphological element (with meaning).

Of the five morphemes identified in (5) above, only one has meaning when it is pronounced in isolation: *erase.* We call such morphemes free morphemes, as they can stand alone. The other morphemes identified above (-ed, re-, er-, and -s) have no particular meaning when pronounced in isolation. Instead, they are bound morphemes, and they become meaningful only when they are attached to a host.

Before proceeding, we pause to note that based on historical facts, it's helpful to split the verbs of English into two major classes: One class comprises the regular (or weak) verbs; to form the past tense of a regular verb, we add -ed at the end of the root. The other class of verbs is called the irregular (or strong) verbs; these are frequently-used verbs which are hold-overs from Old English. The process through which past tense forms are created for these verbs is called ablaut, the technical term for 'shift the quality of the vowel'. Thus we have *break* vs. *broke, take* vs. *took, sit* vs. *sat, give* vs. *gave,* and so forth.

Speakers of Modern English must memorize the past tense forms of the irregular verbs, as the ablaut rule is no longer productive. But we certainly do not have to memorize the past tense forms of the regular verbs, as we are intimately familiar with what is now the productive rule: Add -ed at the end of the verbal root.

Productive rules are those which native speakers employ so often that they produce a great many outputs. In forming the past tense of *blick* from (4) above, you were showing off your knowledge of and your ability to employ the productive rule of past tense formation in English.

But our knowledge of English words is much deeper than hinted at so far. Intuitively, we all know *unhappiness* is one word which consists of three morphemes: the free morpheme *happy* and the bound morphemes *un-* and *-ness.* Likewise, we know *rehospitalized* contains four morphemes (*hospital, re-, -ize, -ed*) and *reinstitutionalizations* contains seven morphemes (*institute, re-, -tion, -al, -ize, -ation, -s*). What may not be so intuitive is that, in each instance, the order of the morphemes is neither random nor subject to change. This statement may not sound surprising until you consider how many possible arrangements exist in each case.

To determine how many orders a given number of elements can occur in, we use the mathematical operation called "factoring." Three elements can be ordered in 3! ways, where 3! is the output of $(1 \times 2 \times 3) = 6$. The six ways the three morphemes of *unhappiness* could be arranged are these:

6.

un - happy - ness	*happy - un - ness	*happy - ness - un
*un - ness - happy	*ness - un - happy	*ness - happy - un

What's significant about the data in (6) is that only a single arrangement of these three morphemes produces a word of English; the other five arrangements produce nonsense. Similarly, the four morphemes of *rehospitalized* could be arranged in 4! = 24 ways, while the seven morphemes of *reinstitutionalizations* could be arranged in an astounding 7! = 5,040 ways. Yet even in these instances, only a single order results in a word of English.

In the following section, we develop a method that accounts for the allowable arrangement of morphemes within a given word of English. There are three important facts to keep in mind as we proceed through the discussion: First, there is no correspondence between syllable and morpheme; thus the word *hippopotamus* consists of five syllables but only a single morpheme, while the word *cats* consists of a single syllable but two morphemes.

Second, there is no necessary correspondence between the morphemes of English and its orthographic system; *scarier* consists of three morphemes: *scare*, *-y*, and *-er*, not *scar*, *-i*, and *-er*. We know the middle morpheme in *scarier* is *-y* rather than *-i*, because of the existence of words such as *scary, scratchy, runny, jumpy,* and so forth.

Third, a given morpheme (whether free or bound), may exhibit phonological alternation, as shown below for English:

7.

	indefinite article	
a	<u>an</u> { apple, onion, eel, eyeful }	<u>a</u> { banana, potato, snake, mouthful }
	past tense *–ed*	
b	jump[t], kiss[t], walk[t], lurch[t]	jab[d], buzz[d], jog[d], judge[d]

Such phonological alternants of various morphemes are called <u>allomorphs</u>. We encounter a range of similar allomorphy throughout this chapter.

With these three facts in mind, we are ready to explore the world of morphology, a world which is generally split into three major types of word formation processes: derivation, inflection, and compounding. These types are detailed in the following sections; each begins with a discussion of the relevant phenomena in English and then enlarges the discussion to consider a range of other languages.

C. Derivational Morphology

The function of derivational morphology is to make new words out of existing words, a process which entails creating a word with a different meaning or one of a different syntactic category than that of the <u>root</u> from which it derives. In English (as in many languages), roots come from only three syntactic categories—N, V, or A—all of which are among the content categories. The most common operation is <u>affixation</u>, the process of combining free morphemes (i.e., roots) and bound morphemes.

C1 Affixation in English

English has two productive affixal operations: <u>prefixation</u>, where the affix is attached at the beginning of the free morpheme, and <u>suffixation</u>, where the affix is attached at the end of the free morpheme:

8.

a	*prefixation*	re - start	ex - spouse	un - happy
b	*suffixation*	start - er	spouse - al	happy - ness

Note of the examples in (8a) that the result of prefixation is to create a word with a meaning different from that of the root: start vs. start again, spouse vs. former spouse, and happy vs. not happy, respectively. But in the examples in (8b) the result of suffixation is to create a word of a different (syntactic) category than that of the root: verb vs. noun, noun vs. adjective, and adjective vs. noun, respectively.

In fact, if we consider a wider range of (productive) affixation in English, we find the same generalizations: Prefixes create words of different meaning while suffixes create words of different category, compared to the roots from which they are derived. Here are some further examples of prefixes to consider:

Table 1: *Some English Prefixes*

prefix	meaning	attach to	examples
anti-	against, opposite	N	anti-hero, anti-depressant, anti-climax
in-	not	A	incompetent, intolerant, indecent, ingrown
mis-	wrong, opposite	V	misidentify, misfire, misplace, mishandle
re-	again	V	rethink, reexamine, restate, redo, reread
un_1-	not	A	unhappy, unpleasant, uneven, unintelligent
un_2-	reverse action	V	untie, unmask, unblock, unclog

Table 1 shows that there is no one-to-one correspondence between sound and meaning in English prefixes. *In-* and un_1- share meaning but are phonologically distinct, while un_1- and un_2- share sound but have different meanings. Further, each prefix listed above is limited to attaching only to roots of certain syntactic categories. Thus, while both *anti-* and *mis-* contain the meaning 'opposite', *anti-* attaches to nouns while *mis-* attaches to verbs; and if we switch the prefixes on *anti-hero* and *misidentify*, for example, the results are gibberish: *anti-identify, *mishero.

But some prefixes have restrictions that go beyond the category of the root they attach to. Un_1- generally attaches only to adjectives that have a 'positive' meaning; compare the examples in Table 1, all of which are fine, with these decidedly weird words: *unsad, *unnasty, *unlopsided, *unstupid. In the same vein, while un_2- attaches to verbs, it cannot attach to just any verb; as *uneat, *uncook, *unhappen, and *unoccur demonstrate, un_2- cannot attach to verbs which denote actions or changes of state which can not be reversed or undone.

We've seen that the prefixes of English are restricted by the category of the root they can attach to, and sometimes even by the meaning of that root. The 'technical' term linguists use for prefixes which have so many restrictions is finicky.

A few of the productive suffixes of English are given in Table 2:

Table 2:   *Some English Suffixes*

suffix	effect	examples
-able	V → A	fixable, readable, teachable, discernible
-(at)ion	V → N	realization, hospitalization, germination
-al	N → A	national, adjectival, sentential, comical
-er	V → N	teacher, eraser, devourer, speaker
-ian	N → A	Grecian, Egyptian, magician, logician
-ist	N or A → N	violinist, phonologist, activist, realist
$-ly_1$	A → Adv	quietly, happily, rapidly, repeatedly
$-ly_2$	N → A	friendly, godly, queenly, brotherly

The second column in Table 2 denotes both the category of the root to which a given suffix attaches and the category of the resulting complex word. For example, *-able* (pronounced [ʌbəl]) attaches to verbs, and suffixation yields an adjective: If I can *fix* something, then it is *fixable*.

English has two suffixes which share sound: $-ly_1$ and $-ly_2$. The meaning of $-ly_1$ is 'in a manner which is'; it attaches to adjectives, turning them into adverbs. Thus, we can say of someone that *she makes quick$_A$ decisions* or that *she decides quickly$_{Adv}$*. In contrast, *-ly$_2$* is a carry-over from the Old English period, when it was the free morpheme *lic* 'like'. Affixal *-ly$_2$* attaches to nouns, turning them into adjectives; if *he has a friendly$_A$ manner*, then *he is acting like a friend$_N$*.

Like their prefixal counterparts, the suffixes of English are finicky and restricted in their distribution. For instance, *-ly$_1$* never attaches to color terms, even though these are adjectives: **redly, *bluely*. And *-ly$_2$* never attaches to nouns that do not refer to humans: **deskly, *dogly*.

But some suffixes are particularly finicky: While *-ian* attaches to nouns, turning them into adjectives, it in general attaches only to nouns which are of Greek origin. But it doesn't attach to all nouns of Greek origin; thus, while *logician* is a perfectly good word of English, **phonologician* and **morphologician* are impossible—even though both of these words contain the string *logician*. Instead, suffixal *-ist* must occur here: *phonologist, morphologist*. Observe that *-ist* can attach to both nouns and adjectives; but, like *-ian*, it is restricted. Thus, while *clarinetist* and *trombonist* are fine, **drummist* and **trumpetist* are impossible; likewise **permissivist* and **suggestivist* are out, though *activist, realist*, and *relativist* are in.

Another way to see just how finicky derivational affixes can be in English is to consider words such as *sing-**er**, appli-**cant**, violin-**ist**, prank-**ster**, magic-**ian***, and *cook-**Ø***. (The symbol " Ø " is the null sign, meaning that nothing is pronounced out loud.) In each instance, the underlined suffix refers to 'one who'—but the derivational morphemes are not substitutable for each other. For example, words such as **sing-cant* and **violin-ster* are completely impossible. English is fairly unusual among the world's languages in allowing the same meaning to be expressed through more than a single derivational morpheme.

C2 Accounting for Derivational Affixes in English

We account for our knowledge of the internal structure of words which contain derivational affixes by generating <u>word trees</u>. In this way, word trees are analogous to the syllable trees we generated in the previous chapter to account for the internal structure of syllables.

Recall that all syllables are headed, by an element called the nucleus. Similarly, words are <u>headed</u> (more accurately, are <u>endocentric</u>; this term means that at least one element in the string is of the same syntactic category as the whole string). While we may intuitively sense that the head of a word is equivalent to its root (the N, V, or A from which the complex word is derived), this turns out not to be the case. Instead, the head of a given derived word is considered to be the morpheme which determines the syntactic category of the complex word.

We've seen that derivational prefixes create words with different meanings than the roots to which they attach, but derivational suffixes are characterized by the ability to create words of different syntactic categories than the roots to which they attach. In the examples below, the head of the complex derived word is underlined:

9.	a	re-<u>think</u>	un-<u>real</u>	ex-president	un-<u>fair</u>
	b	think-<u>er</u>	real-<u>ist</u>	president-<u>ial</u>	fair-<u>ness</u>

It may be surprising to claim that bound morphemes such as *-er, -ist, -(i)al,* and *-ness* should be considered the head of the word in which they occur. But these morphemes play a most crucial role within the word, as they are solely responsible for the resulting syntactic category which arises through the process of suffixation.

Note that the heads of the words in (9) all occur on the right-hand side of the word. To understand the significance of the right-hand morpheme serving as head of the word, consider the morphologically-complex word *renationalization*. This complex word 'contains' the noun *nation*, the adjective *national*, the verbs *nationalize* and *renationalize*. Yet we unerringly classify the entire word as a noun, because of the presence of the right-most morpheme, *-ation*.

There are exceptional cases in which the right-most morpheme does not serve as the head of a derived word: e.g., *de-throne, en-courage, be-head*. However, these prefixes are hold-overs from earlier stages of the language and are not productive today. That is, we no longer have the privilege of prefixing a noun with *de-, en-,* or *be-* and have the result be a verb; **de-lounger, *en-bravery,* and **be-ear* are non-words and cannot mean 'to deprive someone of a lounger', 'to give someone braveness', and 'to cut someone's ear off', respectively. As with the other morphological exceptions encountered in this chapter (e.g., the irregular past tense forms of the strong verbs), words such as *dethrone, encourage,* and *behead* must be specifically learned and memorized by native speakers.

Like syllable trees, word trees show both linear structure (e.g., *re-think,* not **think-re*) and hierarchical structure. There is a notable difference between the two types of trees, however, as the computational process which assembles morphemes into words can handle only two pieces of structure at any one time, a restriction whose effect will soon become apparent.

To schematize the internal structure of a word such as *rethink* requires several steps:

- ▪ Step 1: Strip off the affix, leaving only the root.
- ▪ Step 2: Project the root and label its syntactic category.
- ▪ Step 3: Project the affix and label it.
- ▪ Step 4: Merge (i.e., combine) the projections of the root and the affix together, and project the syntactic category of the entire word.

'Project' here refers to a tree-building operation that requires identifying a morpheme (root and/or affix) and labeling it with its syntactic category, as exemplified immediately below. (The use of the term *project* in morphology is thus in many ways analogous to its use in phonology. Recall in discussing syllable structure, our first operation was "Project the nucleus.")

The four steps outlined above are schematized below for the word *rethink*.

10.

Step 1	re	think
Step 2		V | re think
Step 3	Af_V | re	V | think
Step 4		V /\\ Af_V V | | re think

Note carefully that the affix *re-* 'again' carries a syntactic category label, denoted by the subscript V. This subscript encodes our knowledge that *re-* attaches to verbs, but to words of no other syntactic category. Similarly, the labels of *ex-* and *anti-* would be subscripted with N, *mis-* and *un$_2$-* with V, *in-* and *un$_1$-* with A, and so forth, to denote our knowledge of the categories these affixes attach to.

The word tree for *thinker* would be generated similarly, in four separate steps, only the last of which is provided below. Notice the affix *-er* is marked with the syntactic category label N; this subscript encodes our knowledge that the meaning of this morpheme ('one who') denotes a noun (i.e., an entity rather than an event or action):

11.

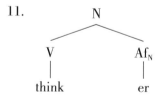

The significant difference between the trees in (10) and (11) relates to the head of each derived word: In the former, the head is the verbal root *think* and the resulting word is also a verb. In the latter, the head is the affix *-er*, and the resulting word is a noun. Most significantly, the head of the word is the morpheme on the right-hand side; that is, the syntactic category of the right-hand morpheme determines the category of the entire derived word.

Drawing word trees for words such as *nationalization,* which contain a number of affixes, is simplified by the fact that the computational system within the morphology module can assemble only two pieces at any one time. The important thing to remember when producing such trees is to start with the root and build structure from the bottom up, one piece at a time. The tree for *nationalization* is given in (12):

12.

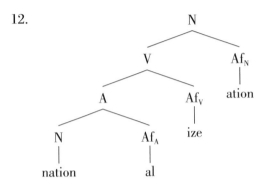

This tree was produced as follows: First, the root *nation* was stripped out, leaving the affixes *-al, -ize,* and *-ation. Nation* was projected as an N, with which Af$_A$ *-al* was merged; the result was the A *national.* Then Af$_V$ *-ize* was merged with the A, resulting in the V *nationalize.* Finally, Af$_N$ *-ation* was merged to the V, resulting in the N *nationalization.* The hierarchical structure of this word is directly reflected in the ordering of the attachment (i.e., merging) of the various morphemes.

Sometimes the internal structure of a morphologically-derived word is not so obvious. Consider the word *unhappiness,* which consists of the root *happy* (an adjective) and the affixes *un-* and *-ness.* Since we can assemble only two pieces at any given time, we must decide which affix we should attach to the root first, the prefix *un-* or the suffix *-ness.* That is, we must determine if we want to attach *un-* to [happy - ness] or if we want to attach *-ness* to [un - happy].

The key to such a problem relates to the *meaning* and *distribution* of the individual morphemes involved. We know *-ness* attaches to a great many adjectives, turning them into nouns: *red-ness, good-ness, sad-ness, slow-ness, deliberate-ness,* and so forth. But we also know (or should at least strongly suspect) that nouns cannot be negated. As a result, words such as **un-ceiling* (to refer to the floor) or **un-leisure* (to refer to work) are completely impossible. Consequently, we must first attach prefixal *un-* to *happy,* deriving the (negative) adjective *unhappy.* Then we can turn the adjective *unhappy* into a noun by attaching suffixal *-ness:*

13.

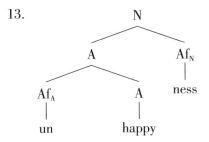

We can rely in part on the meaning of individual morphemes to schematize the internal structure of complex words simply because morphemes are meaningful by definition.

The word tree for *nationalization* was provided in (12). Now consider what the word tree for *renationalization* must look like. Do you think that prefixal *re-* is simply added on top of the structure in (12)? Or must this affix attach somewhere else in the structure? (The solution is provided at the beginning of the answer key for the problems in this chapter.)

The computational process for generating word trees outlined above may appear tedious to you. But it is precisely this step-by-step process of assembling no more than two pieces at a time, mediated by the meanings and distributions of the morphemes involved, that rules out five of the six possible orders for the three morphemes of *unhappiness* as well as 5,039 of the 5,040 possible orders for the seven morphemes of *reinstitutionalizations*, examples noted at the beginning of this chapter. And any computational process which yields such amazing results must be deemed a worthy process.

C3 Other Derivational Processes in English

While affixation is by far the most common derivational process used in English to create new words out of old, the language also employs several other interesting processes.

One such derivational process goes under the rubric <u>stress shift</u>. Stress shift affects a fairly large number of two-syllable words which are interpreted as verbs under one stress pattern but as nouns under another stress pattern. In these examples, stressed syllables are underlined:

14.

a	sub<u>ject</u>	con<u>test</u>	sur<u>vey</u>	per<u>mit</u>	con<u>duct</u>	ex<u>port</u>
b	<u>sub</u>ject	<u>con</u>test	<u>sur</u>vey	<u>per</u>mit	<u>con</u>duct	<u>ex</u>port

The words in (14a) exemplify the <u>iambic</u> stress pattern, in which a stressless syllable is followed by a stressed syllable (cf. Wordworth's *Is <u>this</u> the <u>face</u> that <u>sank</u> a <u>thousand ships</u>?*). And these words can be interpreted only as verbs. In contrast, the words in (14b) exemplify the <u>trochaic</u>

stress pattern, in which a stressed syllable is followed by a stressless syllable (cf., *Jack and Jill went up the hill to fetch a pail of water*). And these words can be interpreted only as nouns.

To see how 'real' these differences in stress patterns are, try pronouncing the words in these sentences with the wrong pattern (the correct pattern is indicated by underlining):

15. a.   That ruler always subjects his subjects to excessive taxes.
     b.   The warden doesn't permit ex-cons to purchase fishing permits.
     c.   Whenever contests end in a tie, Sam always contests the results.

While the number of words subject to stress shift is somewhat limited in the language (as it affects only two-syllable words), English allows a great many words to undergo the derivational process known as conversion (sometimes called zero-derivation). This process is characterized by the absence of accompanying morphological and/or phonological change of any sort, as neither affixation nor stress change occurs. Instead, we simply start with a noun and turn it into a verb:

16. a.   He is my father$_N$; he fathered$_V$ me.
     b.   First she put a saddle$_N$ on the horse, and then she saddled$_V$ the mule.

Among the very wide range of nouns which can be turned into verbs via conversion are these: *mother, sister, brother, butter, phone, mail, email, text, ship, cage, box, crate, brush, comb, saddle, paint, chair, table, board, cough, cry, smile, dance, dream, run, light, trash, swim, roof, eye, elbow,* and *knee.* You could no doubt add another dozen or two to this list with only a few minute's reflection.

The final derivational process of English considered here is acronymy. Acronyms are created by stringing together the first letter(s) in each word of a complex title or descriptive phrase. A few acronyms are provided in (17), where the letters relevant to the acronym are in upper case:

17. a.   NASA   National Aeronautics and Space Administration
     b.   scuba   Self-Contained Underwater Breathing Apparatus
     c.   radar   RAdio Detecting And Ranging
     d.   laser   Light Amplification by Stimulated Emission of Radiation
     e.   taser   Thomas A. Swift's Electric Rifle (a fictional weapon)
     f.   snafu   "Situation Normal: All Fouled Up"

Many governmental entities, such as NASA in (17a), as well as acts passed by governments, are often referred to by their acronyms rather than their full names. Further examples include DOD (Department of Defense), OSHA (the Occupational Safety and Health Act), and TARP (the

Troubled Assets Relief Program). Additionally, some government officials have acronymic titles: POTUS (President Of The United States) and CINCPAC (Commander-IN-Chief, PAcific Command), for example.

One particularly interesting point about acronyms is that we use some of them so frequently that we may forget they started out their existences as acronyms and treat them as simple words instead. Such is certainly the case with *scuba* and *laser,* and perhaps even with *snafu. (Snafu,* in which the last consonant is sometimes claimed to represent a different "f-word" than given in (17f), was presumably coined by U.S. soldiers during World War II to denote their contempt for both the horror of war and the ineptitude of their officers.) Alternatively, we may of course have learned these as simple words (e.g., *taser*), without ever realizing their origins as acronyms.

C4 Derivational Processes in Other Languages

As we've seen, most (but not all) of the derivational processes of English are concatenative processes, in which morphemes are linked together one after the other. While a great many languages have similar processes, some languages have a special type of derivational process that is distinctly non-concatenative. The languages most famous for what is called root-and-pattern morphology are Arabic, Hebrew, and closely related languages.

In such languages, roots consist of nothing other than a series of consonants. These consonants then get inserted into templates or patterns, which consist of vowels and/or consonants to make different words. The most general root is the tri-literal root, that is, a root which consists of three consonants. The following words of Arabic are all based on the root / k t b /:

18.   katab 'to write'   kitaab 'book'   kaatib 'clerk'   maktaba 'bookstore'

Note that the consonants / k t b / appear in that order in each of the words listed in (18); but the patterns into which those consonants get inserted are different in each word. One way to think about how such root-and-pattern systems work is schematized in (19):

19.
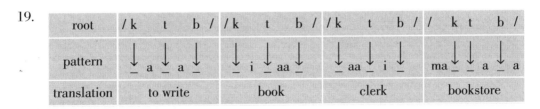

As shown in (19), each consonant in the root simply fills in the appropriate slot in the template, scanning from left to right. Other tri-literal roots of Arabic include / q t l /, from which *qatala* 'he killed', *qaatala* 'he fought and tried to kill', *taqaatala* 'to fight each other', and *ʔiqtatala* 'to fight with one another' are derived; and / ʕ l m / (/ʕ/ is the IPA symbol for a voiceless pharyngeal fricative), from which *ʕalima* 'he knew', *ʕallama* 'he taught', and *taʕallama* 'he taught himself' are derived. These sorts of root-and-pattern systems can in fact become extremely complicated, in ways that extend well beyond the bounds of this text.

Other languages use reduplication to derive new words from old. Reduplication is fundamentally a phonological process, but its application frequently serves to derive new words. In the last chapter, we discovered that both Maidu and Karuk use whole word reduplication, while Dakota and Koasati employ partial word reduplication. In all instances, the result is a new verb, one whose meaning is an intensified version of the non-reduplicated verbal root. The latter examples from Chapter 3 are repeated below. Observe that the (underlined) reduplicant in Dakota attaches at the end of the root and is a suffix. (Recall that the word-final [a] in 'to rustle' is epenthetic.) By contrast, the reduplicant in Koasati attaches inside the root and is an infix:

20.

Dakota	'to cut' [ksa]	→	[ksa-<u>ksa</u>]
	'to be tall' [haska]	→	[haska-<u>ska</u>]
	'to rustle' [xap-a]	→	[xap-<u>xap</u>-a]

21.

Koasati	'to glitter' [cikaplin]	→	[cika-<u>ka</u>-plin]
	'to clabber' [watoplin]	→	[wato-<u>to</u>-plin]
	'to feel a stabbing pain' [waciplin]	→	[waci-<u>ci</u>-plin]

Another language with interesting patterns of partial reduplication which serve derivational purposes is Tagalog. One of these patterns derives new nouns from existing nouns, but with a difference in meaning. While the root noun denotes a product of some sort, the reduplicated version denotes a vendor of that product. The reduplication pattern is shown in (22a) and some examples are given in (22b):

22.

a	Pattern: Reduplicate the initial CV of the root and attach it to the beginning of the root; then prefix *mag* to the reduplicated form		

	root		*final reduplicated form*
b	'pig, pork'	baboy	mag + ba baboy 'vendor of pigs or pork'
	'flower'	bulaklak	mag + bu bulaklak 'vendor of flowers'
	'candle'	kandila	mag + ka kandila 'vendor of candles'

The second pattern from Tagalog derives new verbs from existing verbs; as a result, the meaning of the newly derived verb is intensified (translated below as 'thoroughly verbed'):

23.

a	Pattern: Reduplicate the first two syllables of the root and attach them to the beginning of the root; then prefix *magka* to the reduplicated form		

	root		*final reduplicated form*
b	'broken'	basag	magka + basag basag 'thoroughly broken'
	'damaged'	sira	magka + sira sira 'thoroughly damaged'
	'separated'	hiwalay	magka + hiwa hiwalay 'thoroughly separated'

The examples above demonstrate just how complex reduplication can be; and they also provide further illustrations of the sometimes complex interactions between a language's phonological component and its morphological component.

This ends our overview of such derivational processes as affixation, stress shift, conversion, acronymy, root-and-pattern systems, and reduplication. The next section considers inflectional morphology.

D. Inflectional Morphology

Unlike derivational morphology, inflectional morphology does not create 'new' words (words of different syntactic categories or of different meanings). Instead the function of inflectional morphology is to add grammatical information to an existing word. The types of grammatical information carried through inflectional morphology are always language-specific, and may vary rather dramatically from language to language. Cross-linguistically, the most common process is affixation; in fact, inflection in English is limited to suffixation.

We begin by considering the suffixing inflectional system of English before broadening the discussion to consider other languages and other inflectional processes.

D1   Inflection in English

The inflectional system of Modern English has been described as 'impoverished' compared to its historical antecedents, as it contains precisely eight inflectional suffixes. The eight productive morphemes are listed and exemplified in (24) below. Two of these attach to nouns, four to verbs, and two to both adjectives and adverbs:

24.

	attach to	morpheme	marks	examples
a	N	-s	plural	apes, eagles, walruses
		-s	possessive	cat's paw, dog's ear, horse's tail
b	V	-s	3rd sg present	(He) walks, jogs, lurches.
		-ed	past	(He) walked, jogged, trotted.
		-ing	progressive	(He is) walking.
		-en	past participle	(My car was) stolen.
c	A/Adv	-er	comparative	happier / sooner
		-est	superlative	happiest / soonest

Several important observations must be made of these data; our subsequent discussion in general follows the order of the morphemes presented in (24).

Likely the first point you notice is that it appears English uses the same sound in three different inflectional morphemes, as the plural morpheme, the possessive morpheme, and the third person singular present tense morpheme are all listed as "-s." (Note that we ignore the orthographically-present apostrophe in the possessive suffix.) That these three morphemes sound alike is a relic of the history of the language. What's more interesting is that these three morphemes all undergo the same phonological processes: assimilation and epenthesis. Thus, all three morphemes are voiceless when the word they attach to ends in a voiceless sound (*ape[s]*, *cat[s] paw*, *he walk[s]*), all three are voiced when they attach to a word which ends in a voiced sound (*eagle[z]*, *dog[z] ear*, *he jog[z]*), and all three show up with an epenthetic vowel when the word they attach to ends in a sibilant sound (*walrus[əz]*, *hors[əz] tail*, *he lurch[əz]*). As a result, each of these three morphemes has three <u>allomorphs</u>, as each morpheme undergoes phonological alternation based on the environment in which it occurs. However, irrespective of the allomorphs which occur, the world of morphology allows us to represent each of these three morphemes simply, albeit abstractly, as "-s" as shown in (24).

The label "third singular present tense" requires some explanation. We divide the world of discourse into three persons: first, second, and third. First person refers to the speaker, second person to the one spoken to, and third person to the one spoken about. Further, each person may be singular or plural. These distinctions are clarified below, where the full paradigm of the present tense form of the verb *walk* is given:

25.

	1st person	*2nd person*	*3rd person*
singular	I walk.	You walk.	He walk<u>s</u>.
plural	We walk.	You-all walk.	They walk.

Note that only the third person singular verb is morphologically marked; all other forms of the present tense verb are morphologically unmarked. The *-s* morpheme that occurs is said to mark "subject-verb agreement" as it denotes that the verb "agrees" with the person and number of the subject.

The past tense morpheme is shown in (24) as *-ed*, a form which sometimes differs from the orthography of English. Thus, in *He <u>roast-ed</u> the meat, <u>cut</u> it with a knife, and <u>ate</u> it with relish,* all of the underlined verbs are past tense, yet only one is morphologically-marked with *-ed*. As always, we abstract away from the rules of English spelling and refer to the past tense morpheme as *-ed*, as shown in (24). In addition, notice that the past tense morpheme has three allomorphs: voiceless *walk[t]*, voiced *jog[d]*, and epenthetic *trot[ǝd]*.

The progressive morpheme *-ing* is undoubtedly the most productive suffix in English, as it attaches to every single verb in the language, without exception. That is, it does not distinguish between regular and irregular verbs (*looking, taking*), between transitive and intransitive verbs (*stealing, sitting*), between native and borrowed verbs (*coming, arriving*) or between any other sets of verbs distinguished on any other grounds you might think of. It does, however, have another allomorph, one which occurs in conversational speech, as in *I'm leav<u>in</u>' soon and go<u>in</u>' home.*

The past participle morpheme *-en* is pronounced (and spelled) as such only when it attaches to an irregular verb (e.g., *stolen, broken, taken, eaten*). When it attaches to a regular verb (one subject to the productive rules of the language), it is often spelled *-ed* (e.g., *robbed, fractured, looked, devoured*). However, we here employ the 'archaic' form of this morpheme to avoid confusion with the past tense morpheme *-ed*. One way to decide if a given verbal form represents the simple past tense or the past participle is to see if it can occur alone. With this method, *devoured* in (26a) must be past tense but a past participle in (26b):

26. a. That monster devoured my lunch.
    b. My lunch was devoured by that monster.
    c. *My lunch devoured by that monster.

The comparative morpheme *-er* means 'more' while its superlative counterpart *-est* means 'most'. Both can be attached to many adjectives and adverbs, but with an interesting restriction. This restriction is illustrated in (27) and (28) for adjectives and adverbs, respectively; see if you can figure out why certain forms are just fine while others are weird (those marked " ? ") or impossible (those marked " * "):

27.

blue	bluer	bluest	pretty	prettier	prettiest
purple	?purpler	?purplest	handsome	?handsomer	?handsomest
violet	*violeter	*violetest	beautiful	*beautifuler	*beautifulest

28.

late	later	latest	softly	*softlier	*softliest
often	*oftener	*oftenest	slowly	*slowlier	*slowliest
sadly	*sadlier	*sadliest	frequently	*frequentiler	*frequentliest

In those instances where it's impossible to add the comparative or superlative suffix, we add the word *more* (for comparative) or *most* (for superlative) instead. Thus, *more beautiful* and *most frequently* are perfectly good phrases of English, even though *beautifuler* and *frequentliest* are horrible words. Consequently, it's easy to see that the difference is not related to meaning, as the 'horrible' words are intended to have the same meaning as the good phrases.

The restriction that is applying here is purely phonological, and relates to the number of syllables in the <u>stem</u> of the word (where stem is the root plus affix, if an affix is present). One-syllable stems (e.g., *blue* and *late*) regularly occur with both the comparative and superlative suffixes, three-syllable stems (e.g., *beautiful* and *frequently*) routinely reject them, and two-syllable stems sometimes allow but sometimes reject these suffixes (e.g., ?*purpler* is weird but *oftener* is impossible). One result is that few adverbs show up in comparative or superlative forms, simply because the stems of most adverbs are at least two syllables long. These examples demonstrate yet another instance of interaction between the phonological and morphological modules.

Finally, although this is not shown in (24), observe that inflectional affixes routinely appear outside of derivational affixes, and so may be removed from the root by various derivational affixes. Thus in *nationalizes,* two derivational suffixes (*-al* and *-ize*) intervene between the root and inflectional *-s;* while in *institutionalized,* three derivational affixes (*-tion, -al,* and *-ize*) intervene between the root and inflectional *-ed.*

Before leaving this discussion, you should become aware that the facts presented above provide one way to ascertain the syntactic category of a given word: If that word can be pluralized, it must be a noun. If its past tense form can be produced, it must be a verb. If it has a comparative or superlative form, it must be an adjective or adverb.

Of course, each of these "if p, then q" statements has restrictions: Not all nouns of English have plural forms, as such are lacking in *fish* and *deer* and in many nouns which denote abstractions (e.g., *leisure* and *warmth*). Nor do all verbs have morphologically-identifiable past tense forms (e.g., *hit* and *cut*). And, as already noted, the existence of comparative and superlative morphology is restricted by the phonological system. Nevertheless, it is certainly the case that no noun has a past tense form, no verb has a comparative form, and no adjective (in English) has a plural form. As a result, inflectional morphology can be a helpful, though not fool-proof, way to ascertain the syntactic category of a given word.

D2 Inflection in Other Languages

The inflectional systems of other languages may be much richer than the system of English, by encoding either more information or different types of information than English does.

In Russian, for example, the present tense verb has six different forms, one for each person and each number, as illustrated below for the verb *speak:*

29.

	1st person	*2nd person*	*3rd person*
singular	govorju	govoriʃ	govorit
plural	govorim	govorite	govorjat

The present tense verb forms of Latin and some of its descendants (including Spanish and Italian) pattern similarly to that of Russian, by having six different forms.

In other languages, including such Bantu languages as Swahili, the verb can be marked to agree with both the subject and the object:

30. a. Juma   a-na-ya-taka   ma-embe.
         Juma   3sg-Pres-6-want   6-mango
         'Juma wants the mangoes.'

     b. Juma   a-na-i-taka   n-azi.
         Juma   3sg-Pres-9-want   9-coconut
         'Juma wants the coconuts.'

The first morpheme in each verb, *a*, is glossed as *3sg* and agrees with the third person singular subject, *Juma* (a man's name). The only difference between the verbs in (30a-b) is the third morpheme, which agrees with the direct object in each sentence. In (30a), the direct object is *mangoes*, which is prefixed with a "class 6" morpheme; the verb contains the morpheme *ya*, which agrees with this class 6 object. In (30b), the direct object is *coconuts*, which is prefixed with a "class 9" morpheme; now the verb contains the morpheme *i*, which agrees with this class 9 object.

Nouns in Swahili are grammatically separated into one of a dozen "classes" and every noun in the language is prefixed with the morpheme which corresponds to its "class." Because there are so many of these classes, it's customary to refer to them by number, as in (30).

Other languages which have similar—but less complicated—class systems of nouns usually refer to these classes as "gender" classes. For example, in Spanish, nouns are divided into what are called "masculine" and "feminine" classes:

| 31. | a | *feminine* | mesa | 'table' | razón | 'reason' | noche | 'night' |
| | b | *masculine* | dia | 'day' | balcón | 'balcony' | coche | 'car' |

Significantly, feminine and masculine nouns co-occur with different definite articles:

| 32. | a | la mesa | 'the table' | la razón | 'the reason' | la noche | 'the night' |
| | b | el dia | 'the day' | el balcón | 'the balcony' | el coche | 'the car' |

While it may be tempting to anthropomorphize all nouns in languages such as Spanish, thereby imbuing them with "sex," this temptation is best resisted. On one hand, you should find it difficult to identify a dozen "sexes" to cover the facts of Swahili. On the other hand, you will be forced to explain precisely why the Spanish word for *table* is "feminine" while its counterpart in Russian (*stol*) is "masculine" and the word which Tagalog borrowed from Spanish to denote this entity (*mesa*) has no "sex" at all. Though in some languages, assignment to a given gender class is not completely arbitrary, it is apparent that sometimes such assignment is in fact arbitrary. For example in Latin, the words for *farmer* and *sailor* (*agricola* and *nauta*, respectively) were classified as feminine gender, but (according to the historical record) the vast majority of all farmers and sailors in ancient Rome were men.

The solution to the puzzle is simple: the terms "feminine" and "masculine" are nothing more than labels for grammatical classifications of nouns. But these grammatical classifications—regardless of the labels applied to them—have clear significance in the grammars of the languages in which they appear. We saw such significance in the object-agreement morphemes of Swahili in (30) and in the definite articles of Spanish in (32), where the morphemes are restricted by the class of the noun with which they co-occur.

A final example of languages whose inflectional systems provide information lacking in the inflectional system of English relates to the morphological case-marking of nouns. In English, we can 'see' different cases in most, but not all, pronouns—as shown in the paradigms below:

33.

		subjects (nominative case)		
		1st person	*2nd person*	*3rd person*
a	*singular*	I	you	he, she, it
	plural	we	you	they
		objects (accusative case)		
		1st person	*2nd person*	*3rd person*
b	*singular*	me	you	him, her, it
	plural	us	you	them

Because of the case differences that do exist, we must say *I saw him*, where the subject of the sentence (*I*) is in nominative case and the object (*him*) is in accusative case. In contrast, a sentence such as **Me saw he*, with the subject in accusative case and the object in nominative case, is ungrammatical (likely in all varieties of English).

But such case-marking is completely lacking in nouns, which have invariant forms, regardless of whether they serve as subjects or objects:

34.   a.   Brutus killed Caesar.
      b.   Caesar killed Brutus.

Because of this lack of case-marking on nouns, the word order of English is fairly rigid: The first noun in the sentence is interpreted as the subject, and the noun following the verb is interpreted as the direct object. Changing the order of the nouns, as in (34a-b), changes the meaning of the sentence (in this case, rather dramatically).

Other languages do not suffer such restrictions. In Latin, for example, nouns appeared in one of five morphological cases: nominative (for subjects), accusative (for objects), dative (for indirect objects), genitive (for possessors), and ablative (for the objects of certain prepositions). To keep the discussion simple, we consider only nominative and accusative here:

35.   Brutus-Ø   occidit   Caesar-em.
      Brutus-nom   killed   Caesar-acc
      'Brutus killed Caesar.'

The nominative case-marker in (35) happens to be phonologically-null, but the accusative case-marker is not. As a result, speakers of Latin could always tell "who did what to whom" without relying on the order of the words in a given sentence. And all six orders possible for the three words in the sentence formed perfectly good sentences of Latin, and all meant precisely what the sentence in (35) meant:

36. a. Occidit   Brutus-Ø   Caesar-em.
     b. Occidit   Caesar-em   Brutus-Ø.
     c. Caesar-em   occidit   Brutus-Ø.
     d. Caesar-em   Brutus-Ø   occidit.
     e. Brutus-Ø   Caesar-em   occidit.

Old English also had an extensive system of morphological case-marking for nouns, so that its speakers could distinguish subject from object, for example, based on the form of the noun. Thus, speakers of Old English, like speakers of Latin, were not forced to rely on word order to the extent we speakers of the modern language are.

The various inflectional processes considered so far in this section have all involved some form of affixation. But other processes are possible.

In the previous section, we determined that Tagalog uses certain patterns of reduplication for derivational purposes. Reduplication shows up within its inflectional system as well. In the examples below, reduplication is employed to change a verb from present tense into future:

37.

a	Pattern: Reduplicate the first (C)V of the root, and attach it as a prefix.			
		root		*reduplicated form*
b	'call'	tawag	ta-tawag	'will call'
	'visit'	bisita	bi-bisita	'will visit'
	'enter'	pasok	pa-pasok	'will enter'
	'eat'	kain	ka-kain	'will eat'
	'leave'	alis	a-alis	'will leave'

Some tone languages (most frequently African languages) use tone shift to make inflectional changes. The examples in (38) are from Somali (Chushitic branch of the Afro-Asiatic family). The nouns in the first column are singular, and their (high) tone occurs on the first syllable. The nouns in the second column are plural; as you can see, the tone shifts to the second syllable in the plural forms:

38.

a	'student'	árday	ardáy	'students'
b	'bull'	díbi	dibí	'bulls'
c	'head'	mádax	madáx	'heads'
d	'thief'	túug	tuúg	'thieves'

Hausa (a language of the Chadic branch of the Afro-Asiatic family spoken primarily in Niger and Nigeria) uses differences in vowel length to distinguish among various tense/aspect morphemes. The morphemes glossed 'perfective₁' and 'perfective₂' in the data in (39) are somewhat analogous to present perfect and past perfect in English, as in *I have run* and *I had run*, respectively:

39.

	1sg	*2sgM*	*2sgF*	*3sgM*	*3sgF*	*1pl*	*2pl*	*3pl*
perfective₁	náa	káa	ꞌkín	yáa	táa	mún	kún	sún
perfective₂	ná	ká	kínà	yá	tá	múkà	kúkà	súkà

The first thing you may notice about the data in (39) is that the Hausa forms distinguish not only on the basis of person and number but, in second and third persons singular, also on the gender of the person spoken to or about. But now notice that the difference between perfective₁ and perfective₂ in the first singular, the second singular masculine, the third singular masculine, and the third singular feminine forms is simply the difference in the length of the vowel, which is long in perfective₁ but short in perfective₂.

To summarize this section: The function of inflectional morphology is to add only grammatical information to words (such as plural morphemes to nouns or tense morphemes to verbs), and the most common process used cross-linguistically is affixation. Other processes—including reduplication, tone shift, and differences in vowel length—are available to some languages.

E. Compounding

Compounding is the process of combining two existing words (i.e., two free morphemes) in order to make a third word. Sometimes, compound words have a compositional meaning, as their meaning is based on the meaning of each of their parts. But at other times, the meaning of a compound word may be idiosyncratic by denoting much more than the sum of its parts. Thus, while the compound word *dog house* refers to a house for a dog, the compound word *hot dog* has nothing to do with either heat or dogs; instead, it refers to a type of sausage, a food which may be consumed even if it is cold.

E1 Compounding in English

Putting aside the difference between compositional and idiosyncratic meaning for now, consider the following tables of compound words—for nouns, adjectives, and verbs, respectively—in English. In those instances in which compounding is very productive, the list of example compounds provided is followed by an ellipsis:

Table 3: *Noun Compounds*

members		example compounds
N	N	steamboat, jailbait, doghouse, chalkboard, oil well, fire engine . . .
A	N	highchair, strong box, oval office, yellowtail, smallpox, blue bird . . .
V	N	crybaby, playground, swearword, rattlesnake, jump suit, spoilsport . . .
P	N	underdog, outbuilding, afterthought, inland, downtown . . .

Table 4: *Adjective Compounds*

members		example compounds
N	A	seaworthy, bloodthirsty, dog-tired, nation-wide, brain dead . . .
A	A	true blue, red hot, easygoing, dripping-wet, hardworking . . .
V	A	slap-happy, punch-drunk
P	A	overwide, underripe, above-mentioned, underprivileged, in-grown . . .

Table 5: *Verb Compounds*

members		example compounds
N	V	window shop, spoon-feed, fingerspell, bartend, sunbathe, panfry . . .
A	V	hot-wire, sharpshoot, dry-clean, whitewash, roughcast
V	V	break-dance, slam-dunk, jump-start, drop-kick, blow-dry
P	V	outline, overdo, underfeed, uproot, offset . . .

Clearly, the orthographic system is inconsistent with respect to compounds, which may be written as two separate words (e.g., *window shop*), as one word (e.g., *fingerspell*), or with a hyphen between the two members (e.g., *dry-clean*). However, there are tests we can use to determine whether a given string is in fact a compound word.

For those compounds whose meaning is compositional, we can perform the "is a" test. For example, a *steamboat* "is a" type of boat, a *highchair* "is a" type of chair, and an *outbuilding* "is a" type of building. The "is a" test works best for compounds which are nouns, but it can be extended to adjectives and to verbs—but only if we turn the right-hand member into a noun. In this way, we can say that *true blue* "is a" type of blueness, *seaworthy* "is a" type of worthiness, *spoon-feed* "is a" type of feeding, and *sharpshoot* "is a" type of shooting.

Of course, the "is a" test fails by definition to apply to compounds whose meaning is idiosyncratic: *Hot dog* is not a type of dog and *bloodthirsty* is a type of thirst only in the most metaphorical of senses.

But in such instances, we can rely on the English stress system instead. As noted previously, the stress facts of the language are a much more reliable indicator of a compound word, as in the vast majority of cases, stress falls on the left-hand member; thus, we have the compounds <u>*hot* dog</u> and <u>*bloodthirsty*</u>, rather than *<u>hot *dog*</u> and *<u>blood*thirsty*</u>.

Of potentially more interest is the fact that in all the compounds provided in Tables 3 through 5 the resulting word is of the same category as its right-most member. That is, this set of compounds of English behaves just like those words formed through the (productive) processes of derivational affixation, as the results of both are endocentric words which are headed by the morpheme on the right-hand side. (Recall that *endocentric* means that one piece of the string is of the same syntactic category as is the entire string.)

Word trees for such endocentric compounds can be produced straightforwardly by projecting each individual morpheme, along with its syntactic category; merging the two morphemes; and projecting the syntactic category of the right-most morpheme to the top of the compound word:

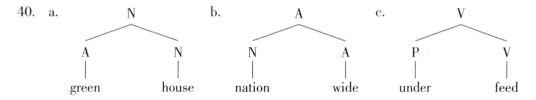

40.   a.   N: A green + N house   b.   A: N nation + A wide   c.   V: P under + V feed

However, not all of the productively-formed compounds of English are endocentric. There are at least two types of <u>exocentric</u> compounds in the language. An exocentric compound is a headless compound, in which the syntactic category of neither of its members shares its syntactic category with that compound word:

41.

a	over$_P$ + weight$_N$	overweight$_A$
b	up$_P$ + keep$_V$	upkeep$_N$
c	make$_V$ + shift$_V$	makeshift$_A$
d	speak$_V$ + easy$_A$	speakeasy$_N$

Note that these compounds fail the "is a" test: a *speakeasy* is not a type of easiness, for example. While *upkeep*, *makeshift*, and *speakeasy* all pass the stress test (with stress on the left-hand member), it seems that both members of *overweight* can be equally stressed.

The second type of exocentric compounds of English is often described as resulting from conversion (i.e., zero-derivation) from the verb-particle construction. The verb-particle construction consists of a verb plus another element which resembles a preposition:

42. The waiter first <u>mopped up</u> the floor, then <u>wiped down</u> the counter.

While *up* and *down* are often prepositions, they must not be prepositions here. For one thing, they do not denote directions: The floor is not up, and the counter is not down (and the same can be said of the waiter). But as prepositions, *up* and *down* regularly denote directions. Moreover, as particles, *up* and *down* are movable, though as prepositions they are not:

43. a. The waiter first <u>mopped</u> the floor <u>up</u>, then <u>wiped</u> the counter <u>down</u>.
    b. The waiter first <u>climbed</u> up the ladder, then went down the stairs.
    c. *The waiter first climbed the ladder up, then went the stairs down.

With this introduction to the verb-particle construction, consider this (non-exhaustive) list of compounds, all of which have the form of [mop$_V$ + up$_P$]$_N$: *run-down, lowdown, kick-back, cook-off, kiss-off, do-over, screw-up, payoff, buyout, pullover, sit-up, layout, sing-along, breakdown*.

Several—often competing—methods for drawing word trees for the exocentric compounds of English have been proposed, none of which is particularly satisfying. We abstract away from considering this complex task here, as it is beyond the bounds of this text.

There are two final points to be made about compounds in English. First, only rarely can the first member of a compound be inflected; when inflection occurs, the left-hand member must be a noun. Thus we have compounds such as *dues payment, systems analyst, thieves market, pants leg*, and *clothes dryer*. Of course, we can pluralize these by suffixing compound-final *-s: dues payments, systems analysts, thieves markets, pants legs, clothes dryers*.

The broader generalization, therefore, is that inflectional suffixes occur productively on the outside of compound words (just as they do on words formed through derivational affixation). Thus we have *doghouses* but not **dogshouse*, and *slam-dunked* but not **slammed-dunk*.

Such was not always the case, however, in the history of the language: The plural of *lady-in-waiting* was (and is still) *ladies-in-waiting* (cf. *lady-in-waitings). But the plural forms of *court martial* and *attorney general* have now been regularized to *court martials* and *attorney generals,* although the older forms, *courts martial* and *attorneys general,* are retained in legal settings.

The second point about compounds is among the most significant, as we can form compounds which exhibit one of the defining features of human language, a feature which sets human language apart from the communication systems of many animals. That feature is recursion, the iterative application of a given rule to the output of that rule. For compounding, the basic rule requires the combining of two words to make a new word. The recursive feature of language allows us to combine the resulting new word with another word to make another new word, and then to combine the newer new word with another word to make an even newer new word, and so forth. This recursive property is illustrated below:

44.   a.   [[toe] [nail]]
      b.   [[toe nail] clipper]
      c.   [[toe nail clipper] accident]
      d.   [[toe nail clipper accident] insurance]
      e.   [[toe nail clipper accident insurance] company]
      f.   [[toe nail clipper accident insurance company] employee]
      g.   [[toe nail clipper accident insurance company employee] benefits]
      h.   [[toe nail clipper accident insurance company employee benefits] manager]
      i.   and so forth . . .

You may find these examples rather humorous; but you should be most impressed with your abilities to both understand the meaning of each and to produce similar examples on your own.

E2 Compounding in Other Languages

Every human language has the ability to make compounds, many of which are analogous to those of English discussed above. For instance, the following examples from Japanese and Mandarin Chinese are both right-headed, endocentric compounds which pass the "is a" test:

45.   a.   Japanese   b.   Mandarin
           hai-zara   hé-mā
           ash-plate   river-horse
           'ashtray'   'hippopotamus'

As the glosses make clear, the Japanese compound "is a" type of plate, not a type of ash; and the Mandarin compound "is a" type of animal, not a body of water.

The English word *hippopotamus* is mono-morphemic (i.e., consists of a single morpheme) for native speakers of English. We borrowed this word from the Greek compound *hippos* + *potamos* 'horse' + 'river', an endocentric compound, but one whose head is on the left-hand side, not the right-hand side.

Other languages which have left-headed compounds include Hebrew and Jacaltec (a Mayan language of Guatemala):

46. a. Hebrew   b. Jacaltec
         tapúax-adama   potx'-m txitam
         apple-earth   kill-er pig
         'potato'   'pig killer' (*'killer pig')

We can use the "is a" test with both: The Hebrew compound, as its gloss demonstrates, "is a" type of food, not a type of dirt. The Jacaltec compound "is a" type of killer, not a type of pig, hence the ungrammatical translation shown.

Finally, while many languages have endocentric compounds, quite a few languages also have exocentric compounds, as illustrated below for French. The example in (47a) consists of [V+A] but the result is an N; and example in (47b) consists of [V+Adv] but the result is another N:

47. a. gagne-petit   b. couche-tard
         gain-small   lie-late
         'low wage earner'   'night owl' (i.e., 'one who stays up late')

To summarize this section: All of the world's languages have rules which allow the formation of compound words. In many languages, the resulting compounds are endocentric, though whether the head is on the right-hand side or the left-hand side is a language-specific choice. Additionally, exocentric compounds also exist in English and in other languages; the syntactic category of an exocentric compound is the same as the syntactic category of neither of its members. While word trees for endocentric compounds are straightforwardly produced, those of exocentric compounds are difficult, perhaps impossible, to draw.

F.   How to Solve Morphology Problems in Languages Other Than English

While there is no absolutely "correct" way to solve morphology problems in languages you're not familiar with, there are certain "do's" and "do not's" that can assist you.

The most important "do" is to search for recurring strings of sound and match them with recurring meanings. Sometimes, meaning is denoted by glosses, making this task relatively straightforward. But other times, you may be forced to puzzle out meaning by referring to translations, rather than glosses. For example, the following words of Turkish are translated, but not glossed:

48. | mumlar 'candles' | toplar 'guns' | adamlar 'men' | kitaplar 'books' |

Yet since all the translations are plurals, and since all of the Turkish data contain the suffix [lar], we can straightforwardly determine that [lar] is the plural morpheme of Turkish—even though we have no glosses to lead us to this solution.

There are a series of "do not's:" First, do not assume that, just because a given morpheme is always bound in English (e.g., past tense -ed) or always free in English (e.g., the definite determiner *the*), morphemes with similar meaning should have similar status in other languages. The data in (49) show that the past tense morpheme is free in both Thai and Koranko (a Niger-Congo language spoken in West Africa); the data in (50) show that the definite determiner is bound in both Swedish and Arabic:

49.   a.   Thai   Boon   tʰaan   kʰaaw   <u>lɛɛw</u>.
               Boon   eat   rice   <u>past</u>
               'Boon ate rice.'

    b.   Koranko   a   <u>ya</u>   kɔlɔmabolɔ   kari.
                3sg   <u>past</u>   tree.branch   break
                'He/she broke a tree branch.'

50.   a.   Swedish   fisk-<u>en</u>   flicka-<u>n</u>   (< flicka-en, but /e/ deletes)
               fish-the   girl-the
               'the fish'   'the girl'

    b.   Arabic   <u>al</u>-qamr   <u>aʃ</u>-ʃams   (< al-ʃams, and /l/ assimilates to /ʃ/)
             the-moon   the-sun
             'the moon'   'the sun'

Second, do not assume that the order of morphemes that occurs in English also occurs in the language you are analyzing. For instance, past tense -ed is always a suffix in English, occurring at the end of the verbal root; but in Swahili, the past tense morpheme precedes the verbal root:

51.   Haji   a-<u>li</u>-ya-taka   ma-embe.
     Haji   3sg-<u>Past</u>-6-want   6-mango
     'Haji wanted the mangoes.'

Third, do not assume that every contrast that shows up in English also shows up in every other language. While most nouns of English have plural forms, all nouns in Cambodian have only a single form, as there is simply no 'plural morpheme' in the language. As a result, lacking a discourse context, nouns are interpretable as either singular or plural:

52. kmeɪŋ   baan   məəl   səphiw.
    child   Past   read   book
    '{A child / some children} read {a book / some books}.'

In a given context, of course, such sentences are generally easily interpreted; if confusion remains, the speaker can always add a number or a quantifier (e.g., *two, some, many, few, all*).

Fourth, do not assume that every contrast that shows up in the language you're studying has a morphological counterpart in English. We've already encountered three interesting examples of such languages: Swahili, Spanish, and Hausa. In example (30), we discovered that Swahili has object-agreement morphemes, in addition to subject-agreement morphemes. In example (32), we saw that the definite determiners of Spanish must agree with the gender class of the noun with which they occur. And in example (39), we found that Hausa's subject-agreement morphemes encode not only person and number, but also gender (in second and third person singular). English lacks all of these forms of agreement.

Finally, do not be surprised if you discover that a given morpheme in a given language has phonological alternants (i.e., allomorphs). Compare these further plural forms of Turkish with those provided in (48). (IPA [y] is a high front round vowel and [ø] is a mid front round vowel.)

53.   ipler 'ropes'   yzler 'faces'   eller 'hands'   køler 'villages'

Then recall the discussion of Turkish vowel harmony from Chapter 3. Which phonological alternant—either [lar], as in (48), or [ler], as in (53)—occurs is the direct result of the operation of the language's vowel harmony rule which requires the vowels in a given to be all front or all back.

Careful consideration of this list of "do's" and "do not's" should help you solve morphology puzzles for many of the world's languages.

G. A Note on Language Acquisition

One of the more fascinating aspects of the acquisition process is just how rapidly our knowledge of our native language grows—most noticeably at a point in our lives when we are too young to be purposely taught much of anything. The growth in our vocabularies (i.e., in the size of the inventory of words in our mental lexicon) exemplifies the speed of this development.

By the age of eighteen months or so, most of us have vocabularies of around fifty words. Many children use nouns which refer to family (*mommy, daddy, baby*), to foods and drinks (*juice, milk, water, cookie, apple*, etc.), and to animals, toys, and other entities in the child's environment (e.g., *dog, ball, blocks, car, bottle, book, shoes*). Verb-like and adjective-like words may also appear at this stage: *hot, all-gone, dirty, up, sit, see, eat, go*. Finally, most children also control a few "personal-social" terms, such as *hi, bye, yes, no, please*.

Over the next few years, a child's vocabulary increases rapidly, at the amazing rate of one word every two hours (Pinker 2000, 3). As a result, by the time children start first grade (around six years of age), the majority have vocabularies in excess of thirteen thousand words. This rapid rate of adding new words continues through adolescence, so that by the time we graduate from high school, we have vocabularies in the range of sixty thousand words. By the time we graduate from college, we've added another vast array of technical and non-technical terms to our vocabularies, as we've encountered new experiences and expanded our knowledge of the world.

One of the most general and truly significant findings that has emerged from an array of diary, observational, and experimental studies of child language acquisition is how easily and readily children figure out and internalize the productive morphological rules of their language. We can tell that children must have internalized such rules based on the "errors" that they make. For instance, many three- to four-year old children acquiring English produce forms such as "foots" (for *feet*) and "goed" (for *went*). Since these forms are not present in the speech of the adults around these children, the only way the children could produce them is through application of the productive rules that generate them.

Two particularly seminal studies have been conducted on the development of inflectional morphology in children acquiring English: Roger Brown's (1973) observational study and Jean Berko's (1958) tightly-controlled laboratory study. Both studies have been replicated numerous times, always with very similar (if not precisely identical) results.

Brown's study involved three (unrelated) children who were between the ages of twenty and thirty-six months at the beginning of the test. These children were audio- and/or video-taped over a period of several years, as they interacted with each other and with adults in naturalistic settings. The most amazing finding of this study is that the acquisition of several inflectional morphemes occurred in the same order for the three children (though the ages at which acquisition occurred varied). This order of acquisition is schematized in Table 6 below. ("Aux be" refers to the use of *be* as an aspectual auxiliary, as in *He is running*.)

Table 6:   *Children's order of acquisition of inflectional morphemes*

order	1	2	3	4	5	6	7
morpheme	-*ing*	plural -*s*	poss. -*s*	*the, a*	past -*ed*	3sg V-*s*	aux *be*

Clearly, the order of acquisition cannot be based purely on sound, as plural -*s*, possessive -*s*, and 3sg V-*s* (i.e., third person singular present tense subject-verb agreement) all sound the same—yet the last is sixth on the acquisition list while the others are second and third, respectively. Moreover, the children's order of acquisition cannot be based on the frequency of the inflectional morpheme usage of the adults around these children, as their frequencies were quite different from the children's order of acquisition, as shown in Table 7.

Table 7:   *Frequency of inflectional morphemes in adult usage*

frequency	1	2	3	4	5	6	7
morpheme	*the, a*	-*ing*	plural -*s*	aux *be*	poss. -*s*	3sg V-*s*	past -*ed*

The most frequently proffered reason for -*ing* being number one in the children's order of acquisition list relates to phonological saliency: The presence of -*ing* always produces an extra syllable, and children more easily recognize whole syllables than they do individual sounds within syllables. The order of acquisition of the other morphemes is often related to the semantic complexity of the morphemes, with those with the least semantic complexity acquired before those with the most semantic complexity. On such an account, plural encodes only number, past encodes only time, and progressive encodes only temporary duration, so these should be higher in the order of acquisition than auxiliary *be*, which encodes number, time, and temporary duration.

In contrast to Brown's naturalistic study, Berko (who now goes by the name Berko-Gleason) conducted formal experiments in a laboratory with fifty-six subjects (twenty-eight boys and twenty-eight girls), who ranged in age from four to seven years. Berko's interest was in testing the children's ability to produce 'allomorph-appropriate' plural and past tense forms. To this end, she created a series of nonsense nouns and verbs and drew a picture for each word. The "nonsense noun" pictures were bird-like cartoons, and the "nonsense verb" pictures showed men performing various actions.

In the "nonsense noun" tests, the experimenter showed a child a picture and said, "This is a wug (or a wuk or a wutch). Now there is another one. There are two of them. There are two __." The child's task was to fill in the blank with the appropriate allomorph of the plural noun; e.g., *wug[z]*, or *wuk[s]*, or *wutch[æ]*. In the "nonsense verb" tests, the experimenter showed a child a picture and said, "This is a man who knows how to spow (or rick or mot). He is spowing (or ricking or motting). What did he do yesterday?" Here, the child's task was to respond with the appropriate allomorph of the past tense verb, e.g., *spow[d]*, or *rick[t]*, or *mot[əd]*.

The importance of this study lies in its reliance on "nonsense" words. The children could not possibly have heard or learned the 'right' plural or past tense forms of these non-existent words; instead they could rely only on their ability to apply phonological rules to a morphological process for words they had never encountered before.

The older children (the 'first-grade' group) out-performed the younger children (the 'pre-school' group) on almost every test; the accuracy of the former group was often in the 80-90% range, while the accuracy of the latter group was sometimes as low as 25%, but sometimes as high as 74%. But the differences didn't stop here, as the accuracy of both groups was highest on the forms which require assimilation in the adult language (e.g., *wug[z]*, *wuk[s]*, *spow[d]* and *rick[t]*), but considerably lower on the forms which require epenthesis in the adult language (e.g., *wutch[əz]* and *mot[əd]*). In fact, many children supplied no affix at all in such instances.

There are at least two possible explanations for this last difference. One explanation would be that the children understood the final consonant of the nonsense noun or verb as the morpheme in question. That is, the children interpreted the final sibilant of the root of a noun such as *wutch* as the plural morpheme (another sibilant) and the final alveolar stop in the root of a verb such as *mot* as the past tense morpheme (another alveolar stop). Consequently, adding another plural or past tense morpheme would be superfluous.

The alternative explanation is this: As discussed in Chapter 3, assimilation occurs frequently in child language. But the use of epenthesis is rare; thus, children tend to simplify consonant clusters by deleting a consonant, rather than by epenthesizing a vowel, even though the latter option would also simplify the original consonant cluster. In the Berko experiments, what these children were doing can be seen as taking full advantage of a process they were already familiar with, even though they were not familiar with the "word" in which that process occurred. That is, they had gleaned parts of the rules for forming plural nouns and past tense verbs and could apply those rules to nonsense words.

We do not choose between these alternatives here.

A whole range of conclusions have been drawn from the "wug test" and its many replicates. The most general conclusion is that drawn by Berko (1958, 150): "It is evident that the acquisition of language is more than the storing up of rehearsed utterances, since we are all able to say what we have not practiced and what we have never before heard."

KEY TERMS AND CONCEPTS

syntactic categories	content (open) category	functional (closed) category
morpheme	free vs. bound morpheme	root (vs. stem)
regular (weak) verb	irregular (strong) verb	productive rule
allomorph	derivation(al)	affixation
prefixation	suffixation	'finicky'
word tree	merge	conversion (zero-derivation)
stress shift	acronym	root-and-pattern morphology
reduplication	infix	inflection(al)
subject(-verb) agreement	nominative case	accusative case
object(-verb) agreement	tone shift	compound(ing)
endocentric	exocentric	recursion

PRACTICE PROBLEMS

1. Determine the number of morphemes in each of the following words:

   a. desert   b. memory   c. processor   d. supplies
   e. power   f. format   g. faster   h. flowchart

2. For the following words, determine the number of morphemes each contains, and list the free and bound morphemes in each. Example: *eraser* contains 2 morphemes; *erase* is free and *-er* is bound

   a. invalid$_A$ b. invalid$_N$ c. Jack's   d. optionality
   e. wicked   f. refurbish   g. inabilities   h. destabilize
   i. deride   j. evidently   k. understand   l. uncomplicated

3. For the following words, determine the number of morphemes each contains, then identify the root, the syntactic category of the root, and the syntactic category of the entire word. Example: *kindness* has 2 morphemes; the adjective root is *kind*; the derived word is a noun

   a. amazement   b. reusable   c. dishonest   d. rhinoceros
   e. carefully   f. historical   g. impersonal   h. uncontrollably
   i. petunias   j. rereads   k. beautiful   l. Baltimore

4. For each of the following words, state whether it is simple or complex; if complex, state whether the affix is inflectional or derivational. Example: *desks* is complex; the affix is inflectional

   a. prettier   b. delight   c. razor   d. stringy
   e. fly   f. stingy   g. reuse   h. fastest
   i. raced   j. burglarize   k. extent   l. actor

5. For each of the following words, identify the syntactic category of the root and the type of inflectional information found. Example: *watched*; root is a verb and *-ed* is past tense

   a. driven   b. sorriest   c. playing   d. arrives
   e. cat's   f. dishes   g. earlier   h. lamps

6. In each of the following sets of words, two words have the same type of affix, one word has a different type of affix, and one word has no affix at all. Underline the affix in each word and identify the one which is different from that of other items in the set. Then identify the word which has no affix at all. Example: {*ovens, lens, hens, listens*}; underline -*s* in *ovens, hens, listens;* identify -*s* in <u>*listens*</u> as different from -*s* in *ovens* and *hens;* and identify *lens* as being affix-less

   a. {greedy, ivory, jealousy, dirty}   b. {leaven, harden, spoken, thicken}
   c. {rider, colder, silver, actor}   d. {candied, shopped, cleaned, candid}
   e. {greener, farmer, nicer, water}   f. {intelligent, intake, incapable, indirect}

7. For each of the following compounds, identify the syntactic categories it is composed of and give another of that type of compound. Give a different example for each. Then draw a word tree for each compound. Example: *bathroom* contains two nouns, as does *movie star:*

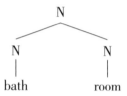

   a. upstairs   b. scarecrow   c. skin-deep   d. slam-dunk
   e. bittersweet   f. rug-rat   g. lunch room   h. outlaw

8. Consider these data from Mende (Niger-Congo family; Liberia and Sierra Leone) and answer the questions which follow:

	translation		translation		translation
[pɛlɛ]	house	[mɔm]	glass	[dɔmi]	story
[pɛlɛi]	the house	[mɔmi]	the glass	[dɔmii]	the story
[kali]	hoe	[hele]	elephant	[kaamɔ]	teacher
[kalii]	the hoe	[helei]	the elephant	[kaamɔi]	the teacher

   a. What is the Mende morpheme meaning 'the'?
   b. If [sale] means 'proverb', what is the form for 'the proverb'?
   c. If [kpindii] means 'the night', what does [kpindi] mean?

9. Use these data from Ganda (Niger-Congo family; Uganda) to answer the questions below:

	translation		translation		translation
[omukasi]	woman	[omusika]	heir	[omusawo]	doctor
[abakazi]	women	[abasika]	heirs	[abasawo]	doctors
[omuwala]	girl	[omulenzi]	boy		
[abawala]	girls	[abalenzi]	boys		

a. What is the morpheme that means 'singular' in Ganda?
b. What is the morpheme meaning 'plural'?
c. If [abalanga] means 'twins', what is the form for 'twin'?

10. These data are from Kanuri (Nilo-Saharan family; Niger and Nigeria). Review the data and answer the questions which follow:

	translation		translation		translation
[gana]	small	[kura]	big	[kurugu]	long
[nəmgana]	smallness	[nəmkura]	bigness	[nəmkurugu]	length
[karite]	excellent	[dibi]	bad		
[nəmkarite]	excellence	[nəmdibi]	badness		

a. Is the affix illustrated here a prefix or a suffix?
b. Is this affix derivational or inflectional?
c. What is the affix?
d. If [kəji] means 'sweet', what is the form for 'sweetness'?
e. If [nəmgəla] means 'goodness', what is the form for 'good'?
f. Draw a word tree for [nəmkurugu] 'length'.

11. Consider these data from Turkish and respond to the questions in (a) through (d):

	translation		translation
[ʃehir]	city	[zilim]	my bell
[ʃehirden]	from the city	[ziller]	bells
[køpry]	bridge	[eve]	to the house
[køpryler]	bridges	[evden]	from the house
[køprylere]	to the bridges	[sesleriniz]	your voices
[køpryde]	on the bridge	[otobysler]	buses
[el]	hand	[elim]	my hand
[elimde]	in my hand	[ellerinize]	to your hands

a. Identify the Turkish morphemes with these meanings: city, hand, bridge, bell, house, voice, bus, from, to, on/in, my, your, plural
b. What is the order of morphemes in the Turkish noun?
c. What do the Turkish words [ʃehirde] and [elleriniz] mean in English?
d. How would you say 'to the buses' in Turkish?

CHAPTER 5

SYNTAX: INSIDE PHRASES AND SENTENCES

While the last chapter explored the internal structure of words, this chapter explores how words are strung together to make phrases and sentences. All languages have rules for combining words together, though the precise nature of those rules may vary from language to language. For instance, in English, the subject normally occurs as the first element in a sentence, the object is last, and the verb occurs in the middle. In contrast, in Tagalog, the verb routinely occurs as the first word in a sentence, but in Japanese, the verb routinely occurs as the last word in a sentence:

1. a. English   Sue <u>wrote</u> a letter, and Bill <u>ate</u> a hamburger.

   b. Tagalog
<u>Sumulat</u>	ang	babae	ng	liham.
wrote	Nom	woman	Acc	letter

   'The woman wrote a letter.'

   c. Japanese
Taroo-ga	hanbaagaa-o	<u>tabeta.</u>
Taroo-Nom	hamburger-Acc	ate.

   'Taroo ate a hamburger.'

The analyses presented in this chapter focus on syntactic phenomena in English to the exclusion of other languages. This choice is not intended to slight other languages in any way; it is based solely on considerations of time and space. We thus use English as a convenient way to illustrate the fundamental hypothesis explored in this chapter: The syntactic module of all languages consists of two parts: (a) detailed information stored in the mental lexicon about the words of our language; and (b) computational rules for combining those words into phrases and sentences.

We explore the mental lexicon in Section B and the computational system in Section C. Before we delve into all the details, we consider in Section A the extent of the knowledge we have of the syntactic system of English.

A. Our Linguistic Competence

As we discovered in previous chapters, we have a great deal of tacit knowledge of the sounds of our native language, of the rules that govern the distribution of those sounds within syllables, of the morphemes of the language, and of the rules that govern the distribution of those morphemes within words. Similarly, we discover in this chapter that we have a great deal of tacit knowledge about the manner in which words can be strung together to make phrases and sentences, that is, of the syntactic system of our native language. This particular type of knowledge is often referred to as our <u>linguistic competence</u>, a label which reflects our abilities to judge some strings of words as <u>grammatical</u> (and others as ungrammatical) and to create and understand new phrases and sentences never before produced.

There are at least three common misconceptions related to our linguistic competence. First, our ability to make grammaticality judgments is in no way related to our past experience(s). That is, we easily judge a string as (un-)grammatical even if we've never encountered that string before. For clarity, consider these examples:

2. a. We saw <u>this movie</u> twice in Rome last year.
    b. *We saw twice <u>this movie</u> in Rome last year.

3. a. a member <u>of Congress</u> with too many teeth
    b. *a member with too many teeth <u>of Congress</u>

Note that the examples in (2a-b) and those in (3a-b) contain precisely the same words; the difference between the (a) and (b) examples is only the order of some of the words. Yet we easily judge the (a) examples as perfectly grammatical and their (b) counterparts as ungrammatical.

Now consider the examples in (4) and (5):

4. a. Who does Moe <u>believe</u> visited Curly?
    b. *Moe <u>believes</u> who visited Curly.

5. a. Moe <u>wonders</u> who visited Curly.
    b. *Who does Moe <u>wonder</u> visited Curly?

We could label the sentences in (4) and (5) a minimal pair, as the only difference between them is the presence of *believe* in (4) vs. the presence of *wonder* in (5). Yet, while (4a) is a perfectly good sentence of English, its counterpart in (5b) is decidedly ungrammatical. Likewise, (5a) is fine although its counterpart in (4b) is impossible.

The (b) examples in (2) through (5) represent what linguists call <u>negative evidence</u>, a type of evidence native speakers simply do not ever encounter (outside of <u>Linguistics</u> classes, that is). Native speakers are never taught not to produce such sentences and never hear anyone else produce such sentences. Yet, without hesitation, we judge them as ungrammatical.

The second misconception about our linguistic competence is that our ability to make grammaticality judgments is based on the meaning of the words uttered or on the context in which those words are uttered. It's straightforward to dispute such a claim. First, there are simply no contexts or situations in which any of our (b) examples in (2) through (5) could be considered grammatical, and our judgments have nothing to do with the meanings of each of the individual words. Second, we can compare our (b) examples to other sentences, such as those in (6); neither of these sentences makes much "sense," yet we judge them grammatical sentences of English:

6.   a.   Colorless green ideas sleep furiously.
     b.   My toothbrush is pregnant again.

The third misconception about our linguistic competence involves "truth." That is, there are some who believe an utterance must be truthful in order to be grammatical. This belief is surely unfounded; both sentences in (7) are grammatical—but only one is truthful:

7.   a.   The Declaration of Independence was signed in 1776.
     b.   The Declaration of Independence was signed in 1976.

The misconceptions cited above are common; but it should be clear by now that our linguistic competence is not rooted in our past experience, in the meaning of a string of words or the context in which those words are uttered, or in the truth of a given sentence. Instead, linguists argue that our linguistic competence arises from the way human brains operate; that is, Language is "hard-wired" into our brains in some fashion, as part of what makes us distinctly human. The label linguists give to this hard-wiring is universal grammar, the part of our brain that provides us with the abilities to produce and understand Language, not a specific human language.

Our linguistic competence, as illustrated above, is a direct consequence of two interacting systems: the system of elements (i.e., the "words") in our mental lexicons and the computational system (i.e., the "rules") which allows us to string those words together to produce phrases and sentences.

Here are three things we 'know' about these two systems. First, we have an extraordinary amount of knowledge about the properties of individual words. For example, we know that different verbs prefer to occur in different types of constructions. That is, some verbs prefer to occur with only a subject; we label such verbs intransitive. Other verbs prefer to occur with both a subject and an object; we label these verbs transitive. Still other verbs prefer to occur with a subject, an object, and an indirect object; these verbs we label ditransitive. Each of these three major classes of verbs is illustrated below, where both grammatical and ungrammatical examples are provided.

8. a. intransitive
       i.   Homer { wept / fell / fainted }.
       ii.   *Homer { wept / fell / fainted } Marge.

    b. transitive
       i.   Bart { praised / abducted / embarrassed / touched } Lisa.
       ii.   *Bart { praised / abducted / embarrassed / touched }.

    c. ditransitive
       i.   Moe { put / placed } a glass on the bar.
       ii.   *Moe { put / placed } a glass.
       iii. *Moe { put / placed } on the bar.

The curly brackets in these examples allow us to consider various verbs simultaneously. If you had no difficulty in judging both the grammatical and the ungrammatical examples in (8), you were exhibiting your knowledge of the differences among the classes of intransitive, transitive, and ditransitive verbs in English. We investigate these differences, among others, in Section B.

Second, we know about the linear order in which words must occur. For English, we know that the subject most generally occurs as the first element in a sentence, while prepositions occur as the first element in phrases which contain them, as exemplified in (9a) and (9b), respectively:

9. a. i.   Cows eat grass.
       ii.   *Eat cows grass.
       iii. *Grass eat cows.

    b. i.   in barns
       ii.   *barns in

If you easily recognized the difference between the grammatical and ungrammatical examples in (9), you were exhibiting your knowledge of the rules which establish the linear order of words in English sentences and prepositional phrases. Other languages may, of course, have other rules; for example, the Tagalog or Irish equivalent of *Eat cows grass* is grammatical in those languages, as is the equivalent of *barns in* in Japanese or Korean. We explore the rules governing the structure of phrases of English in Section C.

You also have (tacit) knowledge of the hierarchical order of phrases and sentences of your native language. Consider these examples from English, both of which have more than a single meaning:

10.   a.   an American history teacher
      b.   Mr. Burns hit the dog with a stick.

The two meanings of (10a) can be paraphrased as: (i) a teacher of American history; and (ii) a history teacher who happens to be an American. Likewise, (10b) has two paraphrases: (i) The dog which Mr. Burns hit was the dog with a stick; and (ii) Mr. Burns used a stick to hit the dog.

    The interesting point about such examples is that the two different meanings each contains cannot be the result of the words, since each has only a single string of words which occur in one linear order. Strings of words with one linear order but two meanings exemplify what is known as structural ambiguity. In Chapter 6, we learn how to assign different hierarchical structures to such examples. For now, it suffices to note that, if you recognized the ambiguity in each of these examples, then you know something about the hierarchical structure of English phrases and sentences.

    In this chapter, we outline a theory—that is, a grammar—for a small part of the English language that will account for our knowledge of both the properties of words and the linear order of words in phrases and sentences. The former is encapsulated in the mental lexicon, the latter in a computational system.

B.   Entries in the Mental Lexicon

Part of what we know when we 'know' a language consists of knowing the meanings of the words of that language, along with various properties associated with individual words and with classes of words. The mental lexicon is the label linguists assign to the giant, dictionary-like repository in our brains of all the words of our language.

    Recall from Chapter 4 that the internal structure of a word may result from the finicky-ness of the morphemes it's composed of (e.g., *logician* is fine, but **phonologician* is not) and/or from historical changes in the productive rules of the language (e.g., past tense *stole* is a hold-over from Old English, while *robbed* obeys the now-productive past tense rule). As a result, the information stored in the mental lexicon must include an array of idiosyncratic information. This static, largely memorized part of our knowledge of language comprises one part of the syntactic module.

    Perhaps most obviously, the sound of a given word must be associated with the meaning of that word. This must be the case, as for the vast majority of words in any language, the connection between sound and meaning is completely arbitrary. As a result, we must, at some point in our lives, connect the sound /sɪt/ with the meaning "to rest on the lower part of the body," and we must memorize (and store in our brains) this sound-meaning set.

    But, as already discussed, we know much more about the words of our language than this. For example, we interpret *disappear* as a verb, and as the type of verb which does not occur with a direct object. Likewise, we interpret *take* as a verb, but as a verb which does not occur without a direct object:

11. a. i.   Moe disappeared.
      ii.   *Moe disappeared the money.

   b. i.   *Moe took.
      ii.   Moe took the money.

We account for this part of our knowledge through <u>lexical entries</u>. By hypothesis, every word of the language has a separate entry in the mental lexicon. Each entry contains the sound, the meaning, the syntactic category, and the idiosyncratic properties of a given word. For *disappear,* its inability to occur with a direct object is listed. The lexical entry for *take* states that it does not occur without a direct object and that it has an irregular past tense form.

In Chapter 4, we classified groups of words into various syntactic categories, which are split into two major classes: the content (or lexical) categories and the functional (or grammatical) categories. Among the content categories are verbs, nouns, adjectives, and prepositions. Some examples of each of these syntactic categories follow:

12.

a	V	die	admire	put	melt	read
b	N	Harry	Nevada	cowboy	wheat	water
c	A	good	tall	old	honest	generous
d	P	in	at	on	to	for

In the following sections, we consider various properties of and lexical entries for each of the content categories, beginning with those of verbs, and we provide both grammatical and ungrammatical examples. Entries for the functional categories are introduced as we encounter them throughout this chapter.

B1 Verbs

We label some verbs intransitive, others transitive, and still others ditransitive. An intransitive verb is one which can appear with only a subject:

13. a. i.   The rabbit appeared.
      ii.   *The rabbit appeared the carrot.

   b. i.   The rabbit arrived.
      ii.   *The rabbit arrived the carrot.

A transitive verb is one which requires a subject and also a direct object:

14. a. i.   Harry touched a cat.
         ii.   *Harry touched.

     b. i.   Anteaters reside in Irvine.
         ii.   *Anteaters reside.

Notice that the syntactic category of the 'direct object' that must follow a transitive verb differs from verb to verb. Thus, while *touch* takes a nominal expression following it, *reside* requires a phrase with a preposition in it. If we try to switch the two, both results are ungrammatical: *Harry touched in Irvine; *Anteaters reside a cat.*

Ditransitive verbs appear with a subject, a direct object, and an indirect object; omission of either the direct or the indirect object leads to ungrammaticality:

15. a. i.   Jack gave a bone to the dog.
         ii.   *Jack gave to the dog.
         iii.   *Jack gave a bone.

     b. i.   Jill put a book on the table.
         ii.   *Jill put on the table.
         iii.   *Jill put a book.

We account for these differences by encoding certain information in the lexical entry for each verb in the language. Each entry in our mental lexicon contains (at least) the following information: (a) phonological information (what the word sounds like); (b) semantic information (what the word means); and (c) syntactic information. The syntactic information is two-fold, as we must encode both the categorial status of the word and the categorial status of the phrase it selects as its complement(s).

The term "complement(s)" in the underlined string at the end of the previous paragraph refers to the fact that some verbs require the presence of further material to *complete* their meaning. That is, the meaning of *touch* is not complete unless the entity which is touched is named; likewise, the meaning of *reside* is not complete unless the location in which residing occurs is named. The complement that *touch* occurs with is the type of phrase we call a Determiner Phrase (DP), while the complement that *reside* occurs with is the type of phrase we call a Prepositional Phrase (PP). The verbs *give* and *put* occur with two complements, both a DP and a PP.

In other words, *complement* is somewhat analogous to both traditional terms "direct object" and "indirect object." Thus syntacticians refer to what are traditionally labeled intransitive verbs as verbs which occur with zero complements, to transitive verbs as verbs which occur with a single complement, and to ditransitive verbs as verbs which occur with two complements.

The complement(s) with which a given verb occurs are listed in what is called the subcategorization frame of that verb's lexical entry. Each verb's subcategorization frame identifies the phrasal category of its complement(s), if any, as this information is a particular, idiosyncratic property of that verb.

Sample lexical entries for *arrive, touch, reside,* and *put* are given in (16) below, where certain facts that we know about each of these verbs is presented in a compressed format. The information in the column labeled *sound* refers to the phonemic (rather than the phonetic) representation of these words. The cells in the column labeled *meaning* consist of words in upper case surrounded by double quotation marks. This representation is not intended to in any way actually reflect the meanings of these words. Instead, it is adopted here only for ease of exposition. Each of these words is a verb, and the syntactic category V is listed in each entry.

The last column contains each verb's subcategorization frame, enclosed in square brackets. The blank denotes the slot in which the verb occurs within this frame; what follows the blank is the syntactic category of the phrase, if any, which a given verb selects as its complement: *Arrive* requires no complement (hence the null sign), *touch* requires a DP complement, *reside* requires a PP complement, and *put* requires both a DP complement and a PP complement, in that order.

16.

	sound	*meaning*	*category*	*subcat. frame*
arrive	/əɹɑɪv/	"ARRIVE"	V	[__ Ø]
touch	/tʌtʃ/	"TOUCH"	V	[__ DP]
reside	/ɹizaɪd/	"RESIDE"	V	[__ PP]
put	/pʊt/	"PUT"	V	[__ DP PP]

If we were being extremely exacting, we would also include here such idiosyncratic information as the irregular past tense form of *put* (which is identical to its present tense form), as this is knowledge native speakers have internalized. We abstract away from such details here, however, as our interest is syntactic rather than phonological or morphological.

There is one more significant point to be made about such lexical entries: Note that no specific mention is made of the subjects of these verbs. This is because all sentences of English require a subject. There is thus no reason to encode such information in every single lexical entry, as the function of lexical entries is to encode idiosyncratic information only.

B2 Prepositions, Nouns, and Adjectives

The other members of the class of content categories—nouns, adjectives, and prepositions—have lexical entries that are analogous to those for verbs. Prepositions such as *in, on, beside, over, above, below, for, with, beyond, around,* and so forth frequently occur with DP complements, as shown in (17). But sometimes, prepositions can occur alone, as shown in (18):

17.   a.   He put the clock { on / beside / over / above } the table.
      b.   She baked cookies { for / with } a friend.
      c.   They went { beyond / around } the barn.

18.   a.   He turned the paper { in / over }.
      b.   She climbed { down / up }.
      c.   We walked { around / along }.

The simplest way to encode the fact that Ps occur with DP complements some times, but not always, is to add parentheses around the DP in the P's subcategorization frame: [__ (DP)]. The parentheses around the DP are shorthand for "optionally."

    Likewise, some nouns may occur with complements; but many nouns lack this ability. Those nouns which may occur with complements fall into two broad sets: titles (such as *prince* and *queen*) and nouns which are derived from verbs (such as *discovery* and *examination*). But in both instances, the presence of a complement to the noun is always optional, though when a complement occurs, it is invariantly a PP:

19.   a.   i.   I met a <u>prince (of France)</u> yesterday.
         ii.   *I met a <u>prince (France)</u> yesterday.

      b.   i.   She mentioned the <u>discovery (of a new vaccine)</u>.
         ii.   *She mentioned the <u>discovery (a new vaccine)</u>.

We assign this subcategorization frame to the nouns in one of these two sets: [__ (PP)].

    But most nouns which fall into the sub-class of common nouns (e.g., *car, artichoke, electricity, water, leisure,* and so forth), as well as proper nouns (e.g., *Henry Hudson, New York City*) do not occur with complements; instead, they much prefer to occur alone. We assign these nouns subcategorization frames that are similar to those of intransitive verbs: [__ Ø].

    Many adjectives—including *tall, green, intelligent, beautiful,* and so forth—occur with no complements and have this subcategorization frame: [__ Ø]. But, as with nouns, there are some adjectives that can optionally occur with PP complements: *{fond / full / tired} (of licorice); interested (in linguistics); suitable (for framing)*. This set of As has this subcategorization frame: [__ (PP)].

B3 Determiners

In the previous paragraphs, we've referenced the category D (for determiner) and mentioned DPs (Determiner Phrases) on several occasions; it's time now to consider this functional category in some detail. "Determiner" is a cover term for four different sub-classes of words in English: articles, demonstratives, quantifiers, and (personal) pronouns:

20.

		English determiners
a	*articles*	(indefinite) a, (definite) the
b	*demonstratives*	this, that, these, those
c	*quantifiers*	some, many, few, all, several . . .
d	*pronouns*	I, me; she, her; they, them . . .

While the words listed in (20) may appear to be a rather eclectic group, these words are all subsumed under a single syntactic category simply because they cannot occur together. That is, we cannot refer to *the those books* or to *a some book* or to *many they* or to any other combination of the words in this set that you might come up with.

The first three sub-classes of determiners shown in (20), articles, demonstratives, and quantifiers, routinely take <u>Noun Phrase</u> (NP) complements; but the last sub-class, pronouns, never occurs with any complement. Abbreviated lexical entries are provided below as representative of each sub-class:

21.

	sub-class	*subcat. frame*
a	articles	[__ NP]
b	demonstratives	[__ NP]
c	quantifiers	[__ NP]
d	pronouns	[__ Ø]

The subcategorization frames in (21) encode our knowledge that pronouns are 'intransitive' DPs, which consist of only a D. The other DPs are 'transitive'; phrases such as *a cat, this dog,* and *many horses* are DPs which contain a D plus an NP complement.

B4 Determining Syntactic Category

Returning to finish up our discussion of the content categories, we consider just how it is that we know that a given word is a V, an N, an A, or a P. There are (at least) three possibilities, the first of which relies on the meaning and/or function of the word. On this (traditional) account, nouns name people, places, or things; verbs refer to actions or states; adjectives modify nouns; and prepositions refer to locations or signal relations between entities.

But such definitions have their limits: For one thing, we'd have to enlarge our definition of noun to include abstractions such as *truth* and *wisdom* and to include unreal entities such as *griffins* and *trolls*. Even more problematic, however, is the fact that a given 'word' can have a variety of meanings and belong to more than a single category; in (22a), *can* is a noun; in (22b) it is a verb; in (22c) the first instance of *can* is a modal auxiliary, the second is a verb, and (reduplicated) *can-can* is a noun that refers to a type of dance:

22.   a. I put the tomatoes in a <u>can</u>.
      b. I <u>can</u> tomatoes every year.
      c. I <u>can</u> <u>can</u> tomatoes while dancing the <u>can-can</u>.

(We consider homophones such as the noun *can* and the modal auxiliary *can* in some detail in Chapter 6.)

As already mentioned in Chapter 4, inflectional morphology can provide more reliable clues to the syntactic category of a given word: Only nouns have plural or possessive forms, only verbs have past tense or progressive forms, only adjectives (and some adverbs) have comparative and superlative forms. Prepositions are the only category (among the content categories) that allow no inflectional affixes at all.

The third way to distinguish the syntactic category of a word is to determine its <u>distributional properties</u>; that is, to consider the categories of the words with which it can occur. For example, we've just seen that many verbs and prepositions can occur with DP complements; but this privilege does not extend to members of other categories:

23.   a. envies$_V$ the clowns
      b. for$_P$ the clowns
      c. *the envy$_N$ the clowns
      d. *envious$_A$ the clowns

Likewise, we've seen that nouns can occur with determiners, but this privilege does not extend to other syntactic categories:

24.   a.   { the / some } clowns$_N$
      b.   *{ the / some } over$_P$
      c.   *{ the / some } arrive$_V$
      d.   *{ the / some } beautiful$_A$

Verbs can occur with modal auxiliaries (*can, could, shall, should, will, would, may, might, must,* and so forth). The modal auxiliaries, as mentioned in Chapter 4, comprise one of the functional categories, I (short for Inflection). We explore their syntax later on in this chapter, delaying discussing their (extremely complex) semantics until Chapter 6. For now, it suffices to note that verbs, but not other content categories, can occur with modal auxiliaries:

25.   a.   { will / must / should } buy$_V$
      b.   *{ will / must / should } clowns$_N$
      c.   *{ will / must / should } over$_P$
      d.   *{ will / must / should } beautiful$_A$

The discussion in this section is summarized in Table 1, which enumerates the categories covered so far along with their possible subcategorization frames:

Table 1:   *Categories and Complements*

category	*may subcategorize for . . .*
V	Ø, DP, PP
N	Ø, (PP)
A	Ø, (PP)
P	(DP)
D	Ø, NP

We discuss the nature of lexical entries further in Chapter 6; but we have sufficient understanding now to use such lexical information to begin to string words together via the computational system in order to make phrases and sentences.

C. The Computational System

This section explores the nature of the computational system, the system which governs the manner in which elements from the mental lexicon can be combined to form phrases and sentences. While the lexicon is filled with idiosyncrasy, the computational system consists of a very few basic operations. Moreover, recall that the computational system in the morphological module is constrained to combining only two morphemes at any given time. The computational system which assembles syntactic phrases and sentences is constrained in precisely the same way; that is, we can combine nothing more than two pieces of syntactic structure at any one time. Some reasons behind this restriction should become clear as we proceed, but full justification for it is left for more advanced work in syntax.

C1 Compositionality

The grammar of every human language is <u>compositional</u>. This statement sounds simple enough, as we are certainly aware that phrases and sentences are composed of words. But the notion of compositionality is rather more complex, entailing three major properties:

- ■   Sentences in all languages are composed of constituents called <u>phrases</u>.
- ■   A given phrase may be composed in turn of one or more smaller phrases.
- ■   The smallest phrase is one composed of a single <u>word</u>.

The first property of compositionality can be clarified with sentences such as these:

26.   a.   A clown praised the acrobat.
     b.   The acrobat praised a clown.

Even though both sentences contain precisely the same words, we interpret them differently, simply because the words—i.e., the phrases *a clown* and *the acrobat*—occur in different orders. As a result, the two sentences have different compositions. Because these sentences have different compositions, we interpret *a clown* as the praiser in (26a) but as the one who is praised in (26b).

The second and third properties of compositionality are demonstrated with this sentence:

27.   A clown with a big nose praised him.

Presumably, you have no difficulty at all in identifying *a clown with a big nose* as the subject of this sentence and hence as the praiser. Now observe that this DP contains an NP (*clown with a big nose*), while the NP contains a PP (*with a big nose*), and the PP contains a DP (*a big nose*).

That is, one phrase contains another phrase, which in turn contains another phrase, thereby exemplifying the second property of compositionality.

Now consider the pronoun *him* in (27), which is intended to refer to and to replace *the acrobat* from (26). This single word is also a phrase. It represents the simplest type of phrase, one which consists of a single word, the third property entailed in the notion of compositionality.

The concept of compositionality plays a fundamental role in syntax, and having a thorough understanding of the three properties outlined above greatly facilitates the balance of the discussion in this chapter.

C2 Parsing Sentences

To parse a sentence means to determine its composition in some detail. One way to accomplish this, in English or any other language, is to work from the "bottom up." Such an analysis begins by identifying the categories of individual words such as nouns, verbs, prepositions, determiners, and so forth, and then works up to larger constituent levels.

To see how this system works, consider the sentence from (26), *A clown praised the acrobat.* Our first task, identifying the syntactic category of each word in this sentence, is straightforward:

28.

D	N	V	D	N
A	clown	praised	the	acrobat

Our second task is to group words together into phrases—that is, into strings of words which "go together" in some sense. The first such string of words we encounter here is *a clown*. There are at least three pieces of evidence we can use to determine that the string *a clown* forms a phrase: First, neither word can appear alone; thus both **A praised the acrobat* and **Clown praised the acrobat* are impossible. Second, we can replace this string with a single word, the pronoun *he* (assuming the clown is male; if the clown referred to is female, the appropriate pronoun would be *she*). Third, the string *a clown* serves as the subject of the sentence. That is, we interpret *a clown* here as the one who is the giver of praise, not as the one who is the recipient of such praise.

The phrase *a clown* is a DP, shorthand for Determiner Phrase. This DP contains two elements: the D *a*, which is the phrase's head, and the N *clown*, which is the head complement. Recall from our discussion of lexical entries that complements, regardless of their categorial status, are by definition phrases. And our discussion of compositionality noted that a phrase can consist of a single word. As a result, *clown* is the N which heads an NP, shorthand for Noun Phrase. Pulling this discussion together gives us the following analysis:

29.

DP				
	NP			
D	N	V	D	N
A	clown	praised	the	acrobat
subject				

The next phrase to consider in this sentence is the string *praised the acrobat*. We can use the same three types of evidence that demonstrated *a clown* is a phrase to demonstrate that *praised an acrobat* is also a phrase. First, none of these words can appear without the other two: **A clown praised; *A clown the; *A clown acrobat*. Second, we can replace this string with the pro-form *do so: A clown praised the acrobat, and then a lion-tamer <u>did so</u>.* Here, we can interpret the pro-form *did so* only as *praised the acrobat*. Third, the string *praised the acrobat* functions as the <u>predicate</u> of the sentence; that is, this string of words delineates the action that the subject of the sentence engaged in.

We call the phrase *praised the acrobat* a VP, shorthand for Verb Phrase. This phrase contains a head, the V *praised,* and its complement, *the acrobat. The acrobat* is another phrase: Neither word can occur alone (**A clown praised the; *A clown praised acrobat*); it can be replaced by a pronoun (*A clown praised {him, her}*); and it functions as the <u>direct object</u> of the sentence, representing the one who is the recipient of the clown's praise.

The acrobat is a DP; it consists of a head (the D *the*) and an NP complement; the NP complement consists of only a head (the N *acrobat*).

We can now add to our analysis from above to delineate the structure of the predicate as well as that of the subject:

30.

		VP		
DP			DP	
	NP			NP
D	N	V	D	N
A	clown	praised	the	acrobat
			direct object	
subject		*predicate*		

Given this "boxy" analysis, we can turn both our subject and our predicate into syntactic trees straightforwardly. In fact, we can even draw 'branches' in the boxes as a sort of intermediate step:

31:

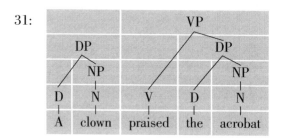

Observe that the labels "subject," "predicate," and "direct object" have disappeared; we return to this point soon. The actual trees that syntacticians draw are provided in (32):

32. a. b.

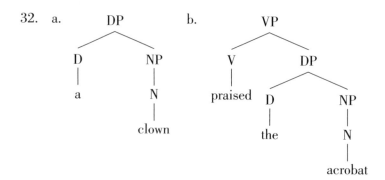

Note carefully that these trees contain precisely the same information that is contained in the "boxy" analysis in (31):

■   The subject DP contains the D *a* (the <u>head</u> of the DP) and an NP (<u>complement</u> to the D); the complement NP contains only the N *clown* (the <u>head</u> of the NP).
■   The predicate VP contains the verb *praised* (the <u>head</u> of the VP) and a DP (the <u>complement</u> to the V); the DP complement contains the D *the* (the <u>head</u> of this DP) and an <u>NP (complement</u> to this D); the NP complement contains only the N *acrobat* (the <u>head</u> of this NP).

Observe also that the syntactic categories of each phrase are the same as the syntactic categories of their heads. This observation entails that syntactic phrases are endocentric. Recall our finding that some compounds of English are endocentric (i.e., headed), while other compounds are exocentric (i.e., headless). The field of syntax is sometimes considered more consistent than the field of morphology, as endocentricity holds of every phrase in every language of the world. Endocentricity requires a one-to-one correspondence between the syntactic category of a given head and the phrase within which that head occurs. Thus, every V occurs within a VP, and every VP is headed by a V; every D occurs within a DP, and every DP is headed by a D; and so forth.

Further, observe that some heads in (32) occur with phrasal complements, as denoted in the lexical entry for each word. Thus, *praise* is a transitive verb which occurs with a DP complement; the articles *the* and *a* are Ds which occur with NP complements. In this way, the information in an element's lexical entry can be said to "guide" its appearance within the computation system.

Syntacticians sometimes use kinship terms as a form of shorthand for describing the relation between various nodes in a syntactic tree. A mother is a node which has one or more daughters; thus, in both (32a) and (32b), DP is a mother with two daughters, (D and NP); in (32b), VP is mother to two daughters (V and DP). The term sister refers to two nodes which share the same mother, thereby denoting the relation between a head and its complement. In (32a) and (32b), D and NP are sisters, as DP is mother to both; in (32b), V and DP are sisters, as both have VP as mother. Note that only female kinship terms are used, a usage consistent with such terms as "mother tongue." These terms will appear in various places throughout this text.

We now need to combine the subject and predicate together to make an entire sentence, a process discussed immediately below.

C3 Merging Subject and Predicate

The "glue" that holds sentences together—and sets sentences apart from other phrases—is called Inflection, an element which denotes tense.

While this choice may initially appear somewhat unusual to you, it arises from two interacting causes. First, from the point of view of morphology, the element which denotes tense is an inflectional element in many (though not all) languages of the world. Second, from the point of view of semantics (i.e., meaning), sentences are considered to be propositions. A proposition is a statement which has a truth value, and truth values are generally rooted in time. The truth value of our current example would be something along these lines: At some point in the past, there was a clown, and this clown engaged in an act of acrobat-praising. Significantly, if a clown had not in fact engaged in acrobat-praising at some point in the past, this sentence would not be true.

We all recognize that the tense of our current sentence is past; its present tense counterpart would be *A clown praises the acrobat.* English is like many of the world's languages in allowing only two tenses: past or present. Because both the past and present tense elements in English are affixes (rather than full words), the element of Inflection that appears here is only an <u>abstract feature</u>. This abstract feature in Inflection is the semantically-rich but phonologically-null element which we represent as PAST. (This feature is shown in the text in small caps as a typographic convenience to denote that it is abstract.) As a result, when we combine subject and predicate, they are "held together" by this feature, which is high-lighted below:

33.   a.   [subject a clown]   (PAST)   [predicate praised the acrobat]

b.

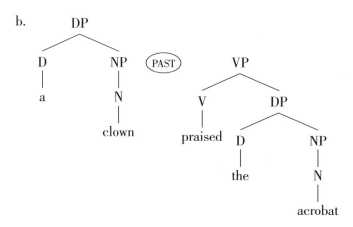

Because I (here, the abstract feature PAST) is a head, it must by endocentricity project all the way to IP. As a result, we can replace the semantic label "sentence" with the syntactic term "IP" (shorthand for <u>Inflection Phrase</u>), a phrase which contains a subject, a predicate, and an element denoting tense.

The internal structure of IP must be more complex than the internal structures of the DPs and the VP we've considered already, as we have two phrases (the subject DP and the predicate VP) to combine with this head. Because the computational system can combine only two pieces of structure at any one time, we cannot simply combine the subject, the feature PAST, and the predicate into a single IP node with three branches.

We have already seen that many heads occur with complements (i.e., phrasal sisters which occur to the right of the head); the predicate VP here projects as complement to I. That is, we merge (i.e., combine) VP as complement (i.e., sister) to I.

But we also need a position in the structure for the subject DP, and this is a position we have not encountered so far, as it is one that precedes the head of the phrase. In order to accommodate both the subject and the predicate into a single phrase, we must first project I to the intermediate level of structure called " I' " (read: "I-bar") before we project all the way to the phrasal level IP. Once we project I to the intermediate I' level, we can merge the DP subject, making it the (left-hand) sister to I'. IP is then mother to the DP subject and to I', as shown in (34).

Projecting this extra level of structure within IP provides us with a position for the subject (left-hand sister to I') and simultaneously allows us combine no more than two syntactic elements at any one time, the fundamental restriction of the computational system. Inspection of hinted at in (34) should clarify why we say that I "mediates between" or acts as the "glue" which holds the subject and predicate together:

34.

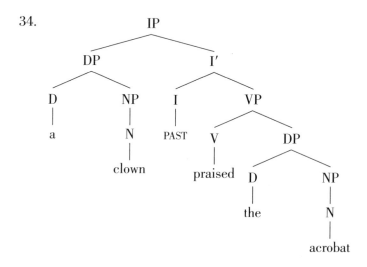

The structure in (34) is the basic structure of all simple, declarative sentences of English. The predicate, which is almost always a VP, is merged as (right-hand) sister to I; and the subject, which is almost always a DP, is merged as (left-hand) sister to I'. In more formal terminology, the VP predicate is the complement of I and the DP subject is the specifier of IP.

We've seen that complement is a broad term which lacks a categorial status, as different heads select phrases of different categories as their complements; in English, complements are always right-hand sisters to heads. The term "specifier" likewise lacks a categorial status. But specifiers differ from complements in their position of attachment. Within IP, specifiers (which are most often, but not always, DPs) are left-hand sisters to I', a position usually abbreviated to "Spec IP." (We'll be adding specifiers in other functional phrases as we proceed.)

Now observe that we are no longer using the quasi-semantic terms "subject," "predicate," and "direct object." While these terms are sometimes useful, there is nothing about the phrase *a clown* that requires it to be a subject and there is nothing about the phrase *the acrobat* that requires it to be a direct object. In fact, we can switch these two phrases around and have another perfectly grammatical sentence, though one whose meaning differs from our current example:

35.   The acrobat praised a clown.

The differences in meaning result from differences in compositionality. In (35), *the acrobat* projects in Spec IP, and *a clown* projects as complement to *praised*.

Let's take a moment to consider other elements which may occur in I. For example, our sentence could be present tense, rather than past: *A clown praises the acrobat*. This sentence would have exactly the same structure as that given in (34)—except that I would be filled with the abstract feature PRES(ENT) instead of the abstract feature PAST.

But English allows another possibility, one in which a modal auxiliary (*can, could, will, would, shall, should, must, may, might* and so forth) occurs instead of an abstract feature. As hinted at in Chapter 4, the modal auxiliaries are instances of category I. Either a modal or an abstract feature can occur in I—but not both at the same time, as the following examples make clear:

36.   a.   A clown might praise the acrobat.
       b.   *A clown { mights / mighted } praise the acrobat.
       c.   *A clown might { praises / praised } the acrobat.

The structure of (36a) would be exactly like that given in (34), except that I would be filled with a word, the modal auxiliary *might* instead of an abstract feature. We could therefore develop the generic tree in (37) to represent the basic structure of any sentence of English:

37.

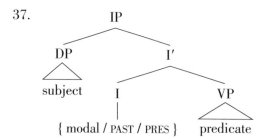

As always, the curly brackets denote "one or another, but only one at a given time," thereby entailing that the head of IP can be filled with only a single element, which may be either a modal auxiliary or an abstract feature.

(Thoughtful readers may be wondering about the structures of sentences such as *A clown is/was praising the acrobat* or *A clown has/had praised the acrobat*. These sentences contain what are called aspectual auxiliaries and denote progressive and perfective aspect, respectively; these have complex structures well beyond the scope of this text.)

C4 The Structures of NP, PP, and AP

In Section B, we noted that some nouns and adjectives and most prepositions can some times surface alone, though at other times they surface with complements. Therefore, we described the subcategorization frames for Ns and As as [___ { Ø , (PP) }] and for Ps as [___ (DP)], where the parentheses denote optionality and the curly brackets denote the different possibilities for different sub-classes of Ns and As. When Ns and As take complements, they are invariantly PPs, while the complements which occur with Ps are always DPs:

38.　a.　{ Princes / Princes of Finland } might some day rule the universe.
　　　b.　Sam fell { down / down the stairs }.
　　　c.　Pam is { afraid / afraid of the snake }.

The structures of the 'intransitive' and 'transitive' versions of the Noun Phrases, Prepositional Phrases, and Adjective Phrases above are schematized in (39a-b), respectively:

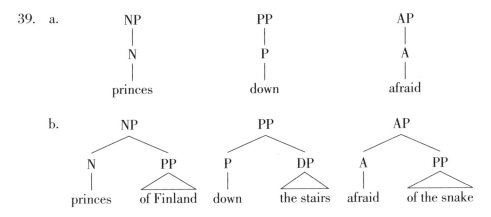

The structures in (39b) introduce the use of <u>triangles</u> (also called coat hangers) in syntactic trees. Triangles are devices for suppressing the internal structure of a phrase. In our current examples, we know what the internal structures of the relevant DP and PP complements look like, so we can suppress their structure. (If you're not sure what the internal structure of the PP *of the snake* is, consider the internal structure of the PP *down the stairs;* the structures are the same.) Triangles are especially useful when the internal structure of a phrase is already known, or not pertinent to a given discussion, or extremely simple (e.g., for a phrase which consists of a single word). But bear in mind that triangles are used only to ignore the internal structure of a phrase; a triangle never entails that a phrase lacks structure.

We can recap our discussion so far as follows: The content categories V, N, P, and A may sometimes occur alone in their phrases or may sometimes occur with a complement phrase. While some transitive verbs occur with DP complements, others occur with PP complements; 'transitive' Ps occur with DP complements, while 'transitive' Ns and As occur with PP complements. We encode this information in the subcategorization frames of the lexical entries of individual words, and we use this lexical information to guide us when we build syntactic structures. Further, in each of VP, NP, PP, and AP, the complement consistently follows the head; thus, the order [head + complement] can be said to characterize the basic word order facts of English.

In addition, we've replaced the traditional term "sentence" with the syntactic term "IP," a phrase headed by the functional category I. I may be filled with either an abstract feature (PAST or PRES) or a modal auxiliary. This functional head routinely takes VP as its complement. In order to make space for the DP subject of a sentence, we first project I to the intermediate I' level and then to the IP level. The DP subject projects in Spec IP, where it is daughter to IP and (left-hand) sister to I'.

These observations of the four content categories and the functional category I are summarized in the following table.

Table 2:   *Summary of Projections so Far*

phrase	*head*	*complement*	*specifier*
VP	V	DP; PP; Ø	none
NP	N	(PP); Ø	none
PP	P	(DP)	none
AP	A	(PP); Ø	none
IP	I	VP	DP

Immediately below, we explore in some detail the internal structure of DPs.

C5 The Structures of DPs

"Nominal expression" is a cover term which encompasses (a) simple pronouns: *he, she, me;* (b) [D NP] phrases: *that cow, some pigs;* (c) proper names: *Jerry, California;* (d) "bare plurals," a label which refers to the plural forms of nouns which occur with no D: *desks, alligators;* (e) abstract nouns: *warmth, leisure;* and (f) possessives: *an alligator's snout.* We already know the structures of the 'intransitive' DPs in which the personal pronouns occur and of 'transitive' DPs such as *that cow.* But we haven't yet considered the other types of nominal expressions noted above, a gap we now fill.

The NPs encountered so far have occurred as complements inside DPs (e.g., *a clown, the acrobat*). But it appears that some NPs occur alone, with no determiner present. This is the case with proper names in English, which prefer to occur with no D, as shown in (40a). And it is also the case with bare plurals as well as with nouns which refer to abstractions and which generally lack plural forms, as exemplified in (40b) and (40c), respectively.

40. a. i. She mentioned { Al / Bob / Cal }.
        ii. *She mentioned the { Al / Bob / Cal }.

    b. i. She mentioned { hospitals / cows / cowboys }.
        ii. *She mentioned { hospital / cow / cowboy }.

    c. i. She mentioned { hospitality / warmth / leisure }.
        ii. *She mentioned { hospitalities / warmths / leisures }.

We could conclude that, since there is no D present in these cases, the NP does occur alone. But this conclusion would over-simplify the issue and be misleading from the point of view of semantic meaning. Semantists consider D the "focal point" of definiteness (or lack thereof). A definite nominal expression is one which refers to or picks out a specific entity or entities which can be identified through the context in which a phrase or sentence is produced. In contrast, an indefinite nominal expression lacks this sort of specific reference and does not pick out a specific entity or entities.

Proper nouns refer to entities which are not only definite but also unique, even though they generally occur without a D. In contrast, abstract nouns and bare plurals are interpreted as indefinites. In the case of abstract nouns, the indefinite interpretation obtains as a direct result of the "abstraction" that the abstract noun denotes. In the case of bare plurals, we usually interpret these expressions not only as indefinite but also as "generic," that is, as referring to an entire set or class of entities rather than to specific entities. Thus, in uttering *She mentioned hospitals,* the speaker is not referring to any specific hospital; instead, "hospitals" here can be interpreted as referring to "all hospitals which have ever existed in the past, all hospitals which exist right now, and all hospitals which will ever exist in the future."

Semantists conclude that the preceding explication entails that proper nouns, abstract nouns, and bare plurals must in fact occur inside DPs, even though we do not pronounce the Ds out loud. The Ds here are instead represented by abstract features, rather analogous to the abstract features PAST and PRES that may occur in I. While we could employ different representations for the "definite-D" that occurs with proper nouns and the "indefinite-D" that occurs with abstract nouns and bare plurals, in this text we use one notation—"e"—to represent both, as shown below. For completeness, the structures of DPs containing a pronoun and an overt D plus NP are also schematized.

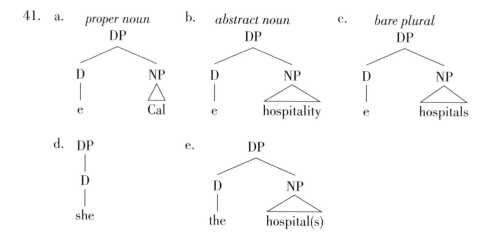

41. a. *proper noun*   b. *abstract noun*   c. *bare plural*

The generalization is that all nominal expressions project as DPs, a situation which obtains for the 'intransitive' DPs in which pronouns project and for all 'transitive' DPs which take NP complements, whether the D is pronounced out loud or not.

We have one more type of nominal expression to consider, possessive DPs such as *John's hat*. Possessive DPs are comprised of the possessor(s), the entity or entities possessed, and (in most instances) possessive (or genitive) morpheme *-s:*

42. a. a student's hat
     b. a student of biology's hat
     c. a student of biology from UCI's hat

The first thing you should notice is that possessive *-s* must not be a simple affix (on a par with plural *-s*, for example), as it doesn't necessarily attach to the possessor: In (42b), we don't interpret *biology* as the possessor of the hat; nor do we interpret *UCI* as such in (42c).

Possessive *-s* is the type of element that attaches to whole phrases, not to a particular word within a phrase, a fact which can be clarified by adding brackets:

43. a. [a student]'s hat
     b. [a student of biology]'s hat
     c. [a student of biology from UCI]'s hat

What precedes possessive *-s* is an entire DP; what follows is an NP. The structure of (43a) is that given below. Observe that the D head of this possessive DP is filled with possessive *-s*, the possessor is in Spec DP, and the possessed is the NP complement to D:

44.

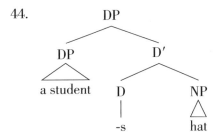

Two points are significant here: First, possessive *-s* is not always pronounced out loud in English; this arises when the possessor is expressed as a pronoun: *{my / your / her} hat.* In such instances, possessive *-s* is still abstractly present. Therefore, to simplify matters, we fill D with possessive *-s* even when it is phonologically-null; that is, as a form of shorthand, we use *-s* to represent the abstract feature [+possessive].

   Second, the structure in (44) allows us to capture a range of parallelisms in English between whole sentences and possessive DPs:

45. a. Fleming discovered penicillin.
     b. Fleming's discovery of penicillin

46. a. That vet examines alligators.
     b. that vet's examination of alligators

In (45a), we interpret *Fleming* as the one who is the discoverer and *penicillin* as the entity that is discovered. Observe that these same interpretations hold in the possessive DP in (45b): The only reading possible in this DP interprets *Fleming* as the discoverer and *penicillin* as the discovered. Given these parallel semantics, we expect to find parallel syntactic structures; and this is precisely what we find:

47. a.

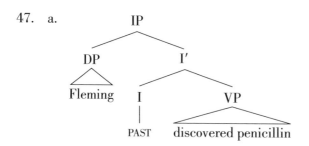

b.

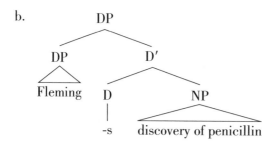

Carefully consider just how syntactically parallel these two structures are:

- Both IP and DP are the projections of functional categories.
- Both IP and DP are headed by abstract features.
- Both I and D occur with complements headed by content categories.
- Both IP and DP allow an intermediate level of structure (I' and D').
- Both IP and DP allow specifiers (i.e., 'subjects').

In these ways, the parallel syntactic structures jibe with the parallel semantics discussed above.

Here is a further set of examples which demonstrate the semantic and syntactic parallelisms between IP and DP:

48. a.

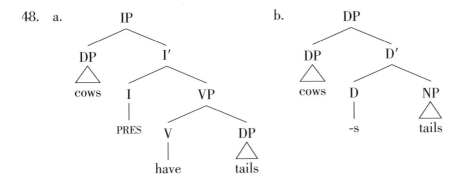

We now enlarge the summary table of projections presented as Table 2 to include the functional category DP:

Table 3:   *Summary of Projections so Far*

phrase	head	complement	specifier
VP	V	DP; PP; Ø	none
NP	N	(PP); Ø	none
PP	P	(DP)	none
AP	A	(PP); Ø	none
IP	I	VP	DP (always)
DP	D	NP; Ø	DP (possessives only)

C6 Sentential Complements

We've limited our discussion of verbs so far to those which occur with DP or PP complements. But some verbs can take an entire sentence as their complement. In English, these verbs fall into two primary classes: verbs of cognition and verbs of saying. Some verbs of cognition are exemplified in (49a-b); (49c) provides some examples of verbs of saying:

49. a. Al { knows / imagines / thinks } that cows have tails.
     b. Cal { wondered / asked } if cows have tails.
     c. Hal { said / reported / claimed } that cows have tails.

Each of the sentences in (49) contains two clauses, a matrix (or upstairs) clause and an embedded (or downstairs) clause. The embedded clause serves as complement to the verb (*know, wonder, say*) in the matrix clause. As a result, these sentences have the same overall structure (i.e., the same overall composition) as the mono-clausal sentences we've already discussed, as they contain a subject and a predicate, and the predicate contains a direct object, which happens to be an entire sentence. This overall structure is schematized below for (49c):

50.

Hal	said	that cows have tails
subject		*direct object*
subject	*predicate*	*predicate*

The structure of (49a) would be the same, though the matrix verb would differ; the structure of (49b) would differ most interestingly by the presence of *if* (rather than *that*) inside the complement to the matrix verb.

The string *cows have tails* in our examples in (49) and (50) is a complete sentence, that is, an IP, just as it is in (48a). But we have a problem now, with the words *that* and *if*, as we have no position in syntactic structure in which to project these words. Here's the solution to our problem: *That* and *if* are of the syntactic category C(omplementizer), a category whose name reflects the fact that Cs are often used to introduce complement clauses—that is, whole sentences which serve as complements to verbs of cognition and to verbs of saying.

C is the last of the functional categories we encounter in this text, bringing our grand total to three. (The other two are of course I and D.) Endocentricity demands that, given an instance of C, we must also have its phrasal projection, CP (Complementizer Phrase). Thus, our sentence in (50) has the following structure, where the upstairs matrix clause and the downstairs embedded clause are separately outlined:

51.

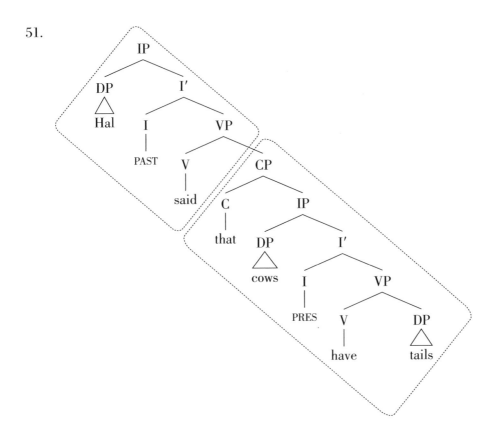

Hal is the subject in (51); what is predicated of *Hal* is the VP *said that cows PRES have tails.* The complement to the verb *say* is the CP *that cows PRES have tails,* and the complement to the C *that* is the IP *cows PRES have tails.* Observe carefully that the embedded IP *cows PRES have tails* has precisely the same structure here as when it appears as an independent sentence, as in (48a).

Note that the structure in (51) represents a further example of compositionality, as the predicate of the complex sentence is composed of a verb plus another sentence; that is, one sentence contains another sentence.

If we were to detail lexical entries for verbs such as *say* or *know,* we would include the possibility of their taking CP complements as well as DP complements (e.g., *Hal said a few words* and *Al knows French*). One way to do this would show the subcategorization frame as [__ {CP, DP}], where the curly brackets denote "one or the other, but not both at the same time." If we were to detail lexical entries for Cs such as *that* and *if,* we would show their subcategorization frame as [__ IP].

The most significant observations made in this section are summarized in Table 4, which enlarges upon the summary previously presented in Table 3. Note that, with respect to specifiers, the content categories pattern alike (as specifiers do not appear here); instead, only the functional categories, I and D, allow specifiers.

Table 4: *Summary of Projections so Far*

phrase	head	complement	specifier
VP	V	DP; PP; Ø; CP	none
NP	N	(PP); Ø	none
PP	P	(DP)	none
AP	A	(PP); Ø	none
IP	I	VP	DP (always)
DP	D	NP; Ø	DP (possessives only)
CP	C	IP	none (so far)

Excursus on Recursion

Recursion refers to the iterative application of a given rule to the output of that rule. In Chapter 4, we discovered that recursion can occur in English compounds (as shown in the examples in (44)). We can also see recursive processes at work in the syntax.

Most languages have various types of recursive properties. For example, in all languages, it's possible to take any sentence, add a word such as *and*, and then add another sentence. And this [sentence + *and* + sentence] routine can be repeated many times. Here's a more interesting example: We know that in English, heads routinely precede their complements; and we know that certain verbs (those of cognition and of saying) can take sentential complements. With these facts in mind, consider the following examples, where the relevant heads are underlined and their complements are enclosed in brackets:

52. a. Beckham plays [soccer].
    b. Socrates proved [that Beckham plays soccer].
    c. Plato only imagined [that Socrates proved that Beckham plays soccer].
    d. Aristotle guessed [that Plato only imagined that Socrates proved that Beckham plays soccer].

e. Descartes <u>knew</u> [that Aristotle guessed that Plato only imagined that Socrates proved that Beckham plays soccer].

f. Kant <u>thought</u> [that Descartes knew that Aristotle guessed that Plato only imagined that Socrates proved that Beckham plays soccer].

g. Wittgenstein once <u>said</u> [that Kant thought that Descartes knew that Aristotle guessed that Plato only imagined that Socrates proved that Beckham plays soccer].

We started with a very simple sentence and embedded it as complement to a verb of cognition; then we embedded the result as complement to another verb of cognition, and so forth. These examples demonstrate the compositional nature of language, a notion which entails that a given phrase can contain another phrase, which can contain another phrase, and so forth. And it is precisely this compositional property of language that lends language its recursive properties.

You might notice that any system which allows recursion has another property—that of <u>non-finiteness</u>. Because language is a recursive system, the length of any sentence (in any language) must be non-finite, if for no other reason than because it can be embedded within a larger sentence, which can then itself be embedded within a larger sentence, and so forth. By extension, then, the number of sentences in any human language must also be non-finite; no matter how many sentences you produce and no matter how long each of those sentences is, there will always be longer sentences and more sentences which you could produce.

As noted in Chapter 4, recursion is one of the defining properties of human language, a property which sets language apart from the communication systems of many animals.

C7 Adjuncts

<u>Adjunct</u> is the technical linguistic term for the traditional label "modifier." Adjuncts are always purely optional elements, and they may be added to provide extra description beyond the core meaning of a given phrase. In English, as in most languages, adjuncts occur most freely with NPs and VPs, and we limit our discussion here to such adjuncts.

Adjuncts, like complements, always project to the phrasal level. But adjuncts differ from complements in several important ways. First, while a given phrase can have several adjuncts, that same phrase allows only a single complement:

53. a. *Col. Mustard killed [Prof. Plum] [Dr. Black].
     b. *the discovery [of penicillin] [of radium]

54. a. Col. Mustard [intentionally] killed Prof. Plum [in the library] [at midnight] [with a hatchet].
     b. the [accidental] discovery of penicillin [at St. Mary's Hospital] [in 1928]

In (53a), we have tried to insert two complements (the bracketed strings) to the verb *kill*, and in (53b) we have tried to insert two complements to the noun *discovery*; both are hopelessly ungrammatical. But we have successfully inserted several adjuncts into the VP in (54a) and into the NP in (54b).

A second way adjuncts and complements differ is this: Adjuncts can often occur in different positions, but complements in general do not have this privilege, as they prefer to be immediately next to the head that subcategorizes for them:

55.   a.   Col. Mustard [intentionally] killed Prof. Plum [with a hatchet] [at midnight] [in the library].
      b.   Col. Mustard killed Prof. Plum [intentionally] [at midnight] [in the library] [with a hatchet].
      c.   *Col. Mustard killed [intentionally] [at midnight] Prof. Plum.

56.   a.   the discovery of penicillin [in 1928] [at St. Mary's Hospital]
      b.   *the discovery [in 1928] [at St. Mary's Hospital] of penicillin
      c.   *the discovery [in 1928] of penicillin [at St. Mary's Hospital]

Because adjuncts can occur in different positions, we need more than a single position in which to merge them. We show this optionality with abstract schematics; " XP " is a variable ranging over VP and NP and the adjunct can precede or follow the phrase it modifies:

57.   a.   b.

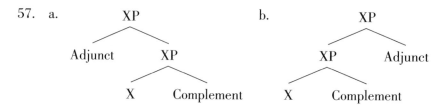

The abstract trees in (57) illustrate the significant structural difference between adjuncts and complements: We know that complements are phrases which are merged as sisters to heads. In contrast, adjuncts are phrases which are merged as sisters to whole phrases. In this way, while complements "complete" the meaning of the head in some sense, adjuncts extend a phrase beyond its core [head + complement] structure.

To see how adjunction works, consider the VPs *often eats tacos* and *eats tacos often;* these VPs are identical up to the site of adjunction, as the Adv(erbial) Phrase *often* may precede or follow the "core" VP:

58.   a.   *often eats tacos*   b.   *eats tacos often*

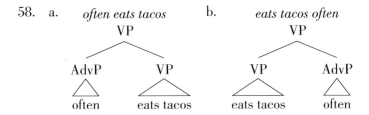

Significantly, the AdvP *often* does not modify only the verb *eats;* instead, it modifies the entire taco-eating activity. Equally significantly, adjoining this AdvP to the VP does not create a new AdvP; if this were the effect of adjunction, then we would expect that IP could take an AdvP complement, but this is clearly not the case, as sentences such as **He {might / PRES} often* are impossible. Instead, the effect of adjunction is to "extend" the VP to which the AdvP is added.

Precisely the same types of effects show up when adjuncts are added to NPs:

59.   a.   *the capped-toothed senator*   b.   *the senator with capped-teeth*

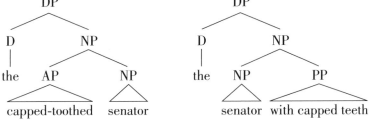

You may wonder why the modifiers here are adjoined to NP rather than to the entire DP. A full response to this problem is beyond the scope of this text. But consider that it is impossible to modify a pronoun: **happy he, *she with capped teeth.* By allowing modifiers on NPs, but not on DPs, we automatically account for this restriction.

You may also notice the categorial status of the adjunct changes, based on whether it appears before the NP, when it occurs as an AP; or after the NP, when it occurs as a PP. Again, a full response to this problem exceeds our current study. Here we note that, in general, English does not allow either pre-nominal PPs or post-nominal APs; **the senator capped-toothed* and **the with capped teeth senator* are both impossible in the language.

Our example in (54b) above appears, at least initially, to be more complex than either of those in (59), because it has three adjuncts, one of which precedes the NP while the other two follow the NP. But once you understand the nature of adjunction, producing its structure is fairly straightforward—providing you start with the "core" NP, the NP which consists of the head and its complement, and then extend this core structure through adjoining one modifier at a time.

Example (54b) is repeated below; its structure is given in (60b), where the NPs are marked with superscripts for ease of exposition:

60.   a.   the [accidental] discovery of penicillin [at St. Mary's Hospital] [in 1928]

   b.

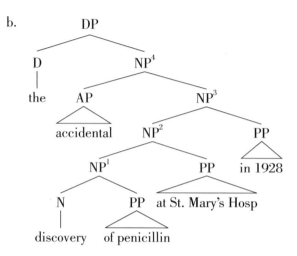

As shown here, the core NP is NP^1, containing the head N *discovery* and its complement, the PP *of penicillin*. Adjoined to this phrase is the PP *at St. Mary's Hospital,* extending NP^1 into NP^2. Adjoined to NP^2 is the PP *in 1928,* which extends NP^2 into NP^3. The AP *accidental* is then adjoined to NP^3, extending NP^3 into NP^4. Finally, the entire NP^4 is merged as complement to the DP headed by *the*.

   Observe that the structure of a sentential counterpart to the nominal expression in (60) has an analogous structure:

61.   a.   Fleming accidentally discovered penicillin at St. Mary's Hospital in 1928.

b.

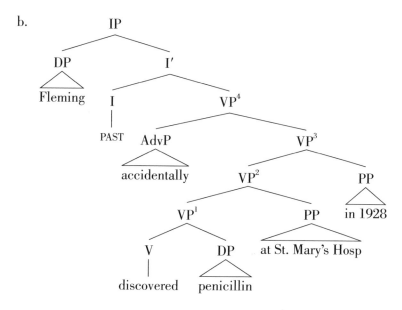

Here again, the crucial part of the VP structure is VP^1, which contains the head V and its DP complement. VP^1 gets extended to VP^2 through adjunction of the PP *at St. Mary's Hospital;* VP^2 gets extended to VP^3 through adjunction of the PP *in 1928;* and VP^3 gets extended to VP^4 through adjunction of the AdvP *accidentally.* Finally, VP^4 is merged as complement to I.

Here are three pieces of advice: (a) Always start with the core [head + complement] structure; (b) practice helps, as the more you practice, the easier it becomes to draw syntactic trees such as those produced above; and (c) make good use of scratch paper.

Let's recap what we've discovered about adjuncts: Adjuncts are optional phrases which may be added to modify either NPs or VPs, in the process extending the NP or VP they merge with. Adjuncts differ from complements in three very significant ways: (a) Adjuncts can iterate (i.e., more than a single adjunct may occur), but complements cannot; (b) adjuncts can often occur in more than one position, but complements are limited to appearing as sisters to the heads that subcategorize for them; and (c) adjuncts are merged as sisters to phrases, but complements are merged as sisters to heads.

We can combine these observations with those given in Table 4 above. Recall the discussion around Table 4, where we noted that only functional categories allow specifiers. What is clarified in Table 5 is that only some content categories (but no functional categories) allow adjuncts. That is, the functional and the content categories differ syntactically, by supporting different types of phrases (specifiers vs. adjuncts).

Table 5:   *Summary of Projections so Far*

phrase	head	complement	specifier	adjuncts
VP	V	DP; PP; Ø; CP	none	yes
NP	N	(PP); Ø	none	yes
PP	P	(DP)	none	no
AP	A	(PP); Ø	none	no
IP	I	VP	DP (always)	no
DP	D	NP; Ø	DP (possessives only)	no
CP	C	IP	none (so far)	no

D. Movement

We've discovered that the computational system is constrained by two major factors: the information contained in the lexical entry of a given word and the ability to merge only two pieces of structure at any one time. While we can therefore generate a very large number of declarative sentences of English, we can generate no interrogative sentences (i.e., questions) in the language. In this section, we develop a means to account for interrogatives of English.

In English (as in all of the world's languages), there are two basic types of questions: In posing a yes/no question, as in (62), the speaker is asking the addressee for an answer in the form of "yes" or "no." In contrast, in posing a wh-question, as in (63), the speaker is asking the addressee to supply an answer that is contentful in some sense.

62. yes/no questions
    a. Should he read this book?
    b. Would she buy a used car from him?
    c. Did you like that movie?

63. wh-questions
    a. What should I read?
    b. Where could she buy a good used car?
    c. Which movie did you like most?

We explore the structure of yes/no questions first, and then return to wh-questions.

D1 Yes/No Questions

The most salient structural point about yes/no questions, such as that in (62a), is that the modal auxiliary precedes the subject. Traditionally, yes/no questions were claimed to be derived from their declarative counterparts from what was called <u>subject-aux inversion,</u> an operation which simply transposed the subject and the auxiliary, so that the latter ended up in front of the former:

64.   He should read this book.

The "movement" schematized in (64) is basically unconstrained, as nothing should prevent inverting the first subject encountered in a given sentence with the first auxiliary encountered:

65.   Any house he could afford would be in a bad neighborhood.

But of course the output of such "movement" is nonsense: *Could any house he afford would be in a bad neighborhood?* For this reason (along with many others), subject-aux inversion has been replaced with an operation that is particular to the computational system within the syntactic module. This operation is called <u>move,</u> an operation which displaces an element from its original position in syntactic structure.

In yes/no questions, the element which "moves" is the element inserted in I, the head of IP; the subject, in Spec IP, does not "move" at all. The position into which this element moves is C, the head of CP. (Recall that clauses embedded under verbs of cognition and verbs of saying are CPs and that C takes IP as its complement, as schematized in (51) above.) The movement operation for our question in (62a) follows:

66.   a.   *before movement*   b.   *after movement*

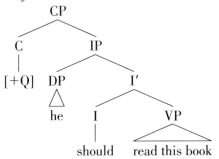
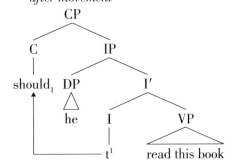

Let's consider the "before movement" structure in (66a) first. The structure of the IP is what we would expect if our sentence was the declarative *He should read this book.* But observe that this IP is embedded under a CP, and the head of that CP is marked with an abstract feature, [+Q]. The presence of this feature ensures that the sentence is intended by the speaker to be interrogative, rather than declarative. And it is this feature which "forces" the auxiliary to move from I into C: Once *should* has raised into C, the addressee can interpret the sentence as interrogative, as the speaker can now pronounce the [+Q] feature of C out loud.

In the "after movement" structure in (66b), *should* has raised from I into C; the arrow shows the path of movement. Significantly, *should* leaves a "trace" of itself in I, abbreviated as "t." The trace and *should* are co-indexed, denoted by the shared subscript "1." This convention allows us to ascertain that *should* started out in I and gives a history of the derivation of this question.

The "before movement" structure in (66a) is sometimes called d-structure, a label which refers to the level of syntactic representation that is based on the information contained in lexical entries (e.g., *should* is of the functional category I), as well as abstract features (e.g., [+Q]), and the basic rules of the computational system.

The "after movement" structure in (66b) is sometimes called s-structure, a label which refers to the level of syntactic representation that is derived from d-structure through the operation move; this level of representation contains traces which are co-indexed with moved elements.

In fact, every sentence, whether declarative or interrogative, has both a d-structure and an s-structure. While these two levels of structure are different in interrogatives (given the movement that occurs), in declaratives the two levels of structure are identical, as there is no movement. This entails that if we were being extremely exacting, we would embed every (declarative) IP under a CP, but one whose head did not carry the [+Q] feature. In general practice, however, this extra level of structure is most generally assumed rather than overtly drawn out, as declarative is considered the default value of a sentence.

There is one final point we must discuss with respect to yes/no questions. Consider the following declarative sentences and their yes/no interrogative counterparts:

67. declarative
   a.   Tom left early.
   b.   Dick sings off-key.

68. interrogative
   a.   Did Tom leave early?
   b.   Does Dick sing off-key?

The important point about these pairs is that the declarative versions have no overt auxiliary; instead only an abstract feature is present in I (PAST in (67a) and PRESENT in (67b)). But in the interrogatives in (68), an auxiliary occurs. This auxiliary is called dummy-DO, a label which differentiates this particular DO from the lexical verb *do* (as in *You should do the dishes*) and from emphatic *do* (as in *I did do the dishes!*). Dummy-DO is empty of meaning; its sole function is to serve as a (phonological) host to an affix in I (either PAST or PRESENT) which would otherwise not be pronounceable.

Because it is empty of meaning, dummy-DO is not present in d-structure; instead it is inserted in s-structure, thereby allowing the addressee to understand that the speaker is asking a question. The structures of (62c)—*Did you like that movie?*—are given below:

69.   a.   *d-structure*   b.   *s-structure*

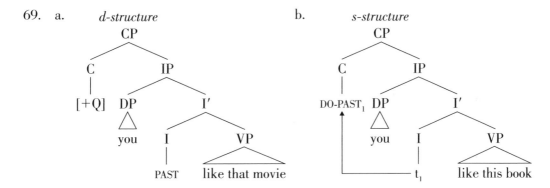

If our question had been *Do you like that movie?*, the feature PRESENT would have been inserted in I in d-structure and DO-PRESENT₁ would appear in C in s-structure. As syntacticians, we are free to leave the actual pronunciation of DO-PAST and DO-PRESENT to the phonological component.

In this discussion of yes/no questions in English, we have introduced two powerful theoretical tools, as we have presented two levels of syntactic representation, d-structure and s-structure, and we have presented move as a syntactic operation. As a result, yes/no questions have these characteristics:

- In d-structure, the question feature [+Q] is merged into C to denote that the sentence is interrogative rather than declarative.
- At s-structure, the element in I (either modal auxiliary or tense feature) moves into C so that the [+Q] feature can be pronounced out loud. This process is referred to as "I-to-C movement."
- If only a tense feature is present in I, dummy-DO is inserted at s-structure, as a tense feature alone is no more pronounceable than is the question feature [+Q].

D2 Wh-questions

Here are some examples of simple wh-questions in English:

70. a. { Who / Which animal } devoured my donut?
    b. { What / Who(m) / Which animal } can you see?
    c. { When / Where / Why / How } did you fix the car?

Wh-questions differ from yes/no questions in various ways. The most obvious difference involves the type of answer expected by the speaker: While the speaker expects "yes" or "no" as answer to a yes/no question, the speaker expects "content" of some sort when posing a wh-question. Sometimes that answer can be a single word or phrase; for example, a possible answer for (70a) might be "Sam" or "that ugly dog." But sometimes the answer can be quite involved; this often occurs in response to "why" and "how" questions.

A second way wh-questions differ from yes/no questions is that they contain a wh-phrase, a phrase that (in English) most often begins with the sequence <wh>; *how* is the exception here.

A third way wh-questions differ from yes/no questions relates to movement: The wh-phrase must occur at the very beginning of the sentence. Failure to move the wh-phrase results in what is called an "echo" question. Echo questions are not actual questions; instead they carry a range of presuppositions, that is, information that is shared (or not shared) by the participants in a discourse. Consider the following very short discourse:

71. a. Speaker A: Sam just bought a big fat pig.
    b. Speaker B: Sam just bought which pig?

Speaker B might well produce the echo question in (71b) if she thought that what Sam wanted to buy was a cute little pot-bellied pig as a pet. Notice also that this echo question must be produced with a great deal of stress and rising intonation at the end of the string. Wh-questions are not subject to either of these restrictions.

While it's clear that wh-questions and yes/no questions are different from each other, it's also the case that they share one significant characteristic, as I precedes the DP subject in both; compare *Should Sam buy a pig?* and *Which pig should Sam buy?*, for example. While I-to-C movement is the only movement operation in yes/no questions, wh-questions involve both I-to-C movement and a second movement operation: that of the wh-phrase to a position preceding C. So we need to ascertain just where in syntactic structure the wh-phrase moves to.

We've already encountered two instances in which a phrase precedes a head and appears in a specifier position: DP subjects routinely appear in Spec IP, and DP possessors routinely appear in Spec DP. The second part of the movement involved in wh-questions is this: the wh-phrase moves into Spec CP. To see how these two movement operations work, consider first the d-structure for *Which pig should Sam buy?* given in (72):

72. *d-structure*

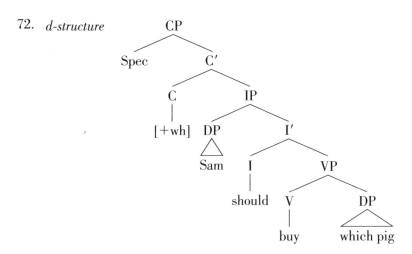

We know that *should* must be inserted in I, as it is a modal of this functional category. We know that I projects to I', making room for merging the subject DP *Sam* in Spec IP; and we know that I takes VP as its complement. Finally, we know that some DP must appear as sister to *buy*, as *buy* is a transitive verb which subcategorizes for a DP complement. In this example, the wh-phrase *which pig* fills this role.

Now note that an abstract feature, [+wh] appears in C. This feature is part of what differentiates wh-questions from yes/no questions: By hypothesis, this feature "forces" the movement of <u>both</u> the modal in I and the wh-phrase in VP. That is, as with yes/no questions, the head of C in d-structure contains an abstract feature, and the grammar of English requires that this feature be pronounced out loud; so I moves into C.

Additionally, the presence of the abstract feature [+wh] in C forces C to project first to the intermediate C' level, in the process allowing the presence of a specifier position within the CP; and the wh-phrase raises into Spec CP. The movements which occur are shown in the s-structure in (73):

73. *s-structure*

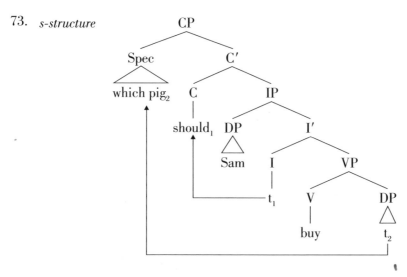

The movement of the modal is identical to that in yes/no questions: It undergoes I-to-C movement and leaves a trace; both the moved modal and its trace have the same index, here "1." In addition, the wh-phrase raises from within VP into Spec CP; it too leaves a trace with which it is co-indexed, and here the index "2" is used. The actual subscripts used are irrelevant; some researchers prefer to use "i" and "j," for example.

What is important, however, is that the trace of the modal and the trace of the wh-phrase have <u>different</u> indices, and that the index of each trace matches that of the element which has moved from the position the trace now occupies. After all, the purpose of the traces is to show what moved where; in our current example, if the trace in I carried the same index as the wh-phrase, we would be forced to conclude—incorrectly—that the wh-phrase is of the functional category I.

The wh-phrase *which pig* is an argument in (72-73), but a given wh-phrase may well project as an adjunct instead. In (74a-b), the d- and s-structure representations for *Where can he buy a piglet?* are schematized:

74. a. *d-structure*

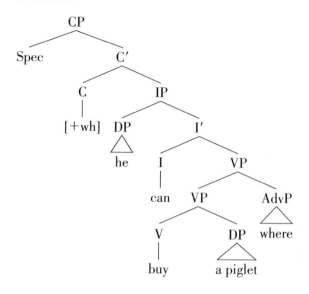

b. *s-structure*

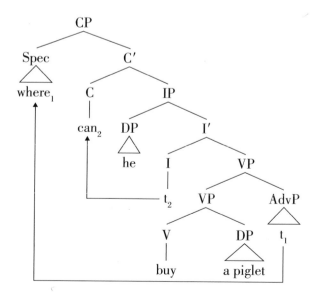

Observe that Spec CP is not labeled with any specific category; this is because wh-phrases come in a range of categories. Many wh-phrase are DPs (e.g., *who, what, which pig*); but *how, when* and *where* are generally AdvPs. The typology of wh-phrases is an interesting topic and is explored in more advanced work in syntax; here, we can safely ignore the subtleties.

One point that we cannot ignore, however, is that dummy-DO occurs in wh-questions for precisely the same reason and through the same mechanisms that it does in yes/no questions: When there is no modal auxiliary in the d-structure, dummy-DO is inserted in s-structure to host the PRESENT or PAST tense affix in I. In this way, the s-structure in (75b) would be derived from the d-structure in (75a), though we leave drawing the trees for each to readers of this text:

75.

a	*d-structure*		[+wh]	Sam	PAST	buy	which pig
b	*s-structure*	Which pig$_2$	DO-PAST$_1$	Sam	t_1	buy	t_2

What we've explored in this section is the operation move, that part of the computational system which displaces an element from the position in which it is inserted in d-structure into some other position in s-structure. In yes/no questions, a single movement occurs, as I must move into C. In wh-questions, we find two movements: I-to-C movement and movement of the wh-phrase into Spec CP. Each instance of movement leaves a trace, which is co-indexed with the element that moves.

We can now complete the summary of projections that we've been developing throughout this chapter, by enlarging Table 5 into Table 6:

Table 6: *Summary of Projections*

phrase	*head*	*complement*	*specifier*	*adjuncts*
VP	V	DP; PP; Ø; CP	none	yes
NP	N	(PP); Ø	none	yes
PP	P	(DP)	none	no
AP	A	(PP); Ø	none	no
IP	I	VP	DP (always)	no
DP	D	NP; Ø	DP (possessives only)	no
CP	C	IP	wh-phrases only	no

E.   A Note on Language Acquisition

We discovered in Chapter 4 that eighteen month old children have a vocabulary of some fifty words, a number which explodes to some thirteen thousand by the time the child enters school. The child's growth in combining words into phrases and sentences parallels her growth in vocabulary. Three main stages of syntactic development have been identified: the one-word stage, the two-word stage, and the "telegraphic" stage.

The one-word stage is characteristic of most twelve to eighteen month old children. Because their vocabularies are limited to some fifty words, they tend to use a single word to express what would be an entire sentence in the adult language. Thus *dada* can mean "I see Daddy" and *up* can mean "I want (to be picked) up." For this reason, this stage is often referred to as the holophrastic (i.e., whole phrase) stage. The amazing thing is that while their utterances are limited to single words, children are quite good at picking out the most informative word from what would be the adult counterpart. That is, the child who wants to be picked up is much more likely to use the word *up* than the word *I* or the word *want* or the word *pick* to express his wish.

Between eighteen and twenty-four months, children enter the two-word stage and begin to utter mini-sentences such as "baby chair" (to mean "The baby is sitting on the chair") and "hit doggie" (to mean "I hit the doggie"). One interesting fact is that inflectional material (plural suffixes on nouns, past tense on verbs, and so forth) is usually completely absent at this stage. Most researchers interpret this lack as suggesting that children at this age have not yet acquired the concept of syntactic categories. Nevertheless, children in the two-word stage still get basic word order correct; thus "hit doggie" can never mean "The doggie hit me."

At around twenty-four to thirty months, children's vocabularies enlarge and their sentences get bigger, though for many children, inflectional material still does not appear. The sentences produced at this stage resemble the style that characterized telegraphs (now an antiquated technology). Western Union charged by the word, so telegraph senders included only the essential content words and omitted all non-essential function words. Because children in this stage of syntactic development tend to lack words from the functional categories, this stage is often called the telegraphic stage. Some examples are provided below; note that word order is completely "adult" and that modifiers now appear:

76.   a.   Car make noise.
      b.   I good boy.
      c.   Man ride bus today.
      d.   Me wanna show Mommy.

It's also at around this stage in their development that most children begin to produce both yes/no questions and wh-questions. While a child may sometimes produce adult versions of questions, sometimes that same child may produce distinctly non-adult questions. For example, in yes/no questions, the child may repeat Inflection, producing it once in its original position (i.e., the position of the trace in the adult language) and once in C (i.e., the position to which I raises in the adult language):

77. a. *Can* he *can* look?
     b. *Did* you *did* came home?

In wh-questions, children almost always move the wh-phrase to the front of the sentence (to Spec CP), but they may or may not move I to C:

78. a. What me think?
     b. What I did yesterday?
     c. Where I should put it?

The vast majority of children move from the telegraphic stage into the adult grammar by the time they enter school, and they do so easily and without formal training. So we should ask just how it is that children acquire the grammar of their language.

It should be clear that children do not simply imitate the adult language that is spoken around them; no adult speaker of English would produce sentences such as those in (76) through (78). It is also the case that reinforcement or feedback by an adult speaker of the language is not the key to the child's acquisition of grammar; here are two frequently cited examples:

79. Adult: Adam, say what I say: Where can I put them?
     Child: Where I can put them?

80. Child: Want other one spoon, Daddy.
     Father: You mean, you want "the other spoon".
     Child: Yes, I want other one spoon, please, Daddy.
     Father: Can you say "the other spoon"?
     Child: Other . . . one . . . spoon
     Father: Say . . . "other".
     Child: Other.
     Father: Spoon.
     Child: Spoon.
     Father: Other . . . spoon.
     Child: Other . . . spoon. Now give me other one spoon?

The child in (80) is both polite and patient—but certainly not receptive to his father's attempts to "correct" his non-adult grammar.

Neither imitation nor reinforcement accounts for the comparative speed with which children acquire the adult grammar, nor for their ability to do so without formal instruction. Instead, by the time most children begin school, they have acquired the basic rules of their language—regardless of whether their parents speak to them constantly or rarely, or whether their parents read to them or play classical music for them, or whether their parents encourage or discourage them from talking. These kinds of facts lead linguists to argue that humans must have a genetic endowment which allows us to acquire, to produce, and to understand Language. The label given to this unique biological ability is <u>universal grammar</u>, as discussed in Section A.

KEY TERMS AND CONCEPTS

linguistic competence	negative evidence	universal grammar
structural ambiguity	mental lexicon	lexical entries
phrases	heads	complements
subcategorization frame	intransitive	transitive
ditransitive	subject	predicate
direct object	indirect object	Determiner Phrase (DP)
Verb Phrase (VP)	Prepositional Phrase (PP)	Adjective Phrase (AP)
Noun Phrase (NP)	compositionality	endocentricity
mother node	daughter node	sister node
proposition	Inflection Phrase (IP)	I' (I-bar) level
specifier	definite vs. indefinite	possessive DP
D' (D-bar) level	Complementizer Phrase (CP)	recursion
non-finiteness	adjunct	yes/no questions
subject-aux inversion	I-to-C movement	d-structure
s-structure	traces	dummy-do
wh-questions	wh-movement	C' (C-bar) level
abstract features (PRESENT, PAST, e, [+Q], [+wh])		
one-word stage	two-word stage	telegraphic stage

PRACTICE PROBLEMS

1. Identify the category (N, V, A, etc.) of each of the words that are underlined in the sentences below, and justify your response in terms of evidence presented in this chapter.

   a. Pamela's heart <u>beat</u> fast and her hands trembled as <u>she</u> listened to the knocking on <u>the</u> front <u>door</u> of her shanty, located <u>near</u> the railroad tracks beside a <u>hobo</u> <u>jungle</u>, and she thought, "That's a <u>bum</u> rap if I ever <u>heard</u> one."

   b. Here's how to make <u>a</u> <u>fortune</u>. Buy fifty <u>male</u> <u>deer</u>. Then <u>you</u> <u>will</u> <u>have</u> fifty <u>bucks</u>.

2. For each of the following phrases, determine the head of the phrase, its complement (if any), and its adjuncts (if any). Then determine the type of each phrase (DP, VP, etc.) Example: *the rat* . . . the head is *the;* the complement is *rat;* there are no adjunct(s); the phrase type is DP

   a. in the barn
   b. the cat in the hat
   c. fond of crisp apples
   d. ran to the store
   e. walked the dog briskly
   f. destruction of that city
   g. ran the store
   h. hastily swept the floor
   i. books with blue covers

3. Each of the phrases below contains a head and a complement. Generate a syntactic tree for each, using triangles for the complements.

   a. some poems
   b. exercise an option
   c. over the river
   d. smoke cigars
   e. fond of apples
   f. the arrival of winter

4. Each of the phrases below contains a head, a complement, and an adjunct. Generate syntactic trees for each, using triangles for complements and adjuncts.

   a. professors of history with white beards
   b. rarely exercise an option
   c. white-bearded professors of history
   d. swept the floor hastily

5. Determine the complement options for the verbs listed below. Do this by thinking of grammatical and ungrammatical sentences containing the verb.

   a. rely   b. watch   c. imagine   d. write   e. wonder

6. Nouns, adjectives, and prepositions also have restrictions on the types of complements with which they can and cannot occur. Determine the complement options for these lexical items:

a. pleasure   b. with   c. contribution   d. at
e. intelligent   f. attraction   g. proof   h. between

7. Generate syntactic trees for these sentences; use triangles to suppress the structure of all single-word phrases and all adjuncts.

a. Abner hid the loot from the hold-up under a mattress.
b. That garbage stinks.
c. Stan hopes that Ollie's daughter becomes a pilot.
d. Nancy proved that aliens exist.
e. Nancy proved the existence of aliens.
f. Sailors must often wonder if they will drown.
g. The salesman hoped those customers would buy a new car from him.

8. Derive the following questions by showing their structures both before movement (d-structure) and after movement (s-structure). Be sure to include co-indexed traces and to insert dummy-DO, as required. Use triangles to suppress the structures of all single-word phrases and wh-phrases.

a. Will the unicorn eat the lilies?
b. Does Gillian like fish?
c. Can my dog stay at your house?
d. What should Gillian do now?
e. Who(m) did David meet?
f. Where did David meet him?
g. Which car did your father sell?
h. Why did he sell that car?

CHAPTER 6

SEMANTICS: ANALYZING MEANING

The fundamental task of semantics is to explain how we convey our thoughts through our utterances in order to provide the content required to fulfill the communicative function of language. This task turns out to be extraordinarily complicated, as it involves a range of technical concepts developed in anthropology, logic, philosophy, psychology, and mathematics as well as in linguistics, many of which are well beyond the scope of this text. Our discussion here provides only a glimpse into our current understanding of how we express meaning and how we understand the meaning of our interlocutors.

This chapter outlines both lexical semantics (the meanings of individual words) and compositional semantics (the meanings of strings of words in phrases and sentences). Compositional semantics explores how syntactic structure contributes to the content of an utterance. Lexical semantics and compositional semantics together contribute to what is called the literal meaning of an utterance.

In contrast to literal meaning, speaker meaning focuses on on-going discourse to analyze how non-grammatical factors such as situational setting and speaker intentions can affect meaning. This chapter introduces one approach to speaker meaning, an approach which attempts to explain our ability to interpret (i.e., to obtain meaning from) words or strings of words which our interlocutors do not express out loud.

A. Meaning Relations: Basic Definitions

We begin our exploration of literal meaning by considering various relations that may hold between two words, or two phrases, or two sentences, or inside a given sentence.

A1 Meaning Relations among Pairs of Words

Our previous discussions of the mental lexicon focused on words as independent elements; as such, we provided each word with its own lexical entry, where its sound, its meaning, and various syntactic properties are listed. We considered the sounds of words in Chapters 2 and 3, the internal structure of words in Chapter 4, and the syntactic properties of words in Chapter 5; but we have not yet considered the meaning of words in any detail. We fill this gap here.

Perhaps one of the most significant aspects of meaning is that much of what we have in mind about a given word is the semantic relation(s) it shares with other words. That is, quite frequently what we know about a given word is not independent of what we know about some other word(s). For example, if asked to define the word *lackadaisical*, we could define it in terms of another word with the same meaning (e.g., "apathetic") or with the negation of a word with the opposite meaning (e.g., "not enthusiastic"). Words which have the same meaning stand in the semantic relation of synonymy; those with opposite meanings stand in the semantic relation of antonymy. We consider these two relations below, along with several other relations one word may share with another.

Synonymy

Synonymy refers to two words which can refer to the same entity, describe the same action or event, provide the same attribute, or describe the same location. As a result, we can find synonyms among each of the content classes (nouns, adjectives, verbs, and prepositions), as exemplified below:

1.

a	car / automobile	corner / niche	room / chamber
b	small / petite	smart / intelligent	yearly / annual
c	buy / purchase	recall / remember	shut / close
d	over / above	under / beneath	near / close

If you consider the pairs of words in (1), you should notice that although it's often possible to substitute one for the other, still some subtle differences in meaning may arise. That is, while both words may describe the same entity, attribute, action, or location, you may find social and/or expressive differences in their meanings. In particular, you may sense that one member of the pair is more formal in some way than the other member. Because of this, you may find that you might prefer to use one rather than the other in a certain discourse setting. For example, if you were trying to impress your neighbor, you might say you were on your way to "purchase an automobile." But if you were trying to bond with your neighbor, you might prefer to mention that you were going to "buy a car." Discourse settings and the rules which govern them form a part of the study of pragmatics; we return to this topic in Section E.

Interestingly, many of the words on the right-hand side of each pair in (1) were borrowed into English from French, primarily between the eleventh and fourteenth centuries, a period which began when the Normans (i.e., French from the coast of Normandy) held sway in England. This period began with the victory of William the Conqueror (known in France as *Guillaume le Conquérant*) over the English troops at the Battle of Hastings in 1066 and lasted well into the Middle Ages. It turns out that when one group conquers another group, the speech of the conquerors often becomes viewed as the "prestige" language, while the speech of those conquered is demoted to "non-prestige" status. Concomitantly, "prestige" words are generally considered more "formal" in some sense than their "non-prestige" counterparts. What we can see of English is that words that were considered "prestige" centuries ago may well retain a sense of formality today.

Phenomena such as those outlined in the previous paragraph are detailed in historical linguistics and socio-linguistics, fields of great interest and relevance to the complete appreciation of any language, and both beyond the scope of the current text.

Antonymy

Antonymy is the opposite of synonymy, as it refers to two words which are opposite in meaning. It's easy to find antonyms among the adjectives, verbs, and prepositions of English, and you can likely come up with many more pairs than are given below. However, outside of gender terms and kinship terms, it is more difficult to find antonyms among nouns; this generalization obtains since we do not usually negate nouns (e.g., we can not refer to the *ceiling* as the *un-floor*).

2.	a	female / male	parent / child	employer / employee
	b	alive / dead	beautiful / ugly	general / specific
	c	buy / sell	remember / forget	find / lose
	d	up / down	over / under	in / out

Some pairs of antonyms are considered binary pairs, as the positive meaning of one entails the negative meaning of the other; for example, *female* entails not male, *dead* entails not alive, *buy* entails not sell, *up* entails not down. Other pairs of antonyms are considered gradable pairs. In a gradable pair, the positive meaning of one does not entail the negative meaning of the other, because there may be words which denote intermediate degrees of meaning between the antonyms. This situation arises most frequently with pairs of adjectives such as *hot* and *cold,* where *warm, tepid,* and *cool* denote intermediate degrees of temperature between hot and cold.

Polysemy

Polysemy is the label given to a single word which has two meanings which are related to each other in some way. It's generally thought that one of the meanings is 'basic' (i.e., original) and the other has been 'derived' by extending or enlarging the basic meaning, sometimes rather metaphorically. Some examples are given in (3):

3.

		original meaning	*extended meaning*
a	diamond	a jewel or gem	place where baseball is played
b	ring	a piece of jewelry	place where boxing occurs
c	bright	shining by emitting light	intelligent
d	deposit	minerals in the earth	money in the bank
e	gem	a jewel	valuable or useful person or thing
f	right	direction (i.e., not left)	correct

In some instances, understanding how the original meaning was extended is straightforward: The layout of home, first, second, and third bases in a baseball field has the same shape as a diamond that has been cut into a certain shape. But in other instances, the meaning extension is not so clear; for example, a ring that is a piece of jewelry is almost always round; but a boxing ring is always square.

Homophony

In contrast to polysemy, homophony refers to a single form which has two or more distinct meanings; that is, to two words which derive from different sources but happen to sound the same. Sometimes, two homophonous words share not only sound but also spelling (sometimes called homographs), as in (4); but sometimes, the two share sound but have different orthographic representations, as in (5):

4.

a	bank	steep side of a river	financial institution
b	to glare	to shine brightly	to stare angrily
c	pen	writing instrument	animal cage
d	bat	flying mammal	club to hit balls with

5.   piece / peace   do / dew   so / sew   write / right

Historical facts are generally the cause of homophony. For example, English borrowed the word *bank* 'steep side of a river' in the twelfth century from the Old Norse word which meant 'ridge'; but English borrowed the word *bank* 'financial institution' in the fifteenth century from the French word which meant 'the table on which financial transactions are carried out'.

Those interested in discovering the origin of words are encouraged to seek out a good, un-abridged dictionary. The twenty volumes and 21,730 pages of (the second edition of) the Oxford English Dictionary provide what is considered the most comprehensive compilation of the words of the English language. Most (university) libraries own this version. A compact web version of the OED, which allows you to search for individual words at no charge, is now available at www.askoxford.com.

Hyponymy and Hypernymy

Hyponymy and hypernymy are terms which relate to hierarchical taxonomies that we hold in mind. A hierarchical taxonomy is a simply a list of elements that is organized in a specific way. One very small representative of a hierarchical taxomony follows:

6.

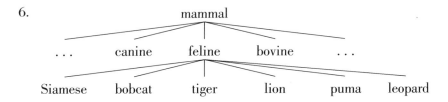

One way to read such as diagram is from the bottom up; for example, we could read (6) in part as "a leopard is a kind of feline; and a feline is a kind of mammal." In doing so, we would be referring to hyponyms, the subordinate term in a hierarchical taxonomy. Alternatively, we could read (6) from the top down: "mammals include felines; and felines include leopards." In this instance, we would be referring to hypernyms, the superordinate terms in a hierarchical taxonomy.

Hyponyms are always the more specific terms, while hypernyms are always the more general terms. But the labels hyponym and hypernym have no meaning unless some sort of taxonomy is involved. Thus, words like *leopard* and *clarinet* never occur in the same taxonomy, and neither can be hyponym nor hypernym for the other.

A great deal of the meanings of the words that we 'have in mind' are related in such taxonomies, including chemical elements (e.g., inert gases vs. heavy metals), musical instruments (e.g., reeds vs. strings), fields of study (e.g., Social Sciences vs. Biology), majors within schools (e.g., Linguistics vs. Economics), as well as the names of countries, states, counties, cities, neighborhoods, and so forth. Hierarchical taxonomies are of great interest to anthropologists, who study how the classification of plants or foods or religious ceremonies might be related to a given culture, and to psychologists, who study how the human brain organizes, remembers, and forgets information.

A2 Meaning Relations That Hold between Phrases and/or Sentences

Various semantic relations can hold between phrases and/or sentences, as well as between words. Here, we explore three of these relations.

Paraphrase

Two phrases or sentences which have the same meaning—that is, which refer to the same event or entity—are in what is called the paraphrase relation. The English word *paraphrase* comes from the Greek word *paraphraizein* 'to explain alongside'; thus, to paraphrase a string of words is to provide an alternate explanation for that string. The paraphrase relation that may exist between two phrases or sentences can be seen as roughly analogous to the synonymy relation that may obtain between two words.

7.

a	a red hat	a hat that is red
b	a gap-toothed senator	a senator with gapped teeth
c	The bottle is half-empty.	The bottle is half-full.
d	Tom gave a bone to the dog.	Tom gave the dog a bone.

Observe that if a speaker can refer to a given hat as 'a red hat', that speaker could also refer to that hat as 'a hat that is red'; both utterances would pick out exactly the same hat. Note also that if it is true that a given bottle is half-empty, it must also be true that that bottle is half-full. In other words, if the phrase or sentence in the first column of examples in (7) is true (i.e., true of a given entity or event), then the phrase or sentence in the second column of examples must also be true.

The mutual truth value that obtains in such examples represents a bidirectional condition. This condition can be abbreviated as A ↔ B, where the two-way pointing arrow is interpreted as "if and only if." Thus, A (i.e., the first column of examples in (7)) is true if and only if B (i.e., the second column of examples in (7)) is also true; and B is true if and only if A is also true.

Here are some further examples of the paraphrase relation:

8. a. i.   Tarzan often ate donuts.
      ii.   Tarzan ate donuts often.
   b. i.   Tom sold a car to Harry.
      ii.   Harry bought a car from Tom.

Note that sometimes, the two sentences in which the paraphrase relation holds contain precisely the same words, as in (8a), where the difference between the two arises only based on the order of the words. Of course, we recognize the AdvP *often* as an adjunct, and we know that adjuncts can occur in different positions, so we expect to find the two sentences in (8a) in the paraphrase relation.

But in other instances, the two sentences contain different words, as in (8b), where we find *sold* and *to* in the first but *bought* and *from* in the second. Significantly, the difference between *sold . . . to* and *bought . . . from* causes a difference in the syntactic positions of *Tom* and *Harry*—yet we unerringly judge these two superficially very different sentences as referring to precisely the same event: In both, *a car* originally belonged to or started out with Tom but ended up with Harry. In Section C, we develop a means to account for our interpretation of two sentences as 'meaning the same thing'.

Entailment

Entailment is a relation that can hold between two sentences, in which the truth of one sentence includes within its meaning the truth of another sentence, as in these examples:

9.   a.   i.   That house is red.
         ii.   That house is not white.

     b.   i.   Rangers killed this bear.
         ii.   This bear is dead.

The truth of the sentences in (i) above entails the truth of their paired sentences in (ii). Thus, if it is true that that house is red, it is also true that that house is not white. Likewise, if it is true that rangers killed this bear, it is also true that this bear is dead.

But notice that the truth of the sentences in (ii) above need not entail the truth of their paired sentences in (i); for example, any house that is not white could be green or blue or yellow or brown; it does not have to be red. Similarly, any number of factors might have caused this bear to become dead, as it might have died from disease or old age or from the after-effects of a fight with another bear; there is nothing in the sentence *This bear is dead* that entails that rangers killed it.

While the paraphrase relation represents a bidirectional condition, the entailment relation represents a unidirectional condition: A $\rightarrow$ B, where A entails B but B does not entail A (i.e., *B $\rightarrow$ A).

Contradict

Contradict is the label given to two sentences when the truth of one sentence implies the falsity of other. That is, if one sentence is true, the other sentence must be false, so that one sentence contradicts the other:

10. a. i.   Betty adores pigs.
        ii.   Betty detests all animals.

    b. i.   Vera is an only child.
        ii.   Olga is Vera's sister.

    c. i.   J.R. Ewing shot Jack Ruby in Texas.
        ii.   J.R. Ewing was in Maine when Jack Ruby was shot.

Contradict requires the simultaneous operation of two unidirectional conditions, both of which make use of the symbol "⌐", meaning 'not'. On one hand, if A is true, then B is false (i.e., not true); that is, A → ⌐ B. On the other hand, if B is true, then A is false (i.e., not true); that is, B → ⌐ A.

For example, if it is true that Vera is an only child, it is false that Olga is Vera's sister. At the same time, if it is true that Olga is Vera's sister, then it is false that Vera is an only child.

A3 Meaning Relations That Hold within a Single Sentence

The two meaning relations considered here hold of single sentences only; but each sentence generally (but not always) contains more than a single clause. The first relation, tautology, refers to any sentence which must be true:

11. a.   If something is a big animal, then it's an animal.

    b.   If you don't get any better, you'll never improve. (attributed to Yogi Berra)

    c.   "It's no exaggeration to say the undecided could go either way." (George W. Bush, in Ohio during the 1988 presidential campaign; cited by Esther B. Fein in a *New York Times* column on July 1, 1992)

    d.   "Anything that happens, happens. Anything that in happening causes something else to happen, causes something else to happen. Anything that, in happening, causes itself to happen again, happens again. It doesn't necessarily do it in chronological order, though." (Adams 1992, 1, 3, 5, 7)

Semanticists deem tautologies such as those in (11) to be "informationally empty," as their truth follows automatically from the meaning relations within the statement and without regard to the context in which they are produced. As a result, it is not possible to empirically test such statements, as their meaning does not depend on or derive from facts of the world. The other types of sentences we've considered so far are open to such empirical testing against facts of the world, however; thus, if we knew the context in which a sentence such as (10b), *Vera is an only child,* had been uttered, so that we could identify Vera, we could ascertain if Vera is in fact an only child.

The opposite of tautology is contradiction, the label given to a single sentence which cannot be true because it contradicts itself:

12.   a.   That's a big animal, but it's not an animal.
      b.   Vera's sister is an only child.

Contradictions (like tautologies) are not open to empirical testing, as their falsity derives automatically from the meaning relations within a given statement, without regard to context. Thus, if Vera has a sister, as entailed by the possessive DP in (12b), then that sister cannot be an only child.

The significance of contradiction traces back to Aristotle, a Greek philosopher of the fourth century BCE, who formulated the Law of Contradiction as a fundamental principle of logic: The same attribute cannot at the same time belong and not belong to the same subject in the same respect (cited in Löbner 2002, 59). Both tautology and contradiction are of interest to philosophers of language and to logicians in general, and both are detailed in various introductory courses in logic and philosophy.

So far, we have considered only a portion of the phenomena which fall under the general rubric of lexical semantics. In the following section, we broaden our discussion of lexical semantics to consider three phenomena related to verbal systems.

B.   Tense, Modality, and Verbal Aspect

This section introduces three types of information contained within the verbal systems of various languages, where "verbal systems" serves as a cover term for both verbs and modal auxiliaries.

B1 Tense

We begin by differentiating between time and tense. <u>Time</u> is a non-linguistic concept, one which is (presumably) universally divided into past, present, and future, as all human beings view time as flowing from the past, through the present, and into the future. In contrast, <u>tense</u> is a linguistic concept, one which refers to the correspondence between our concept of time and the <u>form of the verb</u> in a given sentence. As a result, tense is often reflected in a language's morphological system.

We've already seen that English morphologically marks two tenses, past and present, though we can 'see' present tense only when the verb agrees with a third person singular subject: *Pat jumps* vs. *Pat jumped.*

There is nothing that requires all languages to be like English when it comes to what tense(s) may be morphologically marked. Thus, some languages mark past and nonpast (rather than present and past), as in these Japanese examples:

13. a. Haji-ga   pan-o   taberu.
         Haji-Nom   bread-Acc   eat.nonpast
         'Haji { eats / is eating / will eat } bread.'

     b. Haji-ga   pan-o   tabeta.
         Haji-Nom   bread-Acc   eat.past
         'Haji ate bread.'

Many Native American languages differentiate between immediate past and remote past, as exemplified below by Shasta (a Hokan language spoken in northern California):

14. a. kw-áhussáaʔ   b. p-áhussáaʔ
         imm.past-talk.1sg   remote.past-talk.1sg
         'I talked.'   'I used to talk (long ago).'

Finally, in some languages, a verb can occur with no overt tense marker at all; this example is from Cambodian:

15. Sowan   ŋam   numpaŋ.
     Sowan   eat   bread
     'Sowan { eats / ate / will eat } bread.'

Of course, appropriate adverbial expressions can be added to any sentence in any language, if precision is required and verbal morphology is not available. A speaker of Cambodian could add a time expression such as *tɲai-nih* 'today', *msəl-məŋ* 'yesterday', or *sʔaek* 'tomorrow' to the sentence in (15), for example.

Of some interest is the fact that the English language does not consistently observe a one-to-one relationship between time and tense. Consider these examples:

16.   a.   The train arrives at 8:00 tomorrow morning.
       b.   Cows eat grass.

Regardless of when the sentence in (16a) is uttered, it clearly refers to a future time; yet the verb is in present tense. The sentence in (16b) exemplifies what is called generic time; sentences which are interpreted with generic time are considered to be always true. Thus, (16b) has been true as long as cows and grass have existed, it is true in the present time (even if no cow on earth happens to be eating grass right now), and it will continue to be true as long as cows and grass continue to exist. Yet, once again, the verb appears in present tense.

Readers interested in exploring the intricacies of the interpretation of tenses in English are encouraged to delve into a comprehensive description of the language such as Quirk, Greenbaum, Leech, and Svartik (1985).

B2 Modality

Semanticists divide modality into two broad classes: epistemic modality and deontic modality. Each of these classes is defined and detailed below, primarily with examples from English, a language in which modality is quite frequently expressed through a modal auxiliary (*can, could, will, would, must, should,* and so forth).

Epistemic Modality

Epistemic modality is concerned in general with a speaker's internal system of beliefs; that is, epistemic modality involves what a speaker knows or believes that she or he knows. (The word *epistemic* is derived from the Greek word *episteme* 'knowledge'.) More specifically, linguistic elements used to denote epistemic modality allow a speaker to express varying degrees of commitment to, or belief in, a given statement.

Consider, for example, the following sentences of English:

17.   a.   Sheila left already.
       b.   Sheila must have left already.
       c.   Sheila might have left already.
       d.   Sheila could have left already.

The sentence in (17a) is a statement of fact in which the speaker is committed to the truth of the proposition. It would not be difficult to empirically test this fact to ascertain if the speaker of this sentence had uttered a truthful proposition, though of course such a test would have to be carried out at the time in which the sentence was uttered.

But the sentences in (17b-d) are different; they do not represent statements of fact and are not open to empirical testing. Instead, in these examples, the speaker is expressing varying degrees of commitment to his or her belief in Sheila's departure. And it is the presence of the modal auxiliaries which lead to these varying degrees of commitment, from the strong commitment denoted by the use of *must* in (17b) to the fairly weak commitment denoted by the use of *could* in (17d).

English has other devices for expressing epistemic modality, including adverbial phrases such as *certainly, (quite) probably,* and *perhaps;* the addition any of one of these to (17a) would indicate the speaker's degree of commitment to Sheila's departure. Another device available to English is demonstrated below:

18. a. Dan knows that Sheila has left already.
     b. Dan believes that Sheila has left already.
     c. Dan imagines that Sheila has left already.
     d. Dan wonders if Sheila has left already.

In all examples in (18), the embedded IP is the same: *Sheila has left already.* The difference comes in the matrix verbs—*know, believe, imagine, wonder.* While all of these examples relate something about the state of Dan's internal belief system, the one in (18a) denotes his very strong commitment to Sheila's departure, while the others denote successively weaker commitments on his part.

Now consider the following sentence and try to decide if it is true or false:

19. Dan believes the King of France takes bribes.

On one hand, there is no King of France (whether he takes bribes or not). So the sentence must be false. But on the other hand, the sentence can be true of Dan's internal system of beliefs. To account for the truth of Dan's beliefs, semanticists refer to the notion of possible worlds, worlds which extend beyond the real, actual world. In the world of Dan's beliefs, the sentence in (19) could be true.

Speakers of English can also use modal auxiliaries to open up possible worlds:

20. a. I must have left my keys in the car.
     b. It might be raining in Belfast.

By uttering (20a), I am expressing my belief that my keys are in my car; such a sentence would follow had I driven my car, parked it, and walked a short distance when I suddenly noticed my keys were missing. As a result, based on the state of my knowledge at the time, (20a) could be paraphrased as *I believe I left my keys in the car.* And this sentence could be true of the world of my belief system, even if it turns out in the real world that my keys are not in fact in the car.

The speaker of (20b) uses the modal *might* to set up a hypothetical situation (rain in Belfast); and hypothetical situations exist only in possible worlds, not in the real world. While we could ascertain whether or not it was raining in Belfast at the time of the speaker's utterance of (20b), so that we could judge the truth of the rain-in-Belfast situation, the sentence is deemed always true of the possible world of the speaker's belief system.

The semantic concept of *modality* is closely related to the grammatical concept of *mood.* Some languages morphologically differentiate between indicative mood and subjunctive mood. In such languages, statements of fact (which have truth values in the real world) are encoded with indicative mood; subjunctive mood is reserved for the types of hypothetical situations which exist within a speaker's system of beliefs, that is, in a possible world. The difference is illustrated below with examples from Italian:

21.   a.   Marina   dice   che   Iole   mentisce.
            Marina   says   that   Iole   lies (indicative)

    b.   Marina   pensa   che   Iole   mentisca.
            Marina   thinks   that   Iole   lies (subjunctive)

Observe that the difference in the mood of the verb in the embedded clause is directly related to the meaning of the verb in the matrix clause: In (21a), the matrix verb is *dice* 'says', and the embedded verb *mentisce* is in indicative mood. But in (21b), given the matrix verb *pensa* 'thinks', the embedded verb *mentisca* is in subjunctive mood, denoting that the situation of Iole's telling lies is true of the possible world of Marina's belief system (but may not be true in the real world).

Not all languages which morphologically distinguish between indicative and subjunctive moods do so in precisely the same way that Italian does. Exploring the various uses subjunctive mood serves cross-linguistically is well beyond the scope of this text. It suffices here to note the generalization that subjunctive mood frequently serves to open up possible worlds and thus to examine hypothetical situations.

Deontic Modality

While epistemic modality refers to a speaker's internal belief system, deontic modality refers to the norms, rules, procedures, standards, and so forth, of the cultural and social system in which a speaker lives. Deontic modality often expresses obligation, recommendation, or permission. (The English word *deontic* is derived from the Greek *deonton* 'that which is binding'.)

Deontic modality is often expressed in English through modals, as below:

22. a. You must pay your utility bill on time.
     b. Guests should leave their keys in their cars.

If you encountered (22a) on your electricity bill, you would likely interpret it as an obligation to pay your bill on time (or suffer the consequence of having your electricity cut off). If you encountered (22b) on a sign in the parking lot of the hotel where you were staying, you would interpret it as a rule of the hotel. Both of these examples could be expressed by other means: *You are obligated to pay your utility bills on time* and *It is a rule of the hotel that guests leave their keys in their cars.* But the modals convey the same sense of obligation as do these alternatives, and they do so more succinctly.

The example in (23a) demonstrates the use of a modal to express the speaker's permission, while the modal in (23b) is used to express the speaker's recommendation:

23. a. You can leave your books here.
     b. I loved this book; you must read it!

Note that in (23b), a very brief context has been added to ensure that the second clause is interpreted as a recommendation. Had a different context been added, a different interpretation would obtain for the second clause:

24. The final exam focuses on this book; you must read it!

The second clause of (24) would most likely be interpreted as an obligation, rather than a recommendation, though it also represents deontic modality.

Lacking context, many English modals may be ambiguous between deontic and epistemic modality, as shown in the following examples:

25. Third graders <u>may</u> use pens.
     a. epistemic: Perhaps third graders use pens.
     b. deontic: Third graders have permission to use pens.

26. He <u>can</u> swim after running.
     a. epistemic: I believe he has the ability to swim after he runs.
     b. deontic: I give him permission to swim after he runs.

27. The car <u>must</u> be ready.
     a. epistemic: Surely the car is ready.
     b. deontic: I oblige you to ensure the car is ready.

If we knew the contexts in which such sentences were spoken, we would have little trouble disambiguating deontic and epistemic modality. For example, consider (27) above: Say the time of utterance of this sentence is 4:00 on a given afternoon. I had left my car to be repaired at 9:00 that morning, and the mechanic had promised it would be ready by noon of the same day. The epistemic interpretation is thus readily available, as the utterance would denote my belief that the repairs on my car had been completed as promised.

B3 Verbal Aspect

The term verbal aspect refers to a classification of predicates based on how they unfold in time and represents a further instance in which lexical semantics plays an important role in meaning. This classification is sometimes referred to as the "Dowty-Vendler" classification system, after the philosophers who initially developed it (see Dowty 1979 and Vendler 1967).

The fundamental claims of the Dowty-Vendler system are (a) only four classes of predicates exist in human languages; and (b) all four classes exist in all human languages. These four classes are called accomplishments, achievements, activities, and states; each is defined and exemplified below. As you can glean from the various examples offered, the transitivity of a given predicate plays no role in this semantic classification.

Achievements
Achievements are defined as eventive predicates which always involve change; we view that change as instantaneous and the event as having a distinct endpoint (i.e., a point in time in which the event denoted by the predicate ceases). A few examples are given below:

28. a. Bob arrived.
     b. The bomb exploded.
     c. The army exploded the bomb.
     d. Jill found her glasses.
     e. But Jack lost his hearing aid.

Because each of these predicates—*arrive, explode, find,* and *lose*—involves change, we interpret each as an event with a 'before' and an 'after' part. That is, we interpret (28a) as entailing that Bob was not present 'before' the arriving event, but he was present 'after' the arriving event. Similarly, Jill's glasses in (28d) were missing 'before' the finding event but were not missing 'after' the finding event. And we interpret both the arriving event and the finding event as occurring instantaneously (that is, of having little or no duration).

Accomplishments

Accomplishments are also defined as eventive predicates which always involve change; but we perceive of that change as lasting over a period of time, and of the event as having a particular endpoint. Thus, the primary distinction between achievements and accomplishments is the length of time over which change occurs: instantaneous in achievements but over a period of time with accomplishments.

29. a.   The patient should recover from his illness soon.
     b.   Maria built a birdhouse.
     c.   Frank mops up the floor once a day.
     d.   Moe learned French.
     e.   The clown ate all the apples.

If you think about these examples, you should realize that it takes a period of time to recover from an illness or to build a birdhouse or to mop up a floor. But, you should also realize that to *recover from illness* entails not only a change from 'sickness' to 'health' but also an endpoint to the illness; to *build a birdhouse* entails the creation of a birdhouse from 'non-birdhouse' into 'birdhouse' (i.e., from 'nothing' into 'something'); to *mop up a floor* entails a change in the floor from 'dirty' to 'clean' and that the floor-mopping-up event has ceased.

Notice also that, because accomplishments have an endpoint as one of their features of meaning, we interpret the event as no longer on-going—even if either a modal or present tense occurs, as in (29a) and (29c), respectively.

Activities

Activities are defined as eventive predicates which involve change but have no particular endpoint; as a result, we interpret the event as continuing to occur and the change as on-going:

30. a.   Bob { runs / ran } in the morning.
     b.   Maria { cries / cried } (over nothing).
     c.   Frank { mops / mopped } the floor every day.
     d.   The serf pushed the cart.
     e.   Nero played his fiddle.

While both accomplishments and activities involve change over a period of time, we interpret them differently, as activities (but not accomplishments) lack endpoints to the change. That is, predicates such as *run in the morning* and *mop the floor every day*, as in (30a) and (30c) respectively, do not entail that either the running event or the floor-mopping event has ceased; instead, we interpret such predicates as on-going events, even given the presence of past tense.

We can, however, turn an activity predicate into an accomplishment predicate by adding what is called a <u>measuring out phrase</u>. Measuring out phrases function as endpoints to otherwise on-going activities. Compare the sentences in (30) above with their counterparts in (31) below, where the measuring out phrases are underlined:

31. a. Bob { runs / ran } <u>two miles</u> in the morning.
     b. Maria { cries / cried } <u>for an hour</u> (over nothing).
     c. Frank { mops / mopped } <u>up</u> the floor every day.
     d. The serf pushed the cart <u>into the barn</u>.
     e. Nero played his fiddle <u>until the barn burned down</u>.

Observe that, while measuring out phrases have various syntactic structures, they all serve the same purpose: They function as endpoints to events, in the process turning events we interpret as activities into accomplishments. Thus, we interpret the running event in (31a) as terminating at the two mile mark, the cart-pushing event in (31d) as terminating when the cart is into the barn, and so forth.

States

States are predicates which refer to non-eventive situations which do not involve change as an inherent part of their meaning. A few examples are provided below:

32. a. Bob is tall.
     b. Frank knows { French / how to drive a car }.
     c. Moe belongs in the zoo.
     d. Curly has a new car.
     e. Manny admired the painting.

While it may be true that at some other point in time, Bob is taller than at the time (32a) is uttered, the point here is that a predicate such as *be tall* does not inherently involve change. Instead, such predicates describe a situation at a (given) point in time. Similarly, Frank may at some other time not know how to drive a car; yet at the time of utterance of (32b), Frank's state of knowledge included knowledge of car-driving.

Tests for the Dowty-Vendler Classification System

Various syntactic tests have been designed to tease apart the semantic differences among these four classes of predicates. Here, we consider only four of those tests; when a given test is applied, it picks out one or more classes of predicate as ungrammatical. For ease of explication, only eight predicates will be offered here, two for each of the semantic classifications.

Test #1 involves the ability of a given predicate to occur as an imperative (i.e., a command). As you can see below, this option is not available to states, though achievements, accomplishments, and activities readily occur in the imperative.

Test #1: *Ability to Occur as an Imperative*

achievement	Find my book! Die, you coward!
accomplishment	Rake up the yard! Draw a unicorn!
activity	Run, you fool! Study French!
state	*Stink, you fool! *Know French!

Our second test involves the ability of a given predicate to occur with what is called a subject-oriented adverb. Subject-oriented adverbs include *carefully, deliberately, intentionally,* and so forth; they describe the manner which the subject assumes in carrying out the predicate. Neither achievements nor states can felicitously occur with subject-oriented adverbs, though accomplishments and activities are not so restricted.

Test #2: *Ability to Occur With Subject-oriented Adverbs*

achievement	*Jack intentionally found a book. *Jill deliberately died.
accomplishment	Jack { carefully raked up the yard / drew a unicorn carelessly }.
activity	Jack deliberately ran. Jill studied French intentionally.
state	*Jack deliberately stank. *Jill knew French intentionally.

The third test requires adding what is called a time limit adverbial to a given predicate. Time limit adverbials—*in an instant, in an hour, in ten years*—limit the duration of the predicate which they modify. Time limit adverbials cannot occur with either activities or states, as neither of these classes can be bounded in time (by the definitions of activities and states given above).

Test #3:   *Ability to Occur with a Time Limit Adverbial*

achievement	Jack found his book in a few minutes. Jill died in an instant.
accomplishment	Jack { raked up the yard / drew a unicorn } in an hour.
activity	*Jill { ran / studied French } in an hour.
state	*Jack stank in a minute. *Jill knew French in ten days.

In contrast, <u>time duration adverbials</u>—*for an instant, for an hour, for ten years*—occur felicitously with activities and states, but not with achievements and accomplishments, as these adverbials specify the length of the event denoted by an activity or the situation described by a state.

Test #4:   *Ability to Occur with a Time Duration Adverbial*

achievement	*Jack found his book for a minute. *Jill died for a minute.
accomplishment	*Jack { raked up the yard / drew a unicorn } for an hour.
activity	Jill ran for an hour. Jack studied French for an hour.
state	Jack stank for a whole week. Jill knew French for ten years.

Notice, in particular, the anomaly present when a time duration adverbial occurs with an accomplishment predicate: The only way we can interpret a sentence such as *Jack drew a unicorn for an hour* is to deny that Jack in fact created a drawing of a unicorn, an interpretation which represents a contradiction to the meaning of *Jack drew a unicorn*. (Refer back to Section A2 for the definition of contradiction, if necessary.)

Pulling the fore-going discussion together allows us to see that these four semantic classes of predicates differ from each other syntactically:

Table 1:   *Summary of Tests for Verbal Aspect*

class	imperative?	subj-orient adv?	time limit?	time duration?
achievement	Y	N	Y	N
accomplishment	Y	Y	Y	N
activity	Y	Y	N	Y
state	N	N	N	Y

As mentioned at the outset of this section, the four classes of predicates outlined above are claimed to exist in all languages of the world. I have personally investigated Cambodian, Choctaw (a Muskogean language of Oklahoma and Louisiana), Tagalog, and Turkish and know various other researchers who have investigated a range of other languages. To my knowledge, no language studied so far has provided a counterexample of this fundamental Dowty-Vendler claim.

With the lexical semantics presented in Sections A and B, it's time to turn our attention to compositional semantics, in which syntactic structure plays a role.

C. Accounting for Ambiguity

To many, the word *ambiguity* may carry a range of negative connotations, but to linguists the word simply denotes a single element—either word or string of words—which has more than a single interpretation. Linguists recognize two types of ambiguity: lexical ambiguity and structural (or syntactic) ambiguity.

C1 Lexical Ambiguity

Both polysemy (one word with more than a single meaning) and homophony (two words which sound the same) can lead to lexical ambiguity. Thus, produced in isolation, sentences such as the following contain lexical ambiguity:

33. a. She took a <u>pen</u> and a <u>bat</u> and went to the <u>bank</u>.
     b. Your <u>glasses</u> are on the table.

In (33a), *pen* could refer to a writing implement or to a cage for an animal; *bat* could refer to a stick-like object usually used to hit baseballs or to a flying mammal; and *bank* could refer to a financial institution or to the side of a river. In (33b), *glasses* could refer to containers for drinks or to lenses which correct vision. Most generally, the context in which such sentences are uttered are sufficient for us to glean which meaning the speaker (or writer) has intended.

C2 Structural Ambiguity

Structural ambiguity refers to a phrase or sentence which has only a single linear order of words, but simultaneously has two separate interpretations (i.e., two different meanings). The two different meanings result from the fact that a single linear order of words can have two different <u>hierarchical</u> orders.

In order to understand structural ambiguity, we begin by introducing the <u>Principle of Compositionality</u>:

34.   The meaning of a sentence is determined by two factors:
    a.   the <u>meaning</u> of its component parts (i.e., of the words involved); and
    b.   the <u>manner</u> in which those component parts are arranged in syntactic structure.

Clause (a) of the Principle of Compositionality ensures that the difference between *The dragon killed the monster* and *The dragon kissed the monster* is in the meaning of the words involved, as *killed* and *kissed* refer to very different types of events (and very different outcomes for the monster involved). Clause (b) ensures that the difference between *The dragon killed the monster* and *The monster killed the dragon* results from the manner of the arrangement of the words, as whether a given DP shows up as subject (in Spec IP) or object (as complement within VP) determines our interpretations of killer (the subject) and killee (the object).

Now consider the examples given in (35). Observe that each example contains only a single string of words—yet most of us find two interpretations readily available for the DP in (35a) and for the sentence in (35b):

35.   a.   smart students and teachers
    b.   Bart saw the bear with one eye.

Because only a single (linear) string of words is involved in these examples, clause (a) of the Principle of Compositionality cannot apply. Thus, by default, clause (b) must apply, and we must seek out a way through which we can arrange the same words in different syntactic structures.

The first step required in disambiguating an otherwise structurally ambiguous phrase or sentence is to provide two paraphrases, each of which uses different words and/or different word orders than in the original example but which has the same meaning as the original. (Recall from Section A2 that the paraphrase relation refers to two phrases or sentences which have the same meaning.) Appropriate paraphrases for our examples could be these, though alternate paraphrases are also possible:

36.   a.   smart students and teachers
        i.   students who are smart and teachers
        ii.   smart students and smart teachers

    b.   Bart saw the bear with one eye.
        i.   The bear that Bart saw had one eye.
        ii.   Bart used one eye to see the bear.

Let's begin with the two paraphrases of the DP in (36a); the first paraphrase attributes *smart* only to students, while the second paraphrase attributes this quality to both students and teachers. That is, the AP *smart* modifies only students in (i), but modifies both students and teachers in (ii). Consequently, we can provide two different hierarchical orders for this single linear order of words:

37.   a.

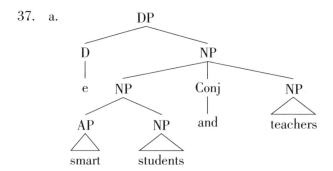

   b.

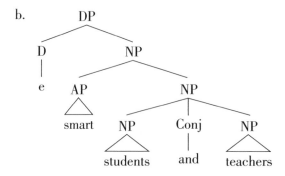

The two conjuncts depicted in (37a) are [smart students] and [teachers], and the AP is attributed to the first conjunct but not to the second conjunct. In contrast, the two conjuncts of (37b) are [students] and [teachers], and the AP is attributed to the entire conjoined structure, not to just one part of this structure. In particular, note that the AP is attached higher in the syntactic structure in (b) than it is in (a).

What we have accomplished is this: We have assigned two syntactic structures for a single string of words; these two structures differ from each other in their hierarchical orders, but the words are arranged in the same linear order in both. As a direct result of having different hierarchical structures, each has its own meaning or interpretation. This finding follows clause (b) of the Principle of Compositionality, which asserts that meaning is determined in part by the manner in which parts are arranged in syntactic structure.

The two syntactic structures available for our example in (36b) are provided below, where the relevant parts of each structure are enclosed in dashed boxes:

38.   a.

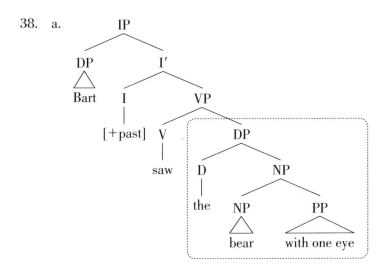

b.

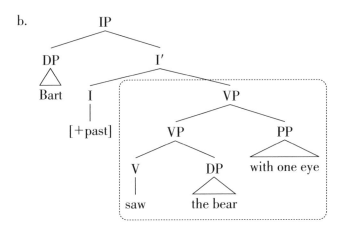

The ambiguity in this sentence is caused by the adjunct PP *with one eye*, which can be adjoined in two different positions in syntactic structure. In (38a), the PP has been merged as sister to, and thus modifier of, the NP headed by *bear*. This structure gives rise to the paraphrase interpretation *The bear that Bart saw had one eye*. In (38b), the PP has been merged as sister to the VP and so modifies the bear-seeing event. And it is this structure which gives rise to the paraphrase *Bart used one eye to see the bear.*

Given a specific context or situational setting, it's likely that neither of the examples of structural ambiguity discussed here would be ambiguous to the one who hears or reads them. One or the other interpretation would be consistent with the on-going discourse and so would be 'discourse appropriate'. What's interesting is that we are so frequently able to pick out the 'discourse appropriate' interpretation, while ignoring the other interpretation.

D. Arguments, Predicates, and Theta Roles

In Chapter 5, we explored the syntactic relationship between a predicate and its arguments (subject, plus sometimes object and/or indirect object). In this section, we explore the relationship between a predicate and its arguments from the semantic point of view.

Semantically, the meaning of a given sentence is the meaning of the subject plus the meaning of the predicate. Subjects generally are entities; predicates are events, activities, or states in which the subject is involved. The formal semantic term for 'sentence' is proposition, a term which denotes a complete thought or statement that can be either true or false—and is true if and only if the predicate accurately describes what the subject is/was engaged in.

The subject is an argument of the predicate; and sometimes, the subject is the only argument of a predicate. This situation holds for the class of predicates we have previously labeled intransitive verbs. Other classes of predicates occur with more than a single argument: Transitive verbs occur with direct objects, ditransitive verbs with both direct and indirect objects.

In Chapter 5, we developed a series of lexical entries for these different classes of verbs. (If you don't remember all the details involved in lexical entries, now would be a good time to review them.) Abstracting away from many details, *sit, occur,* and *disappear* are intransitives which occur with no complement at all; *touch, throw,* and *praise* are transitives which require a DP (object) complement to 'complete' their meaning; and *place, donate,* and *contribute* are ditransitives which require both a DP (object) complement and a PP (indirect object) complement. Abbreviated lexical entries for each of these classes are schematized below, where only subcategorization frames are shown:

39.

verb class	intransitive	transitive	ditransitive
subcategorizes for	[__ Ø]	[__ DP]	[__ DP PP]

With this brief review, consider these sentences, noting that the verbal predicates here— *fear* and *frighten*—are transitives which occur with DP subjects and DP objects:

40.   a.   The children feared the bear.
      b.   The bear frightened the children.

Our problem now is accounting for the ungrammaticality of sentences such as these:

41.   a.   *{ The rock / the eraser } feared the bear.
      b.   *The bear frightened { the rock / the eraser }.

In (41), both *fear* and *frighten* occur with two DP arguments, one the subject and the other the object. Since this is also the case in our examples in (40), it appears that the problem is not a syntactic problem. Instead, it appears that not just any DP will do in such instances.

The problem in (41) is semantic: Rocks and erasers cannot fear and they cannot be frightened. In order to account for the difference between, e.g., the children and the rock, we need to enrich our lexical entries for predicates by adding information that will restrict the class of DPs that may occur with a given predicate.

The information we need to add to lexical entries has been variously referred to as interpretative roles, semantic roles, thematic roles, and <u>theta roles</u>; we use the latter label here.

Before we get into the nitty-gritty of the discussion, you should be aware that linguists do not always agree on the precise number of theta roles; some claim only six or seven theta roles are sufficient, while others argue that a more-finely grained system encompassing ten or twelve theta roles is necessary. In addition, not all linguists agree on the labels used for those theta roles. But linguists do agree on three important points:

- The same set of theta roles is universally available; that is, the same set of theta roles is used by every human language.
- The number of theta roles is in fact quite small, less than a dozen or so.
- Theta roles are assigned by predicates (mostly verbs, but also prepositions) to all arguments of that predicate.

The eight theta roles deemed sufficient for our current study are labeled, defined, and exemplified in Table 2:

Table 2: *Theta Roles*

label	*definition*	*examples*
agent	the entity that performs or initiates an action	*The army* destroyed the town. The town was destroyed by *the army*.
theme	the entity that is affected or that undergoes movement or change of state	The invading army destroyed *the town*. *The curtains* swayed in the breeze. Garfield gave *a bone* to Odie. *The vase* broke.
source	where movement starts	*Garfield* gave a bone to Odie. *Tom* sold a car to Harry. Joe moved from *Irvine* to Mesa.
goal	where movement ends	Garfield gave a bone to *Odie*. Tom sold a car to *Harry*. Joe moved from Irvine to *Mesa*.
location	where an event takes place	Anteaters live in *Irvine*. He was stranded on *a coral reef*.
instrument	the means by which an action comes about	George cut down the tree with *an ax*. *Pollution* killed the tree.
experiencer	the entity that undergoes an emotion or a cognitive event	*The children* feared the bear. The bear frightened *the children*. *Children* know they should avoid bears.
stimulus	the entity that causes an experience	The children feared *the bear*. *The bear* frightened the children.

A moment's reflection on the last two theta roles (which generally co-occur) should help you account for the ungrammaticality of our examples in (41) above: Neither rocks nor erasers can experience an emotion; hence, neither is a possible subject for *fear* nor a possible object for *frighten*.

Observe that particular theta roles are not assigned to particular arguments. Thus the subjects of predicates such as *fear* and *know* are experiencers, while the objects of verbs such as *frighten* and *amuse* have this same role. If you scan through the examples above, you'll note that subjects can also be agents, themes, instruments, or sources, while objects can be themes or locations as well as experiencers or stimuli. What is crucial is this: The theta role with which a given argument is interpreted is a function of the predicate with which that argument occurs. Consequently, we need to enrich our lexical entries to include what is called a theta grid, the list of the theta roles that a given predicate assigns to its argument(s).

Abbreviated lexical entries for a few verbs (chosen as representative of their classes) are given below:

42.

verb	subcat. frame	theta grid
'die'	[__ Ø]	<theme>
'smile'	[__ Ø]	<agent>
'hit'	[__ DP]	<agent, theme>
'reside'	[__ PP]	<agent, location>
'amuse'	[__ DP]	<stimulus, experiencer>
'adore'	[__ DP]	<experiencer, stimulus>
'donate'	[__ DP PP]	<agent, theme, goal>
'place'	[__ DP PP]	<agent, theme, location>

As always, subcategorization frames are enclosed in square brackets, with the phrasal category of the argument required to follow a given verb listed. When no argument is required (i.e., when the verb is intransitive), the null sign is listed; when more than a single argument is required (i.e., when the verb is ditransitive), the phrasal categories of both complements are listed in the order in which they occur.

Theta grids are enclosed in angled brackets, a convention widely assumed among linguists. Significantly, while subcategorization frames refer only to the complements of a given predicate, the information contained in theta grids refers to all arguments of that predicate, including its subject. Consequently, the number of labels contained in a given theta grid will always be one greater than the number of phrasal categories listed in a predicate's subcategorization frame.

As you can ascertain from (42), *die* takes no complement and assigns the theme theta role to its subject (as the meaning of this verb entails a change of state). In contrast, *smile* assigns the agent role to its subject (as we interpret a smiler as one who is performing an action). *Hit* and *reside* are both transitive verbs which assign agent to their subjects; but while *hit* assigns theme to its DP complement (which is certainly affected by being the object of *hit*), *reside* requires a PP complement, to which it assigns the location theta role. *Donate* and *place* are both ditransitive verbs which assign the agent role to their subjects and the theme role to their DP objects, as these DPs are interpreted as undergoing movement (e.g., *donated some money to a charity* and *placed the forks on the table*). While *donate* assigns goal to its PP complement, *place* assigns location to its PP complement.

Prepositions also have the ability to assign theta roles to their complements. While English contains a great many prepositions which license the location theta role (e.g., *in, on, over, around, near, above, under,* and so forth), some theta roles are assigned by only a few prepositions. For example, goal is routinely assigned by *to,* source by *from,* and instrument by *with.* The lexical entry for a preposition contains a subcategorization frame and a theta grid, just as the lexical entry for a verb does. A primary difference between the two types of entries arises from the fact that prepositions do not take 'subjects' and thus display a one-to-one correspondence between the number of theta roles listed in their theta grids and the number of arguments listed in their subcategorization frames:

43.	*preposition*	*subcat. frame*	*theta grid*
	'in'	[__ DP]	<location>
	'to'	[__ DP]	<goal>
	'from'	[__ DP]	<source>
	'with'	[__ DP]	<instrument>

One straightforward way to show which theta role is assigned to which argument by which predicate makes use of labeled arrows, as follows, where the arguments have been underlined for clarity:

44.   Col. Mustard hit Dr. Black with a hammer from Ace Hardware in the den.

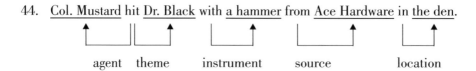

agent   theme   instrument   source   location

The schematization in (44) indicates that the transitive verb *hit* has two theta roles (agent and theme) to assign, and it assigns its agent role to *Col. Mustard* and its theme role to *Dr. Black.* The preposition *with* has only one theta role (instrument) to assign, and it assigns that role to *a hammer.* The preposition *from* assigns its single theta role (source) to *Ace Hardware,* and the preposition *in* assigns its single theta role (location) to *the den.* (The alternative to the labeled-arrow schematization, potentially long prose paragraphs, is eschewed here.)

We have two final but most important points to consider with respect to theta roles. The first involves the labels given to various theta roles. Consider the following sentences:

45. a. Garfield gave a bone to Odie.
     b. Tom sold a car to Harry.

In Table 2, the subjects of both *give* and *sell* are shown as receiving the source theta role, as both verbs involve movement of the object (theme) from the subject (source) to the indirect object (goal). Certainly, both subjects here could also be labeled as agents, as both giving and selling involve volitional activities which the subject performs and/or initiates. This complication is one reason linguists don't necessarily agree on labels. For our purposes, because such verbs always involve movement, we identify such subjects as sources, rather than agents.

The second point about theta roles that requires attention involves the paraphrase relation. When we discussed the paraphrase relation in Section A2, we noted that we sometimes interpret two sentences as 'meaning the same thing', even if those sentences have different verbs and the arguments of those verbs appear in different syntactic positions in the sentences. Our examples in (8b) are repeated below.

46. a. Tom sold a car to Harry.
     b. Harry bought a car from Tom.

Observe that the verb in (a) is *sell,* while that in (b) is *buy;* while *Tom* is the subject of (a), *Harry* occupies this position in syntactic structure in (b); and *Harry* appears inside a PP in (a), but *Tom* appears in this position in (b). But regardless of all these differences, we still impute the same meaning to these two sentences, as referring to the same 'cognitive event'.

The reason we interpret these sentence as representing the same cognitive event is directly related to the theta roles each argument receives. In both, *a car* is the theme, the argument which undergoes movement, a role it receives from either *sell* or *buy*. In (46a), *Tom* receives the source role from *sell* and *Harry* the goal role from *to*. In (46b), *Harry* receives the goal role from *buy* and *Tom* the source role from *from*. The assignments of all theta roles in both sentences are schematized in (47):

47. a. Tom sold a car to Harry.

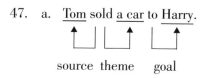

source theme   goal

b.   Harry bought a car from Tom.

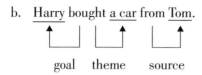

goal   theme   source

What is consistent in these sentences is not which argument is subject and which indirect object; rather what is consistent is the theta role each receives. As a result of the consistency of theta roles received by the various arguments, we interpret these two superficially very different sentences as having the same meaning. This consistency of theta roles received contributes greatly to our ability to paraphrase.

E.   A Taste of Pragmatics

Pragmatics is the sub-field of semantics which focuses on the context in which a given utterance is produced and on speaker meaning (i.e., what a speaker intends to convey) rather than on the types of semantic meaning we've considered so far. Thus, a primary function of pragmatics is to ascertain how we understand each other in on-going discourse.

It turns out that much of what we understand from on-going discourse consists of things that are in fact not overtly stated, as shown in the mini-conversation below:

48.   Speaker A: Have you seen Jim?
      Speaker B: His car is parked in front of Pat's house.

Given the yes/no question posed by Speaker A, we might expect Speaker B to respond with a simple "yes" or "no" instead of with a statement regarding the location of Jim's car. Yet we readily understand Speaker B's response as entailing "no"—even though there is no "no" in the response. We do this through inference, the process of drawing a (frequently but not invariantly logical) conclusion from one or more propositions put forward. In our current example, Speaker B's response comprises the proposition put forward.

It appears that our inferential abilities are grounded in our wanting to preserve coherence in our conversations; that is, we seem confident that our interlocutor will be able to interpret our contribution to a given conversation, even if that contribution is not in the (syntactic) form our interlocutor expects.

In order to account for our inferential abilities in conversation, the philosopher Grice (1975, 1978) developed what he called the Cooperative Principle, a principle meant to explain how an addressee interprets a speaker's utterance:

49. Speaker meaning can be calculated on . . .
    a.   the basis of semantic information; and
    b.   the assumption that speakers are behaving rationally and cooperatively.

The first part of the Cooperative Principle entails that the meaning of an utterance such as *Sam bought a new car* is calculated on the basis of lexical and compositional semantics, as discussed in Sections A through D above.

The second part of the Cooperative Principle is the interesting part, as it claims that, as addressees, we assume that those who speak to us are behaving both rationally and cooperatively. In order to define "rational and cooperative" behavior, Grice developed four maxims (i.e., guiding principles) of conversation:

50. Grice's Maxims
    a. Quality: Make your contribution one that is true rather than false.

    b. Quantity: Provide the information required for the purposes of the conversation, but no more.

    c. Relevance: Make your contributions relevant.

    d. Manner: Be clear and orderly in your talk.

On Grice's view, listeners assume that those speaking to them understand these maxims and (unless there is evidence to the contrary) are adhering to them. To get a full grasp on the Gricean system, it's helpful to consider various discourses which emphasize one maxim over the others. The following example emphasizes the maxim on relevance:

51. Speaker A: Can I borrow $10.00?
     Speaker B: My purse is on the dining table.

Based on the assumption that Speaker B is acting "rationally and cooperatively," Speaker A interprets the response as obeying the maxim on relevance and therefore infers that the answer is "Yes, you can borrow $10.00"—even though these words are not uttered by Speaker B. Grice refers to such inferences as conversational implicature. By the second part of the Cooperative Principle, implicatures are part of speaker meaning, and speaker meaning is part of the overall meaning of a given utterance.

Here's an example which emphasizes the maxim on manner:

52. Jack climbed up the hill and fetched a pail of water.

If you ask yourself which event occurred first—hill-climbing or water-fetching—you'll likely conclude that the hill-climbing event occurred prior to the water-fetching event, even though no words such as *before* or *then* are present in the sentence to provide this time frame. If this is your conclusion, then you are assuming the speaker of this utterance has presented the information in a clear and orderly manner, with the first event mentioned representing the first event which occurred.

The following conversation focuses on the maxim of quantity:

53. Speaker A: Did you drink all the beer in the fridge?
    Speaker B: I drank some.

The maxim of quantity, which regulates the amount of information provided, leads Speaker A to the implicature that Speaker B did not drink all of the beer, so that Speaker B's response means "no." Of course, Speaker A must also assume Speaker B is obeying the maxim of quality; that is, that Speaker B is telling the truth rather than telling a lie.

Quite often, more than a single maxim is involved in a given discourse. Consider, for example, the mini-discourse first presented in (48), and repeated below:

54. Speaker A: Have you seen Jim?
    Speaker B: His car is parked in front of Pat's house.

The Gricean analysis would be this: If Speaker B did not expect Speaker A to understand his response, then Speaker B would be violating the maxims on quality (the information provided is true), on quantity (the information provided is sufficient), and on relevance (the information provided is pertinent). Because Speaker A assumes this "rational and cooperative" behavior on Speaker B's part, Speaker A makes the implicature that Speaker B's response means "No, I have not seen Jim"—even though this information is not represented in Speaker B's contribution to the conversation.

In the next example, a context is added, representing information shared by the interlocutors:

55. Context: The three students in a given class are Harpo, Chico, and Groucho.
    Speaker A: Which students passed the exam?
    Speaker B: Harpo and Chico.

Speaker A understands that Groucho did not pass the exam, even though Groucho's name is not included in Speaker B's utterance. This understanding follows, on the Gricean view, because Speaker A assumes that Speaker B is obeying the maxims on quality (it's true that Harpo and Chico passed the exam), on quantity (only the names of the exam-passers are mentioned), and on relevance (it's pertinent to the question to mention Harpo and Chico). Therefore, Speaker B draws the conversational implicature that Groucho did not pass the exam.

Sometimes, it's considered "rational" for the speaker to violate one maxim in order to obey another; and the speaker can inform the hearer of this. Consider the following possible utterances:

56.   a.   I'm not at liberty to give you all the details. (that is, I will violate the maxim on quantity in order to obey the maxim on truth)

   b.   I probably don't need to say this, but . . . (that is, I will violate the maxim on quantity in order to obey the maxim on relevance)

   c.   I know this is irrelevant, but . . . (that is, I will violate the maxims on relevance and quantity in order to obey the maxim on quality)

   d.   I hope I can relate all the details of the robbery right, cause when that guy stuck that gun in my face . . . (that is, I will violate the maxim on manner in order to obey the maxim of quality)

More interestingly, speakers can also choose to intentionally violate a given maxim but without informing the hearer of this choice. Grice refers to such intentional violation as <u>flouting</u> a maxim. Consider the following exchange:

57.   Speaker A: Can you pass the salt?
   Speaker B: Yes.

Most of us would interpret Speaker A's question here as a polite way of requesting that Speaker B pass the salt. But, as discussed in Section C, the modals of English are semantically quite complex; what Speaker B is doing here is responding only to the "physical ability" meaning of *can*, in the process flouting the maxims on quantity (by not including sufficient information) and on relevance (by providing "impertinent" rather than pertinent information).

In the following discourse, Speaker B flouts the maxim on relevance:

58.   Speaker A: Does this skirt make me look fat?
   Speaker B: It's a beautiful color.

Even though (perhaps just because) Speaker B flouts a maxim, the implicature is clear: "Yes, that skirt makes you look fat."

The Gricean system of conversation can be applied to written as well as to spoken communication. Consider the following situation: Asked to provide a recommendation for graduate school for a former student, the professor writes:

59.   Mr. Jones writes well, attends lectures regularly, and dresses nicely.

On Grice's view, the recipient of this recommendation assumes that the professor is obeying the maxims on quality (by being truthful) and on relevance (by mentioning writing well and regular attendance). But that recipient also ascertains that the professor is simultaneously flouting the maxim on quantity by providing too much information. This holds, as dressing nicely is not an attribute required for admission into graduate school. Again, the implicature is clear: "Do not admit this student to your graduate school."

As a final exemplification of how Grice's system works, consider Hamlet's responses in the following discourse (<u>Hamlet</u>, Act II, Scene 2; adapted from Neilson and Hill, 1942, 1061):

60.   Polonius: What do you read, my lord?
      Hamlet: Words, words, words.
      Polonius: What is the matter, my lord?
      Hamlet: Between who?
      Polonius: I mean, the matter you read, my lord.
      Hamlet: Slanders, sir; for the satirical rogue says here that old men have grey beards, that their faces are wrinkled, their eyes purging think amber and plum-tree gum, and that they have a plentiful lack of wit, together with most weak hams: all which, sir, though I most powerfully and potently believe, yet I hold it not honesty to have it thus set down; for yourself, sir, should grow old as I am, if like a crab you could go backward.

In this passage, Hamlet is pretending to be insane and his responses are intended to be confusing, rather than responsive to Polonius' questions. His first response violates the maxim on quantity, by not providing sufficient information. His second response flouts the maxim on relevance by "misinterpreting" the meaning of *matter* as referring to an affair between two people rather than to the topic of his reading. His last rambling response flouts the maxim on manner, as it is anything but clear and orderly. Additionally, since Hamlet's intention here is to pretend to be insane, his entire contribution to the discourse can be said to violate the maxim on quality.

Grice's system likely does not hold for all conversations between all speakers. In particular, discourse may be in part governed by social and/or cultural considerations which Grice ignores. Nevertheless, it is a most interesting system which provides a range of insights into numerous discourse phenomena.

F.   A Note on Language Acquisition

Children move from the babbling stage, in which no 'words' are associated with any particular meaning, to having vocabularies in the range of thirteen thousand words by the time they start school. So it's clear that children manage to imbue a great many strings of sounds with particular meanings in only a few years. The central question considered here is this: How do children come to associate sound with meaning?

It's been widely reported in the acquisition literature that, regardless of culture or language, children begin by first acquiring the semantics of nouns, so that nouns comprise between 50% and 75% of the words produced by children in the fifty word stage. By the time children reach the six hundred word stage, the percentage of nouns produced goes down, while the percentage of verbs produced rises from under 10% to at least 25%.

To account for such differences in the acquisition of nouns and verbs, Bruner (1978) proposed a two-part hypothesis: The meanings of nouns are acquired through a word-to-world mapping procedure, while the meanings of verbs are acquired through a sentence-to-world mapping procedure. Each of these procedures is discussed below.

Acquisition of Nouns

The word-to-world mapping procedure allows children to associate a given word with the entity they perceive in the world when someone uses that word. On Bruner's view, toddlers establish joint attention with adults at the moment an adult speaks, so that the two share 'focus of attention' at the time of utterance. As a result, the child recognizes a convergence between the object focused on and the label produced. Thus, when an adult says "Look at the cat!", the child associates the string of sound [kʰæt] with the feline which is the focus of the adult's and the child's joint attention at the moment.

The simplicity entailed in word-to-world mapping has a certain intuitive appeal; but its simplicity leads to three major problems. First, given "Look at the cat!", how does a child understand that the adult is in fact referring to the entire feline, rather than to its whiskers or its ears or its paws? Second, how does a child generalize the meaning of a word like *cat* to other instances of such animals? Third, children also acquire nouns which refer to things that cannot be pointed to or perceived in the world and so cannot be the 'focus of attention' in Bruner's sense (e.g., *day, bed-time, truth*); in fact, by around twenty-one months of age, half of the nouns children produce fall into this last category.

To fill in these gaps in Bruner's hypothesis, Markman (1994) proposed that children make assumptions (that is, have biases) about how words are used. To account for the first problem noted above, Markman proposed what she labeled the Whole Object bias:

61.   <u>Whole Object bias</u>: A novel label is likely to refer to the whole object and not to its parts, substances, or other properties.

The Whole Object bias leads a child to assume that the novel word *cat* (in "Look at the cat!") refers to the entire animal, not just to its tail or whiskers or paws.

Once a child has established a whole object label for a particular object, the child must extend that label to other similar objects, and she does so, on Markman's account, through assuming the Taxonomic bias:

62.   <u>Taxonomic bias</u>: Labels refer to objects of the same kind rather than to objects that are thematically related.

"Thematically related" objects are those which are linked by some sort of causal, temporal, or spatial relation. For example, *cow* is linked to *milk,* since cows give milk; *baby* is linked to *crib,* since babies sleep in cribs. "Taxonomically related" objects are those which belong to the same superordinate category (as discussed in Section A above). Cats, cows, and elephants all belong to one superordinate category, animals; water, milk, and orange juice all belong to another superordinate category, drinks.

Markman argues for the Taxonomic bias as follows: Given pictures of a cat and an elephant, the child who knows the word *cat* (based on the Whole Object bias) but not the word *elephant,* will use the label *cat* for both, as the child assigns both to the same taxonomic category. Both anecdotal reports and various experimental studies appear to back up this argument.

To account for the fact that at some point, children do distinguish between *cat* and *elephant,* Markman argued that children also follow the Mutual Exclusivity bias:

63.   <u>Mutual Exclusivity bias</u>: Words are mutually exclusive . . . (and) . . . Each object will have one and only one label.

The two parts of the Mutual Exclusivity bias are intended to account for two facets of the acquisition of the meaning of a noun. First, it asserts that, since cat and elephant are different objects, they must have different labels, even though they share the superordinate category animal. Second, it accounts for the whole vs. part distinction, as follows: At some point, the child assumes that a given word does not refer to the Whole Object, but to only a part of that object. As a result, when the child hears a new word in the presence of a known object—for example, *tail* in the presence of the (known) object *cat*—the child assumes the novel word refers to a part of the cat, not the entire animal, since the meaning of the words *tail* and *cat* must be mutually exclusive.

A word-to-world mapping procedure, supplemented with Markman's biases, may be of some help to children acquiring the meanings of nouns. But it provides no such assistance in acquiring the meanings of verbs. For that, we turn to Bruner's notion of sentence-to-world mapping.

Acquisition of Verbs

The meaning of a verb may be difficult (sometimes impossible) to observe or to point to and may even be removed from the speech situation. For example, "You broke the vase" can only be uttered after the event of vase-breaking, while "Please hand me that paper" must be uttered prior to the paper-handing event.

Bruner's sentence-to-world mapping entails that, to a large extent, the acquisition of the meaning of a verb depends not on the physical environment in which the verb is uttered but on the syntactic environment in which the verb occurs. In a series of works, Gleitman and colleagues extend Bruner's hypothesis by exploring what they refer to as the "syntactic cuing of verb meaning." (See Gleitman 1990 and Gleitman and Gillette 1995.)

The account developed by Gleitman and colleagues rests on two inter-related assumptions: (a) There is a certain correlation between syntax and semantics; and (b) children are biased to expect just such a correlation. In particular, given a verb with two arguments, children are biased to assume the first argument mentioned (the subject) receives an agentive type of theta role while the second argument mentioned (the object) receives the theme role. Given the presence of both agent and theme, children then are biased to infer that the verb has a causative meaning, in which the agent causes something to happen to someone or something. For example, consider the following sentence:

64.   John { naxed / praked / sperged } the glass.

Even though the child cannot ascertain the precise meaning of verbs such as *nax, prake,* and *sperged,* still the child is biased to interpret John as the agent who caused something to happen to the theme, the glass.

In contrast, if only a single argument occurs with a given verb, that verb must lack the causative meaning. Thus the verbs in sentences such as the following entail only that Bill has engaged in some activity:

65.   Bill { gorped / sibbed / stogged }.

Two very different research paradigms demonstrate that children do interpret causative and non-causative verbs differently and that they use syntactic cuing to do so. One set of experiments used the preferential looking paradigm; in this paradigm, a child simultaneously views side-by-side video screens, each displaying a different event, but only one of the events is consistent with a sentence that is presented aloud. The experimenter then measures the length of time the child's eye gaze is fixed on each of the video screens; the assumption here is that children gaze longer at the display that is consistent with the sentence presented orally.

Naigles (1990) administered this paradigm to children as young as two years of age, using sentences with nonce verbs, one in a syntactically causative construction, the other in a syntactically non-causative construction:

66.   a.   The duck is { gorping / sibbing } the bunny.
       b.   The duck and bunny are { gorping / sibbing }.

The display consistent with the sentence in (a) might show the duck hitting the bunny, while that for the sentence in (b) might show the two characters playing together. Naigles' finding was that the length of the children's gaze matched the causative/non-causative distinction; that is, that given the sentence in (a), children gazed longer at the display that showed the duck causing something to happen to the bunny than at the display in which the duck was not causing such.

A very different research paradigm that bears on the acquisition of verb meaning is reported on in Landau and Gleitman (1985). The subjects in this experiment were three-year old children who were congenitally blind; the focus of experiment was on verbs such as *look* (i.e., verbs which assign the agent theta role to their subjects) compared to perception verbs such as *see* (i.e., verbs in which the subject is interpreted with the experiencer theta role). When asked to "look at the chair," the blind children used their fingers to explore the entire chair. But when asked to "see the chair," the children simply touched it with their finger tips.

To understand how congenitally blind children could possibly interpret the meaning of (action/agentive) *look* vs. (perception/experiencer) *see*, Landau and Gleitman analyzed the speech of their mothers. What they found was that these two verbs appeared in different syntactic contexts: *Look* was used for commands, but *see* was never used this way: *Look at this mess! *See this mess!* Further, the two verbs had complements of different syntactic categories: *Look*'s complement was routinely a PP, while *see*'s complement was routinely a DP.

The over-riding conclusion is that the syntactic information associated with verbs is available to learners and that this syntactic information facilitates the acquisition of the meanings of verbs, thereby lending support to Bruner's initial hypothesis.

The hypotheses and experiments reported above contribute greatly to our understanding of how children acquire the meanings of nouns and verbs, but have little to say about the acquisition of other syntactic categories. Further investigation of these most interesting topics is well beyond the scope of this text.

We end this discussion of meaning by pointing out how children play with language. By the age of three or four, most children have developed sufficient meta-linguistic ability to start producing riddles, jokes, and puns. This ability seems to reach its peak around age eight and is often referred to as 'third grade humor'. Two examples, both frequently cited in the literature (without attribution), are given below:

67. Question: Why is 6 afraid of 7?
     Answer: Because 7 ate 9!

68. Emily: Hey Daddy! What do you do when your nose goes on strike?
     Daddy: I don't know, Emily. What *do* you do when your nose goes on strike?
     Emily: You picket!

If you chuckled at these (as I did), you were reacting to the children's abilities to recognize "homophones" (*ate* vs. *eight, picket* vs. *pick it*) and to use them unexpectedly for humorous effect.

KEY TERMS AND CONCEPTS

synonymy	antonymy	polysemy
homophony	hyponymy	hypernymy
taxonomic hierarchy	paraphrase	entailment
contradict	tautology	contradiction
lexical ambiguity	structural ambiguity	Principle of Compositionality

theta roles: agent, theme, source, goal, location, instrument, experiencer, stimulus

theta grid	time vs. tense	generic time
epistemic modality	deontic modality	possible worlds

verbal aspects: accomplishment, achievement, activity, state

measuring out phrase	subject-oriented adverb	time limit adverbial
time duration adverbial	Cooperative Principle	conversational implicature

Grice's Maxims: quality, quantity, relevance, manner   flouting a maxim

word-to-world mapping   sentence-to-world mapping

PRACTICE PROBLEMS

1. For each of the following, identify the meaning relation that exists given the words, phrases, or sentences provided; example: *test / exam are synonyms*

   a. parent / offspring
   b. a solver of equations with trivial solutions
   c. Mary sang an aria. / It was an aria that Mary sang.
   d. Sam is a widower, and Sam has no wife.
   e. A Great White shark bit that swimmer. / That swimmer is injured.
   f. George gave some books to Sally, yet Sally has no books.
   g. Nancy baked salmon for dinner. / There's nothing to eat for dinner.

2. Each of these sentences is ambiguous. State whether the ambiguity is <u>lexical</u> or <u>structural</u>; provide an <u>unambiguous paraphrase</u> (phrase or sentence) for each of the possible meanings.

   a. Cold beer and wine are what we want.
   b. Congress passed a dangerous drug bill.
   c. The nutty professor left the key in his office.
   d. He met the woman standing by the water cooler.
   e. He promised to leave yesterday.

3. For each of the following, underline all the DPs; then use labeled arrows to identify the theta role assigned to each DP and the element which assigns that theta role.

   a. The boys walked from school to the park.
   b. Which shoes did you buy at the store?
   c. Sally mailed a package to her nephew.
   d. The minister enthralled the congregation from the pulpit.
   e. John had always wondered if Martians would frighten him.

4. Classify the following sentences as exemplifying either deontic or epistemic modality:

   a. Dogs may not ride on this bus.
   b. Fish can swim.
   c. Susan believes the earth is flat.
   d. You must come to the meeting today.

5. Identify each predicate below as exemplifying one of these semantic classifications: state, activity, accomplishment, or achievement:

    a. Sam recognized his friend.
    b. The quick brown fox sneezed.
    c. Humpty fell down the stairs.
    d. Sally owns a dog named Spot.
    e. The dinosaurs died out.
    f. Leslie drew a perfect circle.

6. Consider the following short conversations. Determine which of Grice's maxims are obeyed or flouted and what the implicatures are:

    a. Context: Overweight husband and his not overweight wife at home.
           Husband: Let's go out for some ice cream.
           Wife: There's some great fruit salad in the fridge.

    b. Context: Two friends in conversation; both know John and Susie, that John drives a yellow Beetle, and that John knows Susie.
           Speaker A: Where was John last night?
           Speaker B: Well, there was a yellow Beetle parked outside Susie's place this morning.

Keys to Selected Problems

Chapter 2

1. a. his / <u>hiss</u>   b. <u>fuss</u> / fuzz   c. <u>bath</u> / bathe   d. edge / <u>etch</u>
    e. beds / <u>bets</u>   f. <u>walked</u> / jogged   g. <u>light</u> / lied   i. <u>wick</u> / wig

2. a. fricative   race/breath/bush/bring/breathe/tough/<u>though</u> /rave/<u>hate</u>
    b. nasal   pant/range/rang/dumb/dump/<u>knee</u>/deaf/<u>gnu</u>/pneumonia
    c. stop   pill/lip/lit/graph/<u>crab</u>/dog/hide/laugh/<u>back</u>/hike
    d. lateral   nut/<u>lone</u>/ball/bar/rob/one/run/bare/bale
    e. approximant   <u>we/you/were/lone/one/run/yell/roll/your</u>

3. a. fricative   <u>race/breath/bush</u>/bring/<u>breathe/tough</u>/though/<u>rave</u>/hate
    b. nasal   pant/range/rang/<u>dumb</u>/dump/knee/deaf/gnu/pneumonia
    c. stop   pill/<u>lip</u>/<u>lit</u>/graph/<u>crab</u>/dog/<u>hide</u>/laugh/back/<u>hike</u>
    d. affricate   <u>much</u>/back/edge/ooze/chews/<u>touch</u>/tough/just/push
    e. rhotic   nut/lone/ball/<u>bar</u>/rob/one/run/<u>bare</u>/bale

4. a. velar   knot/<u>got</u>/lot/<u>cot</u>/hot/pot/gnat/lack/tug/<u>ghost</u>/tough
    b. labiodental   <u>fat</u>/cat/that/mat/chat/<u>vat</u>/wife/live/with/by/width
    c. alveolar   zip/nip/lip/sip/tip/dip/pill/pat/pad/par/hiss/his
    d. post-alveolar   lurch/lush/cough/lunge/touch/<u>choose</u>/huge/<u>juice</u>/<u>sugar</u>

5. a. bilabial   mat/gnat/sat/bat/rat/pat/<u>map</u>/<u>nab</u>/dad/<u>tam</u>/tar
    b. alveolar   zip/nip/lip/sip/tip/dip/<u>pill</u>/pat/pad/par/hiss/his
    c. dental   pie/guy/shy/thigh/thy/high/<u>with</u>/<u>width</u>/height/<u>length</u>
    d. post-alveolar   <u>lurch</u>/<u>lush</u>/cough/<u>lunge</u>/<u>touch</u>/choose/huge/juice/sugar

6. a. [tʰ]   b. [h]   c. [n]   d. [k]   e. [tʃ]   f. [s]

7. a. [z]   b. [m]   c. [f]   d. [s]   e. [t]   f. [d]

8. a. [ʔ]   b. [z]   c. [g]   d. [tʃ]   e. [j]   f. [t]
    g. [ŋ]   h. [h]   i. [ð]   j. [v]

9. [z]   voiced alveolar fricative   [v]   voiced labiodental fricative
    [ʤ]   voiced post-alveolar affricate   [k]   voiceless velar stop
    [m]   voiced bilabial nasal   [pʰ]   voiceless, aspirated, bilabial stop
    [θ]   voiceless dental fricative   [w̥]   voiceless labiovelar glide

10. b. tag   d. pending   e. appall   f. careful

11. a. [ng] should be [ŋ]   b. [c] should be [k]   c. [sh] should be [ʃ]
     d. [s] should be [z]   e. [θ] should be [ð]   f. [j] should be [ʤ]
     g. [x] should be [ks]   h. [ð] should be [θ]

12. a. [ʌ]   b. [ə]   c. [ʌ]   d. [ə]   e. [ə]   f. [ʌ, ə]   g. [ʌ]   h. [ə]

13. a. diphthong   sat/sot/set/<u>soy</u>/seat/soot/sate/sit/<u>sight</u>/sought/sew/suit/<u>souse</u>
     b. front   <u>sat</u>/sot/<u>set</u>/soy/<u>seat</u>/soot/sate/<u>sit</u>/sight/sought/sew/suit/souse
     c. back   sat/<u>sot</u>/set/soy/seat/<u>soot</u>/sate/sit/sight/<u>sought</u>/<u>sew</u>/<u>suit</u>/souse
     d. high   sat/sot/set/soy/seat/<u>soot</u>/sate/<u>sit</u>/sight/sought/sew/<u>suit</u>/souse
     e. low   <u>sat</u>/<u>sot</u>/set/soy/seat/soot/sate/sit/sight/sought/sew/suit/souse
                      (NB: If you pronounce *sot* and *sought* alike, both have low vowels)
     f. round   sat/sot/set/<u>soy</u>/seat/<u>soot</u>/sate/sit/sight/<u>sought</u>/<u>sew</u>/<u>suit</u>/souse
                      (NB: If you pronounce *sot* and *sought* alike, neither has a round vowel)
     g. tense   sat/sot/set/<u>soy</u>/<u>seat</u>/soot/<u>sate</u>/sit/sight/sought/<u>sew</u>/<u>suit</u>/souse

14. a. [i]   b. [i]   c. [i]   d. [i]
     e. [u]   f. [u]   g. [u]   h. [u]
     i. [ɔ] or [ɑ] j. [ɔ] or [ɑ] k. [ɔ] or [ɑ] l. [ɔ] or [ɑ]
     m. [ʊ]   n. [u]   o. [ʊ]   p. [ɑʊ]

17. a. [ɑ] should be [æ]   b. [o] should be [ɔ] or [ɑ]   c. [e] should be [ɛ]
     d. [o] should be [ɑ]   e. [i] should be [ɪ]   f. [æ] should be [ə]

Chapter 3

1. a. trees   e. fox

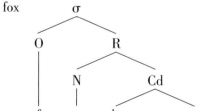

h. aisle

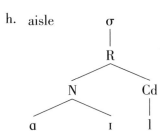

j. width (could be [wɪdð])

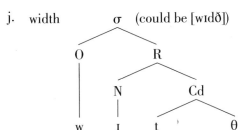

3. Arabic: [h] and [ʔ] are separate phonemes; there are four minimal pairs in the data; e.g., [habba] / [ʔabba]

4. Russian: [l] and [lʲ] are separate phonemes; there are two minimal pairs in the data; e.g., [lat] / [lʲat]

5. Bemba: [s] and [ʃ] are allophones of a single phoneme; [ʃ] occurs only preceding [i]; [s] occurs elsewhere

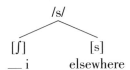

6. Brazilian Portuguese: [d] and [ʤ] are allophones of a single phoneme; [ʤ] occurs only preceding [i]; [d] occurs elsewhere

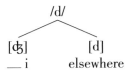

7. English: [t, θ, p, f, s] following the diphthong condition the change; the relevant feature shared by these consonants is voiceless

8. Tamil: [ɯ] occurs only when the preceding V is not round (otherwise, [ʊ] occurs)

9. English: a. [p, t, k]   b.   [p, t, k]   c.   [p, t, k]

                    d. [p, t, k] form a natural class: the set of voiceless stops

10. Old English: [f] / [v]:   [v] occurs only between voiced segments, but [f] is not so restricted
                     [h] / [x]:   [h] occurs only word-initially, but [x] is not so restricted
                     [n] / [ŋ]:   [ŋ] occurs only when the following segment is a velar stop; but [n] is not so restricted

11. Basque: a. [b, β] are voiced Labials; [b] is a stop, [β] is a fricative
                        [d, ð] are voiced Coronals; [d] is a stop, [ð] is a fricative
                        [g, ɣ] are voiced Dorsals; [g] is a stop, [ɣ] is a fricative

                    b. fricatives [β, ð, ɣ] are found only between vowels
                        stops [b, d, g] are found word-initially as well as inside words, both before and after other consonants

                    c. [b, β] are phonetically similar and in complementary distribution; they represent allophones of a single phoneme, /b/
                        [d, ð] are phonetically similar and in complementary distribution; they represent allophones of a single phoneme, /d/
                        [g, ɣ] are phonetically similar and in complementary distribution; they represent allophones of a single phoneme, /g/

                    d.

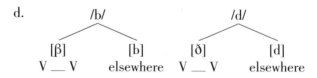

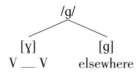

                    e. i. /pugo/   ii. /dedat/   iii. /gubar/   iv. /ambud/

12. for (5), Bemba: /s/ → [ʃ] / __ i
     for (6), Brazilian Portuguese: /d/ → [ʤ] / __ i

13. a. English: <u>assimilation</u>, in which a normally voiced fricative shares the laryngeal status of the following voiceless stop

     b. Greek: <u>dissimilation</u>, in which the second in a string of two consonants which share manner of articulation changes its manner (from stop to fricative, or fricative to stop)

     c. Japanese: <u>assimilation</u>, as voiceless obstruents become voiced when between vowels (and thus share laryngeal status with the voiced vowels)

     d. Russian: <u>deletion</u>, in which alveolar stops disappear when their presence would yield sequences of three or more (Coronal) consonants

     e. English: in (i) and (ii), <u>assimilation</u>, as the past tense forms in (i) all end in [d] and the roots all end in voiced sounds, while those in (ii) all end in [t] and the roots all end in voiceless sounds; in (iii), <u>epenthesis</u>, as the past tense forms here end in [əd]

Chapter 4

The word tree for *renationalization* follows; note that *re-* is not simply added on to the top of *nationalization* (cf. (12) in the text). The reason: *re-* 'again' cannot attach to nouns.

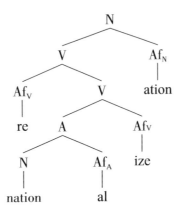

1. a. 1   b. 1   c. 2   d. 2
    e. 1   f. 1   g. 2   h. 2

2. a. 2: bound in; free valid
    b. one
    c. 2: free Jack; bound -s
    d. 4: free opt; bound -tion, -al, -ity
    e. one
    f. one
    g. 4: free able; bound in-, -ity, -s
    h. 3: free stable; bound de-, -ize
    i. one
    j. 2: free evident; bound -ly
    k. one
    l. 3: free complicate; bound un-, -ed

3. a. 2: root amaze is a verb; amazement is a noun
    b. 3: root use is a verb; reusable is an adjective
    c. 2: root honest is an adjective; dishonest is an adjective
    d. 1: root is a noun
    e. 3: root care is a noun; carefully is an adverb
    f. 2: root history is a noun; historical is an adjective
    g. 3: root person is a noun; impersonal is an adjective
    h. 4: root control is a verb; uncontrollably is an adverb
    i. 2: root petunia is a noun; petunias is a noun
    j. 3: root read is a verb; rereads is a verb
    k. 2: root beauty is a noun; beautiful is an adjective
    l. 1: root is a noun

4. a. complex; inflectional
    b. simple
    c. simple
    d. complex; derivational
    e. simple
    f. simple
    g. complex; derivational
    h. complex, inflectional
    i. complex, inflectional
    j. complex, derivational
    k. simple
    l. complex, derivational

5. a. verb, past participle
    b. adjective, superlative
    c. verb, progressive
    d. verb, 3 sq present tense
    e. noun, possessive
    f. noun, plural
    g. adverb, comparative
    h. noun, plural

6. a. same: greedy, dirty; different: jealousy; none: ivory
    b. same: harden, thicken; different: spoken; none: leaven
    c. same: rider, actor; different: colder; none: silver
    d. same: shopped, cleaned; different: candied; none: candid
    e. same: greener, nicer; different: farmer; none: water
    f. same: incapable, indirect; different: intake; none: intelligent

7. a. upstairs: P + N, as is downtown   b. scarecrow: V + N, as is swearword

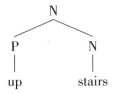

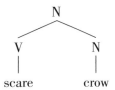

c. skin-deep: N + A, as is sky-blue   d. slam-dunk: V + V, as is break-dance

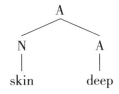

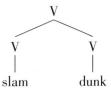

8. Mende: a. [i]   b. [salei]   c. 'night'

9. Ganda: a. [omu]   b. [aba]   c. [omulanga]

10. Kanuri: a. prefix   b. derivational   c. [nəm]
               d. [nəmkəji]   e. [gəla]   f.

N

Af_N   A
| |
nəm   kurugu

11. Turkish: a. city [ʃehir]; hand [el]; bridge [køpry]; bell [zil]; house [ev]; voice [ses];
                   bus [otobys]; from [den]; to [e]; on/in [de]; my [im]; your [iniz];
                   plural [ler]
               b. root + plural + possessor + post-position
               c. [ʃehirde] 'in the city'; [elleriniz] 'your hands'
               d. [otobyslere]

Chapter 5

1. a. beat: verb; she: determiner (pronoun); the: determiner (article); door: noun; near: preposition; hobo: noun used as a modifier; jungle: noun; bum: noun used as a modifier; heard: verb

    b. a: determiner (article); fortune: noun; male: noun used as a modifier; deer: noun; you: determiner (pronoun); will: modal; have: verb; bucks: noun

2. a. head: in; complement: the barn; PP
    b. head: the; complement: cat in the hat; DP
    c. head: fond; complement: of crisp apples; AP
    d. head: ran; adjunct: to the store; VP
    e. head: walked; complement: the dog; adjunct: briskly; VP
    f. head: [e]; complement: destruction of that city; DP
    g. head: ran; complement: the store; VP
    h. head: swept; complement: the floor; adjunct: hastily; VP
    i. head: [e]; complement: books with blue covers; DP

3. a.   b.   c.

4. c.   d.

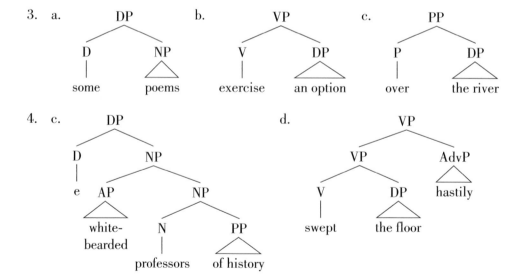

7.   a.

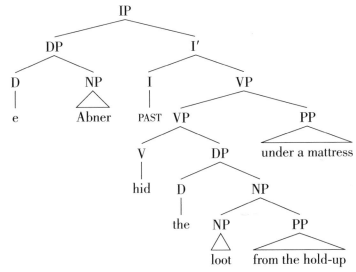

b.

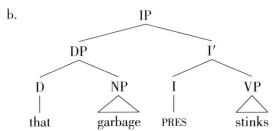

d.

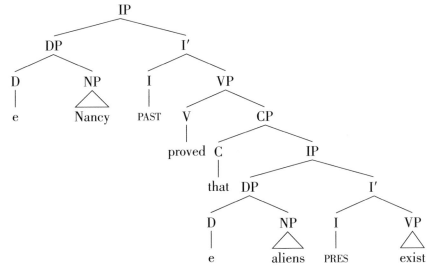

8. b. *d-structure*

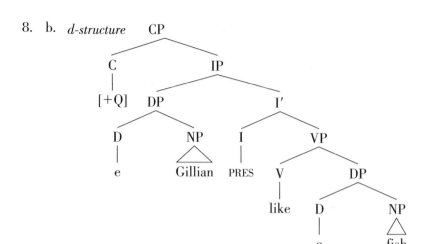

s-structure

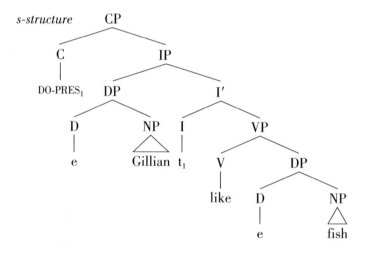

c.   only s-structure shown here; *can* has moved from I to C

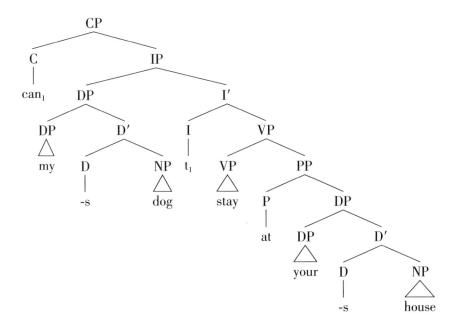

f.   d-structure shown here; dotted lines mark what moves where in s-structure

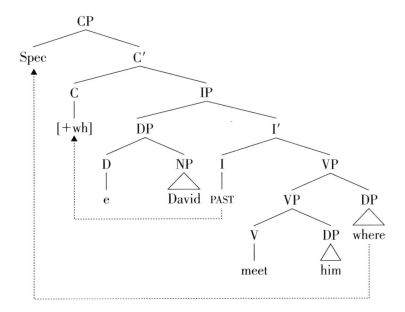

Chapter 6

1. a. antonyms   b. structural ambiguity   c. paraphrase
   d. tautology   e. entailment   f. contradiction
   g. contradict

2. a. structural: i.   We want wine and cold beer.
                  ii.   We want wine and beer that are both cold.

   b. structural: i.   The bill Congress passed was about dangerous drugs.
                  ii.   The drug bill Congress passed was dangerous.

   c. lexical: The professor left in his office . . .
                  i.   the answer key to an exam
                  ii.   the key to the door lock

3. a. The boys walked from school to the park.

              agent   source   goal

   d. The minister enthralled the congregation from the pulpit.

   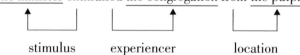

            stimulus   experiencer   location

   e. John had always wondered if Martians would frighten him.

           experiencer   stimulus   experiencer

4. a. deontic   b. epistemic   c. epistemic   d. deontic

5. a. achievement   b. achievement   c. achievement
   d. state   e. achievement   f. accomplishment

6. a. Husband assumes wife is obeying quality (there is fruit salad in the fridge) but is violating relevance (as the information provided is "impertinent"); the implicature is: husband needs to lose some weight.

    b. Speaker A assumes Speaker B is obeying quality (there was a yellow Beetle parked outside Susie's place), quantity (this fact is sufficient to answer the question), and relevance (the fact is pertinent); the implicature is: John was at Susie's place last night.

References Cited

Adams, Douglas. 1992. *Mostly harmless.* New York: Harmony Books.

Berko, Jean. 1958. The child's learning of English morphology. *Word* 14: 150-177.

Boysson-Bardies, B. de and M. M. Vihman. 1991. Adaptation to language: Evidence from babbling and first words in four languages. *Language* 67: 297-319.

Brown, Roger. 1973. *A first language: the early stages.* London: George Allen and Unwin.

Bruner, J. S. 1978. From communication to language: A psychological perspective. in *The social context of language,* ed. Ivana Markova, 255-287. New York: Wiley.

Chomsky, Noam. 1957. *Syntactic structures.* The Hague: Mouton & Co.

Dowty, David R. 1979. The semantics of aspectual classes of verbs in English. Chapter 2 of *Word meaning and Montague grammar,* 37-132. Dordrecht: Reidel.

Eimas, P., E.R. Siqueland, P.W. Jusczky, and J. Vigorito. 1971. Speech perception in infants. *Science* 17: 303-306.

Gleitman, Lila R. 1990. The structural sources of verb meaning. *Language acquisition* 1: 3-55.

Gleitman, Lila R. and Jane Gillette. 1995. The role of syntax in verb learning. in *Handbook of child language,* eds. P. Fletcher and B. MacWhinney, 413-428. Oxford: Blackwell.

Grice, H. Paul. 1975. Logic and conversation. In *Syntax and semantics. Volume 3: Speech acts,* ed. Peter Cole and Jerry Morgan, 43-58. New York: Academic Press.

Grice, H. Paul. 1978. Further notes on logic and conversation. In *Syntax and semantics. Volume 9: Pragmatics,* ed. Peter Cole, 113-128. New York: Academic Press.

Ladefoged, Peter. 2001. *A course in phonetics. Fourth Edition.* Fort Worth: Harcourt Brace Publishers.

Landau, Barbara, and Lila R. Gleitman. 1985. *Language and experience: Evidence from the blind child.* Cambridge: Harvard University Press.

Löbner, Sebastian. 2002. *Understanding semantics.* London: Arnold.

Markman, Ellen M. 1994. Constraints children place on word meaning. in *Language acquisition,* ed. Paul Bloom, 154-173. Cambridge: MIT Press.

Naigles, Leticia. 1990. Children use syntax to learn verb meaning. *Journal of child language* 17: 357-374.

Neilson, William Allen, and Charles Jarvis Hill, eds. 1942. *The complete plays and poems of William Shakespeare.* Cambridge: Houghton Mifflin Company.

O'Grady, William, John Archibald, Mark Aronoff, and Janie Rees-Miller. 2005. *Contemporary linguistics: An introduction.* Fifth Edition. Boston: Bedford/St. Martin's.

Pinker, Steven. 1994. *The language instinct: How the mind creates language.* New York. William Morrow and Company, Inc.

Pinker, Steven. 2000. *Words and rules: The ingredients of language.* New York: Perennial.

Quirk, Randolph, Sidney Greenbaum, Geoffrey Leech, and Jan Svartik. 1985. *A comprehensive grammar of the English language.* New York: Longman.

Tomlin, Russell. 1986. *Basic Word Order: Functional Principles.* London: Croom Helm.

Vendler, Zeno. 1967. Verbs and times. Chapter 4 of *Linguistics in philosophy,* 97-121. Ithaca: Cornell University Press.

Werker, J.F., J.H. Gilbert, K. Humphrey, and R.C. Tees. 1981. Developmental aspects of cross-language speech perception. *Child development* 52: 249-355.

Other Introductory Textbooks

Akmajian, Adrian, Richard Demers, Ann Farmers, and Robert Harnish. 2001. *Linguistics: An Introduction to Language and Communication.* Cambridge: MIT Press.

Bergman, Anouschka, Kathleen Hall, and Sharon Ross, eds. 2007. *Language Files: Materials for an Introduction to Language and Linguistics.* Tenth Edition. Columbus: Ohio State University Press.

Fasold, Ralph, and Jeff Connor-Linton, eds. 2006. *An Introduction to Language and Linguistics.* Cambridge: Cambridge University Press.

Fromkin, Victoria, Robert Rodman, and Nina Hyams. 2007. *An Introduction to Language.* Eighth Edition. Boston: Thompson Wadsworth.

O'Grady, William, John Archibald, Mark Aronoff, and Janie Rees-Miller. 2005. *Contemporary Linguistics: An Introduction.* Fifth Edition. Boston: Bedford/St. Martin's.

Index